Helena Gomm & Jon Hird

Inside Out

Teacher's
Book

MACMILLAN

Macmillan Education
Between Towns Road, Oxford OX4 3PP, UK
A division of Macmillan Publishers Limited
Companies and representatives throughout the world

ISBN 0 333 97587 1 (International Edition)
ISBN 0 333 99905 3 (Level II)
ISBN 0 333 99906 1 (Level II Pack)

Text © Sue Kay, Vaughan Jones and Philip Kerr 2002.
Text by Helena Gomm and Jon Hird.
Design and illustration © Macmillan Publishers Limited 2002.

First published 2002

Project management by Desmond O'Sullivan, ELT Publishing Services.
Edited by Celia Bingham.
Designed by Ann Samuel.
Cartoons on p10 reproduced by kind permission of *Private Eye* and
Cartoonstock.
Cover design by Andrew Oliver.

Printed and bound in Spain by Edelvives

2006 2005 2004 2003 2002
10 9 8 7 6 5 4 3 2 1

Introduction

At the heart of 'Inside Out' is the belief that the most effective conditions for language learning come about when students engage in activities on a personal level rather than just 'going through the motions'. Engagement can be triggered by anything from understanding and smiling at a cartoon to talking at length to a partner about the last time you went dancing and had a good time.

Teaching strategies

All the strategies employed in *Inside Out* aim to promote learning by focusing on personal engagement, both intellectual and emotional. This helps ensure that we never lose sight of meaning as the key ingredient in effective language learning. As Rod Ellis remarks: 'It is the need to get meanings across and the pleasure experienced when this is achieved that motivates second language acquisition.'

Accessible topics and tasks

Each unit is built around a set of two or three related topics. They provide an interesting and wide-ranging selection of subjects about which most students have something to say. However, as Penny Ur explained many years ago: 'The crux is not *what* to talk about, but *why* you need to talk about it.' The tasks in *Inside Out* have been designed to set up opportunities for genuine communicative exchanges.

Grammar awareness / Grammar practice

The course covers the main grammar areas you would expect in a pre-intermediate course book. In some cases the grammar may be completely new to students. In others it will be a further exploration of structures they have met before.

We recognise that learning grammar is a messy, non-linear process – often a case of two steps forward, one step back. All the research suggests that a student's internal grammar is in a permanent state of flux. The constant restructuring necessary to incorporate new rules into the system can adversely affect language already 'learnt'. A typical example is the student who learns *bought* as the past form of *buy* but then starts to over-generalise the regular *-ed* inflection for marking the past tense and uses the incorrect form *buyed* for a while. This characteristic of language learning is perfectly natural and mirrors the process children go through when mastering their native tongue.

We feel that the key to learning grammar then, is to provide students with as many opportunities as possible for meaningful practice. Practice makes perfect. It is only through frequent manipulation of form that students begin to increase the complexity of their output – use more grammar – and in doing so, improve their ability to communicate effectively.

To provide appropriate grammar study, *Inside Out* includes regular 'Close up' sections. These follow a three stage approach: language analysis; practice; personalisation.

1 Language analysis

The language analysis stage promotes 'noticing' of language features and usage. The language to be 'noticed' almost always comes out of a larger listening or reading text where it occurs naturally in a wider context. We do not believe that self-contained, pre-fabricated example sentences are a good starting point for analysis. At this point students are encouraged to articulate and organise what they know, and incorporate new information.

This stage will work both as individual study or as pair/groupwork. In general, we recommend pair/groupwork as this provides a forum for students to exchange and test out ideas before presenting them in the more intimidating arena of the whole class.

Unlike other books which use the 'guided discovery' approach to grammar, we have generally avoided gap fills and multiple choice questions. Research showed us that most students are unenthusiastic about using these techniques to study grammar. This may be because they associate them with testing rather than learning. Instead, we provide questions and discussion points.

2 Practice

In the practice activities students manipulate or select structures, testing their theories. As they do this, they also become more comfortable with the grammar point.

The sentences in this section are designed to be realistic and meaningful rather than relying on invented scenarios about imaginary people. In our study of form, we do not believe that it is necessary to completely abandon meaning. Many of the sentences can be applied to the students' own lives, and this facilitates the next stage.

3 Personalisation

The personalisation stage is not a conventional free practice, where students, for example, take part in a role play which 'requires' the target structure. As Michael Lewis has pointed out, very few situations in real life actually require a particular structure. Furthermore, when they are faced with a challenging situation without time to prepare, many students will, naturally, decide to rely on what they know, rather than what they studied half an hour ago. For these reasons, personalisation is based on actual examples of the target structure. Students apply these examples to their own lives, opinions and feelings. Very often the sentences or questions from the practice stage are recycled for the personalisation. For example:

- Replace the names in the sentences in 1 to make the sentences true for you.

- Work with a partner. Ask the questions in 2. Give true answers.

• Work with a partner. Which of the statements in 3 do you agree with?

All the Close up sections are supported by Language reference boxes, which give accurate, clear explanations backed up with examples. These appear in the unit, right where they're needed, rather than being tucked away at the back of the book.

Contemporary lexis in context

The valuable work done over the years on various dictionary corpora has informed us that approximately 2,000 words account for nearly 75% of all English usage. A primary objective for a pre-intermediate student, then, is to learn these 'top 2,000'.

In *Inside Out* the lexis we focus on is always presented in context and is related to the themes and topics in the unit. Vocabulary is first of all highlighted in exercises which draw attention to it, then recycled in back-up exercises. The Workbook provides further recycling, as do the photocopiable tests in the Teacher's Book. The exercises encourage students to deal with lexis as part of a system, rather than as a list of discrete words. There are a variety of tasks which focus on collocation, connotation and social register.

Personalised speaking tasks

Inside Out is filled with speaking tasks. Their main purpose is to develop fluency. While they are not intended principally as grammar practice, they are linked to the topics, lexis and grammar in the unit so as to include opportunities for students to turn input into output.

The tasks do not require complicated classroom configurations. They are easy to set up and enjoyable to use. Most of them encourage the students to talk about things that actually matter to them, rather than playing roles or exchanging invented information. Personalised, authentic tasks challenge and engage students, and this encourages linguistic 'risk taking': Can I use this word here? Is this how this structure works? Research into second language acquisition suggests that when students take risks they are experimenting, testing theories about how the language works and restructuring their internal language system accordingly. This is an essential part of language learning.

Anecdotes

There are also extended speaking tasks, where students tackle a longer piece of discourse. We've called these 'Anecdotes'. They are based on personal issues, for instance, memories, stories, people you know. When you learn a musical instrument, you can't spend all your time playing scales and exercises: you also need to learn whole pieces in order to see how music is organised. Anecdotes give students a chance to get to grips with how discourse is organised. We have found the following strategies helpful in getting our students to tell their anecdotes.

1   Choose global topics that everybody can relate to

One of the main objectives of an Anecdote is to encourage students to experiment with and hopefully grow more competent at using language at the more demanding end of their range. It therefore seems only fair to ask them to talk about subjects they know something about. With familiar subject matter students can concentrate on how they are speaking as well as *what* they are speaking about. The twelve Anecdote topics in *Inside Out Pre-intermediate* have been carefully selected to appeal to the widest range of students whilst at the same time, fitting in to the context of the unit.

2   Allow sufficient preparation time

Students need time to assemble their thoughts and think about the language they will need. The Anecdotes are set up through evocative questions. Students read or listen to a planned series of questions and choose what specifically they will talk about; shyer students can avoid matters they feel are too personal. This student preparation is a key stage and should not be rushed. Research, by Peter Skehan and Pauline Foster among others, has shown that learners who plan for tasks attempt more ambitious and complex language, hesitate less and make fewer basic errors.

The simplest way to prepare students for an Anecdote is to ask them to read the list of questions in the book and decide which they want to talk about. This could be done during class time or as homework preparation for the following lesson. The questions have check boxes so that students can tick the ones they are interested in. Ask them to think about the language they will need. Encourage them to use dictionaries and make notes – but not to write out what they will actually say. Finally, put them into pairs to exchange Anecdotes.

A variation is to ask the students to read the questions in the book while, at the same time, listening to you read them aloud. Then ask them to prepare in detail for the task, as above.

Alternatively, ask the students to close their books – and then to close their eyes. Ask them to listen to the questions as you read them aloud and think about what they evoke. Some classes will find this a more involving process. It also allows you to adapt the questions to your class: adding new ones or missing out ones you think inappropriate. After the reading, give them enough time to finalise their preparation before starting the speaking task.

3   Monitor students and give feedback

It is important for students to feel that their efforts are being monitored by the teacher. Realistically, it is probably only possible for a teacher to monitor and give feedback to one or two pairs of students during each Anecdote activity. It is therefore vital that the teacher adopts a strict rota system and makes sure that everyone in the class is monitored over the course of a term. Constructive feedback helps students improve their delivery.

4 Provide a 'model anecdote'

It is always useful for the students to hear a model Anecdote at some stage during the Anecdote activity. The most obvious model is you the teacher. Alternatively you might ask a teaching colleague or friend to talk to the students. In several cases there is a model Anecdote on the audio cassette / CD accompanying *Inside Out* which you can use.

5 Repeat the same anecdote with a new partner at regular intervals

Consider going back to Anecdotes and repeating them in later classes. Let the students know that you are going to do this. This will reassure them that you are doing it on purpose, but more importantly, it will mean that they will be more motivated to dedicate some time and thought to preparation. When you repeat the task, mix the class so that each student works with a new partner, i.e. one who has not previously heard the Anecdote.

Another approach outlined by Michael Lewis et al. in *Teaching Collocations* (page 91) is to reduce the time allowed to deliver the Anecdote each time it is repeated: in the first instance the student has five minutes; for the second telling they have four minutes; and the third three minutes.

Repeating complex tasks reflects real interactions. We all have our set pieces: jokes, stories. And we tend to refine and improve them as we retell them. Many students will appreciate the opportunity to do the same thing in their second language, and research by Martin Bygate among others has shown that given this opportunity they become more adventurous and at the same time more precise in the language they use.

You can also use the Anecdotes to test oral proficiency and thereby add a speaking component to accompany the tests in the Teacher's Book.

Realistic reading

In theory, no matter how difficult a text may be, the task that accompanies it can be designed to be within the competence of the student, i.e. 'grade the task not the text'. But conversations with students and teachers and many years in the classroom have convinced us that this is an insight of only limited value. However easy the task, students are quickly disillusioned by an incomprehensible text.

At the other extreme, many of the texts that have appeared in ELT coursebooks in the past have obviously been written merely in order to include examples of a given grammatical structure. Texts like this are often boring to read and unconvincing as discourse.

The solution adopted in *Inside Out* has been to base all reading texts on authentic modern sources, including magazines, novels, newspapers, websites and personal communications. Where necessary, the source texts have been edited and graded so as to make them challenging without being impossible. The texts have been selected not only for their language content but also for their interest and their appropriacy to the students who will use this course.

Varied listening work

The listenings include texts specially written for language learning, improvisations in the studio and semi-authentic recordings. There are dialogues, conversations, monologues and classic pop songs. There is a variety of English accents – British, American, Irish, Australian, Scots, North Country – and some examples of non-native speakers. The tasks are designed to develop real life listening skills.

Pronunciation improvement

Work on particular areas of sound, stress and intonation is integrated into units as appropriate.

Motivating writing practice

The coursebook contains six structured writing tasks which offer the students opportunities to get to grips with a variety of formats: narrative, descriptive, formal and informal letters, application forms and reports.

This is backed up by a self-contained writing course which runs through the Workbook.

Components

Each level of *Inside Out* includes a Student's Book, a Teacher's Book, a Workbook, Class Cassettes and CDs, a Workbook Cassette and CD, and a photocopiable Resource Pack. There is also a Resource site on the internet at www.insideout.net

Student's Book

The Student's Book covers about 90 hours of classroom teaching. It is made up of sixteen main units (1–4, 6–9, 11–14 and 16–19) and four review units (5, 10, 15 and 20). The units do not follow a rigid template: the flow of each one comes from the texts, tasks and language points in it.

The book includes all the tapescripts, plus a list of verb structures, a glossary of grammatical terminology, a guide to the phonemic alphabet, and a list of irregular verbs.

Class Cassettes (2) and CDs (3)

These have all the listening materials from the Student's Book.

Workbook

The Workbook provides revision of all the main points in the Student's Book, plus extra listening practice, pronunciation work and a complete self-contained writing course.

Workbook Cassette and CD

This contains listening practice and pronunciation work, plus recordings of some of the reading texts.

Teacher's Book

In this book you'll find step-by-step notes and answers for every exercise. These include closed-book activities to warm the class up before beginning a new set of work. The tapescripts are included in the body of the notes for easy reference.

For every one of the main units there is a one-page photocopiable test, for use as soon as you finish the unit or a couple of weeks later. There are longer mid-course and end-of-course tests which go with the four review units (5, 10, 15 and 20).

At the beginning of the book there is a Zero unit. This consists of two parts.

The first part is a quiz about the Student's Book to help familiarise students with it: how language is described, the kinds of activities they will do, how the list of contents works, what they can find at the back of the book.

The second part is a Student profile. It aims to discover something about each student's language learning history and reasons for studying English, for example, for an exam, for academic studies, for work reasons, out of personal interest, etc. Students can fill the form out individually or by interviewing each other in pairs. The Student profile is similar to needs analysis, which has been used in business English for many years. But it is not only business students who have reasons for learning. General English students also have needs and wants. Knowing about them will help you to plan lessons, to use the coursebook more appropriately and to get to know your students better.

Resource Pack

The Resource Pack contains thirty-seven photocopiable worksheets designed to supplement or extend the Student's Book. The worksheets are based on the themes and grammar points in the book and are linked to the book unit by unit. They were written for this project by ten different ELT teachers. They are very varied, but one thing they have in common is that they provide practical, useful classroom practice. There are full teaching notes for every worksheet.

Resource Site and e-lessons at www.insideout.net

The *Inside Out* website is a constantly updated resource designed to supplement the Student's Book with a guide to useful websites and a topical weekly e-lesson which you can receive free of charge by subscribing online at *www.insideout.net*

Over to you

If you have any comments about *Inside Out* you can contact us via the *Inside Out* website at *www.insideout.net*. Your opinions will help to shape our future publishing. We look forward to hearing from you.

Zero unit answers

(Page numbers refer to the Student's Book.)

1 a) Twenty.

b) They are review units (pp 28, 58, 88, 118).

2 a) Unit 8 *Rich* (p 46)

b) Unit 16 *Lifestyles* (p 99)

c) Unit 5 *Review 1* (p 28)

d) Unit 6 *Shop* (p 38)

e) Unit 7 *Job* (p 45)

3 a) Collocation refers to words that frequently occur together.

b) jazz (p 131)

c) Do you like your city? (p 133)

4 Future forms: *(be) going to* and present continuous (p 50)

5 a) Unit 4 *Fit* (p 25)

b) Unit 19 *Wheels* (p 113)

6 Reginald Kenneth Dwight. (p 5)

7 80,000 – but two million tourists come in the summer. (p 77)

8 A giraffe. (p 100)

Join us online at www.insideout.net

The *Inside Out* website is a huge teacher resource designed to supplement and enrich your teaching with a wealth of fresh, topical, up-to-the-minute material. And it's all FREE!

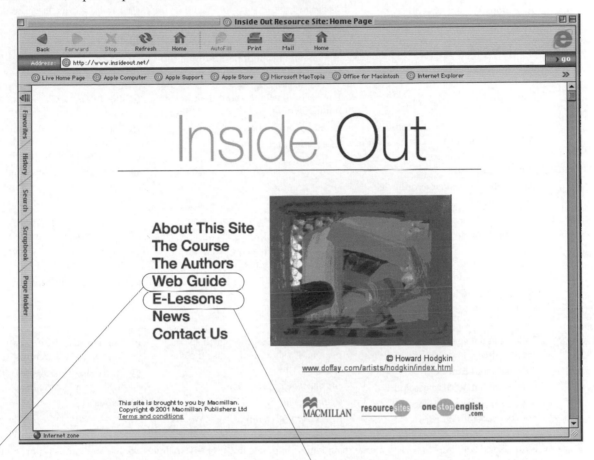

Click on **Web Guide** to add an extra dimension to your teaching.

For every unit in the Student's Book there are direct links to a variety of carefully-selected websites. They provide you with a truly limitless supply of extra supplementary material.

You'll never be stuck for ideas again!

Click on **E-lessons** to receive a free weekly lesson from the *Inside Out* team.

Once you've registered, *English Inside Out* arrives in your E-mail inbox every week. Up-to-date and topical, the E-lessons cover a wide range of topics, including famous people, current events and events in history.

A great start to the week!

(And don't forget to check in the E-lesson Archive for any E-lessons you might have missed.)

Feedback from teachers on the *Inside Out* website.

★ 'I'm really satisfied with the service you provide. Every week I receive enjoyable activities to do with my students. Congratulations!'

★ 'Your site has proved to be of great use in my classes, and my students really enjoy using the material I take to class. Thank you for helping us, teachers, with so many attractive ideas.'

★ 'Thanks again for the materials! You saved me a lot of time this week!'

★ 'I'm astonished by the website and happy to have chosen *Inside Out*.'

★ 'The book is very interesting, and the topics are up-to-date. I find the E-lessons fascinating.'

★ 'All your free lessons are much appreciated and heavily utilised by the staff of this Centre in our general English classes.'

Find out more at: www.insideout.net

0 Zero unit

Book quiz

Look through your book and find the answers to these questions.

1 a) How many units are there in the book?

_____

b) Why are Units 5, 10, 15 and 20 different?

_____

2 Look at the list of contents. In which unit can you:

a) listen to a song called *Money*?

_____

b) read about '104 things to do with a banana'?

_____

c) talk about dating?

_____

d) listen to two men talking about shopping?

_____

e) write a letter of application for a job?

_____

3 Look at the back of the book.

a) Complete this sentence from the Grammar glossary on page 131:

Collocation refers to words that ...

_____

b) Which word illustrates /dʒ/ in the table of phonetic symbols?

_____

c) Complete this question from the beginning of tapescript 07:

Do you like _____?

4 Which grammar structure is dealt with in the Language reference section in Unit 8 *Rich*?

_____

5 Look at the list of contents. Decide which units you think these pictures are in and then check in the unit.

a) _____

b) _____

6 What is Elton John's real name?

_____

7 What is the population of 'Party island' Ibiza?

_____

8 Which animal can last longer without water – a camel or a giraffe?

_____

Student profile

- **Name**

  _____

- **Have you studied English in the past?**

  No ☐ Yes ☐ → When and where? _____

- **Have you got any English language qualifications?**

  No ☐ Yes ☐ → What are they and when did you take them? _____

  _____

- **Do you use English outside the class?**

  No ☐ Yes ☐ → When do you use English and where? _____

  _____

- **Are you studying English, or in English, outside this class?**

  No ☐ Yes ☐ → Please give details _____

  _____

- **Do you speak any other languages?**

  No ☐ Yes ☐ → Which ones? _____

  _____

- **Why are you studying English?**

  I need it for work.

  No ☐ Yes ☐ → What do you do? _____

  _____

  I need it to study.

  No ☐ Yes ☐ → What are you studying? _____

  Where? _____

  I'm going to take an examination.

  No ☐ Yes ☐ → What examination are you going to take? _____

  _____

  When? _____

  For personal interest.

  No ☐ Yes ☐ → What do you like doing in your free time? _____

  _____

Photocopiable

1 Me Overview

The topic of this unit is personal information, particularly people's names, and the grammar focus is on asking questions.

Students start by listening to a woman talking about all the different names she is called by members of her family. This provides revision of vocabulary for family members and aims to get students talking about names in their own families. They listen to some common English names and identify the ones with different long vowel sounds.

The topic is then widened to look at what names students like or dislike and why their parents chose their names. They read a text about famous people who have changed their original names or given their children unusual names. Students' explore the various reasons why people choose particular names.

The subject then changes to how easy it is to remember people's names, and students try a quick memory test using photographs. They then read an article giving some tips for improving your memory which they can also apply to remembering new English words and expressions. They look at some of the vocabulary that can be used to describe people and practise using structures with *look* and *look like*. Next students are introduced to A.L.I.C.E. a computer robot which can answer questions, and this leads into some grammar work on questions: word order in questions and subject questions.

Students then do some work on the song *Stand By Me* before being introduced to an Anecdote, a feature which occurs throughout the book and provides guided extended speaking practice.

Section	Aims	What the students are doing
Introduction page 4	*Listening skills*: listening for specific information	Listening to a woman talking about the different names people call her, and matching them to people.
	Lexis: family words	Talking about names of family members and typical names in your country.
	Pronunciation: long vowel sounds	Identifying the odd one out in lists of common English names.
What's in a name? page 5	*Reading skills*: reading for specific information	Reading a text about famous people to find what the links between them are.
	Conversation skills: fluency work	Talking about how people choose names for their children.
	Lexis: words from the reading text	Completing sentences with words from the reading text.
I never forget a face pages 6–7	*Conversation skills*: fluency work	Talking about techniques for remembering people's names and doing a memory test.
	Reading skills: reading for gist	Matching headings to sections of a text about memory techniques.
	Lexis: describing people	Examining structures with *look* and *look like* and practising describing people.
Meet A.L.I.C.E. page 7	*Reading skills*: reading for gist	Reading a conversation with a computer robot and putting the words in questions in the right order.
	Listening skills: listening to check answers and identify stressed words.	Identifying and practising using the correct stress in questions.
Close up page 8	*Grammar*: word order in questions; subject questions	Identifying the differences in word order between statements and questions. Practising putting the words in questions in the correct order and discussing appropriacy of questions.
		Recognising the difference between subject and object questions and practising asking questions.
Stand By Me page 9	*Listening skills*: listening for detail	Identifying extra words in the lyrics of the song, *Stand By Me*.
		Interpreting the meaning of the song.
	Conversations skills: fluency work	Anecdote: talking about a person who is important to you.

1 Me Teacher's notes

Closed books. Whole class. Write on the board a list of the first names of some of the members of your family and draw an empty family tree. Tell the students that these people are all related to you and they must ask yes/no questions (such as *Is Joe your brother? Is Mary Joe's wife?*) to find out how they are related. If your students don't know many words for family members, list the relevant ones in another section of the board for them to use in their questions. Students who get a *yes* answer to their questions can come up to the board and write in the name in the correct place in the family tree.

If you have time or wish to repeat the activity in a later class for revision, get students to do the same with their family tree for other members of the class to ask questions.

Listening (p 4)

1 🔲 **01 SB p 133**

Focus students' attention on the photo of Susan. Ask them how old they think she is and what kind of person she is. Explain that the first time you play the recording, all they have to do is to identify the name she doesn't like.

Play the recording and allow students to discuss their answers in pairs before checking with the class. Ask if anyone can remember who calls her Maggsie and why (her schoolfriends, because her surname is Maggs).

> 🔲 **01**
>
> My first name's Susan, but the only person who calls me Susan is my dad. Oh, and my sister when she's angry with me, but fortunately that doesn't happen very often now. Most of my friends call me Sue, and so do the people I work with. My old friends call me Maggsie, because my surname is Maggs, and I was always called Maggsie at school. I hated it.
>
> Of course, there's only one person who calls me Mum, and that's my son, but when he's with his friends he calls me Sue.
>
> My mum calls me Sweetheart, and my best friend calls me Suzanne because she's French. My Japanese sister-in-law calls me Suki – apparently, Suki means 'loved one' in Japanese, so that's really nice.
>
> My husband calls me Bunny, but that's another story ...

2 Go through the instructions with the class, then play the recording again. Students match people in Susan's life (*a–h*) with the names that they call her (*1–8*). Allow them to compare answers before checking with the class.

> a 2 b 8 c 6 d 1 e 5 f 3 g 4 h 7

3 Students write down the different names that people call them (or have called them in the past). Encourage them not only to tell their partner about these and who uses the names, but also to say which ones they like and dislike. In a feedback session, find out if there are any interesting nicknames in the class.

Lexis: family words (p 4)

1, 2 Pairwork. Students copy and complete the table with the first names of people in their families, adding more headings and names as necessary. Point out that the Language toolbox has some useful words for talking about family relationships.

3 Make sure students understand the questions before they discuss them in their pairs. When they have finished, put pairs together to form groups of four to compare their findings. If you have a multinational class, try to compile a list of typical names for each country. Are there any names that are popular in more than one country? Are there any names that are popular in one country and exist, but are unpopular or out of fashion, in another? Find out if any of the names have a special meaning.

Long vowel sounds (p 4)

1 🔲 **02 SB p 4**

If your students are familiar with phonemic symbols, you might like to ask them to pronounce the symbols first before you play the recording.

Play the recording and ask students to identify the odd one out in each group. Also ask them to identify which group the odd ones out should go into, but do not check answers at this stage.

2 🔲 **03 SB p 133**

Play the recording for students to check their answers to 2. (This recording has all the names correctly categorised.) Then play it again for them to repeat the names. As a final check, ask students to re-write the groups so that all the names have the same vowel sound.

> 1 Sue 2 Burt 3 Laura 4 Margaret 5 Denise

03

1 /ɔ:/ Paul George Laura Dawn

2 /u:/ Julie Ruth Luke Sue

3 /ɑ:/ Charles Margaret Barbara Grant

4 /i:/ Peter Eve Denise Keith

5 /ɜ:/ Shirley Bernard Earl Burt

What's in a name? (p 5)

Groupwork. Students decide what name they would give the baby girl in the photograph and discuss favourite names for boys. They then talk about how their parents chose their names. In a feedback session, put all the names chosen for the girl on the board and ask the class to vote on the best. Ask groups to report back to the class on any unusual stories they heard about how they got their names.

Reading (p 5)

1 See if the students have any ideas on what links these people before they read the article. You might also like to elicit from the class who these people are and why they are famous. (Elton John is a pop star; David Bowie and Madonna are pop and film stars; Marilyn Monroe was a film star and Demi Moore is one; Bill Clinton is former president of the USA.)

Give students plenty of time to read the article and allow them to discuss their answers before checking with the class.

a) They changed their names.

b) They gave unusual names to their children.

c) They named their children after places.

Note: It may not be obvious to students why Reginald Kenneth Dwight sounds so unsuitable a name for a famous pop star to a native English speaker. You may need to explain that fashions in names change and certain names can take on unexpected connotations and associations in the eighteen years or so between the time when the parents choose names for their baby and when that child wants to enter a particular profession. To many British people, the name Reginald sounds very old-fashioned and boring. Kenneth is also out of fashion now and sounds too serious and studious to fit the image of a pop star, and Dwight is a fairly common name, but perhaps rather odd-sounding and certainly unglamorous.

It might be interesting to ask whether any famous people from the students' own cultures have changed their names for similar reasons and how the original names sound to students of other nationalities.

Students may be interested in the following information.

Top ten girls' and boys' names in England and Wales in 1996.

Girls		Boys
Sophie	1	Jack
Jessica	2	Daniel
Chloe	3	Thomas
Emily	4	James
Lauren	5	Joshua
Rebecca	6	Matthew
Charlotte	7	Ryan
Hannah	8	Samuel
Amy	9	Joseph
Megan	10	Liam

Top ten girls' and boys' names in England and Wales fifty years ago.

Girls		Boys
Margaret	1	John
Patricia	2	David
Christine	3	Michael
Mary	4	Peter
Jean	5	Robert
Ann	6	Anthony
Susan	7	Brian
Janet	8	Alan
Maureen	9	William
Barbara	10	James

2 Students work individually to mark the reasons with a tick or a cross according to whether they appear in the article or not. Check answers with the class.

✔: a, b, d, e, g, h

✗: c, f

3 Pairwork. Ask students to make a note of any other reasons they can think of. In a class feedback session note all the suggestions on the board. Then ask students if any of these reasons account for why their parents chose their names.

Lexis (p 5)

1 Students should complete the sentences individually at first, but allow them to compare answers in pairs or groups before checking with the class.

a) sounds b) make c) feel d) call
e) after f) idea

2 Pairwork. Students ask each other about the items in Exercise 1 and report back to the class on anything interesting they have learnt about their partners.

I never forget a face (p 6)

Warm-up

Bring to class a tray with around twenty common objects (which your students will know the words for) on it, covered with a cloth. Tell the students that you are going to test their memories: they have thirty seconds to look at the tray and should try to memorise what is there. Uncover the tray and let them look. When the thirty seconds are up, cover it again with the cloth.

Ask the students not to talk to anyone, but to write down all the objects they can remember. The winner is the one with the longest list. Ask students how they remembered the objects. Did they remember the position of each one? Did they note the first letter of the name of each one? Did they form a visual picture of the tray? Ask how many people thought in English as they did the activity.

1 Focus students' attention on the title of this section. Ask them if they are good at recognising people they have perhaps only met once before, and, if they can remember their faces, can they also remember their names. Ask students who claim to be good at remembering names to describe the techniques they use.

2 Students look at the faces and names for thirty seconds, then turn to page 124. Find out who found it easiest to remember all the names and again, ask them to try to explain what techniques they used.

Reading (p 6)

1 Go through the headings with the class before they read the text and try to match them to the different paragraphs. You may need to explain that *making associations* means making connections between one thing and another. For example, it is said that waiters can often remember who ordered which dish in a restaurant by making associations between the way the people look and the dish they have ordered, so if a fat person orders fish, they make a mental picture of a big fat fish, etc.

When students have read the text and found an appropriate heading for each paragraph, check answers with the class and ask them if they think this advice would work for them.

> 1 c   2 a   3 e   4 d   5 f   6 b

2 Pairwork. Students discuss the questions. In a feedback session, make a list of all the suggestions for ways of helping to learn and remember new English words and expressions. Encourage students to try some of these and report back later on how well they work.

Lexis: describing people (p 7)

1 Give students a few minutes to decide which nouns, noun phrases and adjectives complete sentence *a* and which sentence *b*. Encourage them to say the sentences aloud to get a feel for what sounds right. Check answers with the class.

> a) friendly, intelligent, shy, very young, middle-aged, stressed out, intelligent, about sixty, Greek, fit, a bit tired, rich
>
> b) a banker, a typical mum, a doctor, a waiter, a Swedish au pair, a student, a retired police officer

2 Elicit answers to the questions and then ask students to make up a few more sentences using *looks* and *looks like*.

> *Look(s)* + adjective
> *Look(s) like* + noun

3 Students work individually to write their sentences. Remind them not to include the names of the people, but to leave a space or a line. Go round and encourage them to use a mixture of both *looks* and *looks like* in their sentences.

4 Students exchange sentences and complete the ones they have received. They should check answers with the person who wrote the original sentences.

5 Repeat the activity with students writing sentences about three members of the class. Discourage them from writing anything embarrassing or offensive. They then exchange with a partner and try to fill in the correct names.

Meet A.L.I.C.E. (p 7)

1 Give students time to read the responses and establish who A.L.I.C.E. is. Do not check answers at this stage.

Optional activity

Students might like to take the letters of their own names and make words from them to describe themselves. (Obviously this will only work if students have fairly long names.)

2 Students work alone or in pairs to put the words in the questions in the right order. Do not check answers at this stage.

3 🔲 **04 SB p 133**

Play the recording for students to check their answers to Exercises 1 and 2.

If you have time and access to the internet, the class might be interested in visiting A.L.I.C.E. at www.alicebot.org.

> A.L.I.C.E. is a computer robot at www.alicebot.org.
> 1 What does your name mean?
> 2 Where were you born?
> 3 Where did you grow up?
> 4 What do you look like?
> 5 What do you do?
> 6 Do you like your job?
> 7 Can you speak any foreign languages?
> 8 Are you married?
> 9 Have you got any children?
> 10 Who created you?

A.L.I.C.E. is an award-winning chat robot at www.alicebot.org. She's intelligent and funny and has won prizes for being the most human-like computer. She was created by Dr Richard S. Wallace. Six thousand people a month chat to A.L.I.C.E. Some people spend up to four and a half hours a day chatting online with her, and some have even said they prefer her to their own girlfriends. Here is a typical conversation.

(A = A.L.I.C.E.; Q = Questioner)

A: Hi. My name's A.L.I.C.E.

Q: What does your name mean?

A: It means Artificial Linguistic Internet Computer Entity.

Q: Where were you born?

A: I was born in Bethlehem, Pennsylvania.

Q: Where did you grow up?

A: I think I grew up in San Francisco.

Q: What do you look like?

A: I'm blue and I've got one wheel.

Q: What do you do?

A: I talk to people on the web.

Q: Do you like your job?

A: Yes, I have a passion for my work!

Q: Can you speak any foreign languages?

A: No, I only speak English at the moment, but I'd like to learn.

Q: Are you married?

A: No, I am single. How about you?

Q: Have you got any children?

A: No, but you can download me and make A.L.I.C.E. clones for yourself!

Q: Who created you?

A: Dr Richard S. Wallace – he is very, very clever! He's also very kind and generous. In fact he's one of the most ...

Q: Yeah, yeah, okay, A.L.I.C.E., Thank you.

4 Ask the students to underline the words in the questions that they think are stressed before they listen to the recording again. Encourage them to work with a partner and to say the questions out loud to get a feel for what sounds right.

Then play the recording for them to check their answers and repeat the questions.

1 What does your name <u>mean</u>?
2 Where were you <u>born</u>?
3 Where did you <u>grow</u> up?
4 What do you <u>look</u> like?
5 What do you <u>do</u>?
6 Do you like your <u>job</u>?
7 Can you speak any foreign <u>languages</u>?
8 Are you <u>married</u>?
9 Have you got any <u>children</u>?
10 Who <u>created</u> you?

5 Pairwork. Put students in pairs with people they don't know well. If this is impossible, you might like to suggest that they invent characters for themselves or choose a famous person to be. Students use appropriate questions from 2 to interview their partners and should also make up some more questions of their own. Point out that there are some useful structures in the Language toolbox. They should then report back to the class.

Close up (p 8)

Questions: word order

1 Pairwork. Students look at the table and discuss the questions. Check answers with the class. If you have a multilingual class, ask several members to explain how questions are formed in their languages. Remind students to look at the Language reference section for more information on word order in questions.

a) Statement word order: subject + verb. Question word order: verb + subject.

b) When there is no auxiliary (present simple and past simple).

c) Students' own answers.

2 You might like to get individual students around the class to change the statements to questions and then put students in pairs to practise asking the questions.

a) Are you hungry?
b) Do you smoke?
c) Can you play the guitar?
d) Have you been to Disneyland?
e) Where do you live?
f) What is your favourite colour?
g) When did you leave school?
h) How many CDs have you got?

3 Ask students to write the words in the questions in the correct order and then check answers. Do not get them actually to ask anyone these questions.

a) How old are you?

b) Do you believe in life after death?

c) How much do you weigh?

d) Have you ever stolen anything?

e) How much money do you earn?

f) How many partners have you had?

4 Groupwork. Students discuss which of the questions in 3 can be asked in the various situations. In a feedback session, find out how much agreement there is around the class and how far the answers depend on the different cultures the students come from.

Subject questions (p 8)

1 Focus attention on the diagram and go through the explanation with the class. Elicit the difference in word order between object and subject questions and ask students to make up further examples of each. Point out that you don't use an auxiliary with a subject question. There is more information about subject questions in the Language reference section. Remind students to use this reference to help them with and remind them of various language points.

Subject questions have the same word order as statements (subject + verb). Subject questions do not use *do, does, did*.

2 Pairwork. Students turn to their respective pages and follow the instructions.

Student A

a) Who created Sherlock Holmes?

b) Who did JK Rowling create?

c) Who created Tarzan?

d) What did Alexander Fleming discover?

e) Who invented the telephone?

f) Where did Elvis Presley live?

g) Who built the Taj Mahal?

h) What did the French football team win in 1998?

Student B

a) Who did Arthur Conan Doyle create?

b) Who created Harry Potter?

c) Who did Edgar Rice Burroughs create?

d) Who discovered penicillin?

e) What did Alexander Graham Bell invent?

f) Who lived in Graceland?

g) What did Shah Jahan build?

h) Which team / Who won the World Cup in 1998?

Stand By Me (p 9)

Song

Students may be familiar with this song. Although it is quite old (it has been recorded many times), it was used relatively recently in the film of the same name, which students may have seen.

1 Encourage students to read the lines aloud to see which words don't sound right and disrupt the rhythm. Do not check answers at this stage, but allow students to compare notes in pairs or groups.

2 🔲 **05 SB p 9**

Play the recording for students to check their answers. If they would like, play it again for them just to listen and enjoy.

a) good   b) Disney   c) flashing   d) probably
e) ever   f) up   g) blue   h) over   i) rocky   j) out
k) big   l) up

🔲 **05**

Stand By Me

When the night has come,
And the land is dark,
And the moon is the only light we see,
No, I won't be afraid,
Oh, I won't be afraid,
Just as long as you stand, stand by me.

So darlin', darlin', stand by me, oh stand by me.
Oh stand, stand by me, stand by me.

If the sky that we look upon
Should tumble and fall,
Or the mountains should crumble to the sea,
I won't cry, I won't cry,
No, I won't shed a tear,
Just as long as you stand, stand by me.

So darlin', darlin', stand by me, oh stand by me.
Oh stand now, stand by me, stand by me.

And darlin', darlin', stand by me, oh stand by me.
Oh stand now, stand by me, stand by me.
Whenever you're in trouble,
Won't you stand by me, oh stand by me.
Oh stand now, oh stand, stand by me.

3 Allow students to discuss the question in pairs and report their views back to the class.

Best interpretation: c).

4 Pairwork. Give students time to consider the question before they have to start speaking. You might like to ask them to do this at home and come to the next class ready to share their stories with a partner.

Anecdote (p 9)

See the Introduction on page 4 for more ideas on how to set up, monitor and repeat Anecdotes.

1 📼 **06 SB p 133**

This is an example of an Anecdote, a feature you will find throughout the course, where students are trained in extended speaking and asked to talk in a structured way about personal experience.

Initially, students simply listen to Tom and tick the topics he talks about. Allow students to compare their answers in pairs before you check with the whole class.

> Tom talks about: the person's full name; when they met; where they live; how often he sees him; why he's important to him; his best qualities; what he doesn't like about him; the last time he saw him.

📼 **06**

Dave Carter's my best friend. We met when we were five years old because our parents were friends and we went to the same school. He works in a different city now, so I only see him at weekends and during the holidays. He's important to me because he knows me so well. We have a really good laugh together and we enjoy the same things – football, clubbing, girls, the usual stuff. When I'm feeling down or when I need to talk to somebody, I can always call him. Recently, I had girlfriend problems and he was great – he's a really good listener. He just lets you speak and he listens. But he isn't perfect! He's always late for everything and he never says sorry. Never! The last time I saw him was last weekend. We arranged to meet at four o'clock to play football, and he arrived at half past six! It was nearly dark! Oh well, nobody's perfect, are they? He's still a really good mate.

2 Pairwork. Students note down as much information as they can remember about what Tom said. Allow them to compare notes with another pair if they wish. Then play the recording again for them to check their answers.

3 Pairwork. Give students plenty of time to decide who they are going to talk about and to choose the topics they want to include. They then take turns to talk about the person to their partner.

Test

At the end of each unit there is a photocopiable test. Use it at the end of the unit, or a couple of lessons later. Allow about 30 minutes for it. It scores 40 points: to get a percentage, multiply the student's score by 2.5. You may not wish to use a grading system, but if you do this is a possibility.

35–40 = A (excellent); 25–34 = B (good); 20–24 = C (pass)

To make the text more complete, add an oral and / or a written component. For example, ask students to talk in pairs about a person who is important to them and / or write a description of a person in the class.

> Scoring: one point per correct answer unless otherwise indicated.
>
> **1**   1 looks   2 looked like   3 looked   4 looks like
>
> **2**   1   chose   2 named   3 make   4 feel   5 sounds
>   6   calls
>
> **3**   1   door, sport
>   2   new, shoe
>   3   arm, car
>   4   free, keep
>   5   bird, work
>
> **4**   1   step-father   2 niece   3 half-sister   4 uncle
>   5   daughter   6 ex-husband   7 grandmother
>   8   brother-in-law
>
> **5**   1   were you
>   2   is
>   3   do you
>   4   chose
>   5   you have
>   6   Have you
>   7   do you like
>   8   do you
>   9   is
>   10 did you start
>   11 was
>   12 is (Leonardo di Caprio)

1 Me Test

Name: _____   **Total:** _____ /40

---

1 Vocabulary – describing people *4 points*
<u>Underline</u> the correct alternative.

1   She **looks / looks like** very friendly.

2   He **looked / looked like** a student.

3   They all **looked / looked like** exhausted.

4   She really **looks / looks like** my sister.

2 Vocabulary – verb collocations *6 points*
Complete the dialogues with verbs in the box. Put the verb in the correct form.

| call   choose   feel   make   name   sound |

A: Who (1) _____ your name?

B: My mum. I was (2) _____ after my grandad.

*   *   *

C: We need to (3) _____ a decision about what to do for Peter's birthday.

D: Well, it's his 18th, so we need to do something to make him (4) _____ really special.

*   *   *

E: Good-looking and rich! She (5) _____ really nice. What's her name again?

F: Nicola – but everyone (6) _____ her Nic.

3 Long vowel sounds *10 points*
Put two more words with the same vowel sound into each group.

| arm   bird   car   free   door   keep   new   sport shoe   work |

1   /ɔː/ saw, _____ , _____

2   /uː/ blue, _____ , _____

3   /ɑː/ far, _____ , _____

4   /iː/ sea, _____ , _____

5   /ɜː/ sir, _____ , _____

4 Vocabulary – family words *8 points*
Write the male or female equivalents.

1   _____ step-mother

2   nephew _____

3   half-brother _____

4   _____ aunt

5   son _____

6   _____ ex-wife

7   grandfather _____

8   _____ sister-in-law

5 Questions *12 points*
Complete the questions to a famous person.

1   'Where _____ born?'
    'Hollywood.'

2   'When _____ your birthday?'
    '11th November.'

3   'Where _____ live?'
    'Los Angeles.'

4   'Who _____ your name?'
    'My mother chose it. I'm named after Leonardo da Vinci.'

5   'Do _____ a nickname?'
    'Yes, I do. My friends call me "The Noodle".'

6   '_____ got any bad habits?'
    'Yes, I've got several bad habits. For one, I bite my nails.'

7   'What kind of music _____ ?'
    'I like all kinds of music, but the Beatles are my favourite.'

8   'What _____ do in you spare time?'
    'I play pool and basketball.'

9   'Who _____ your favourite actor?'
    'Jack Nicholson.'

10 'When _____ acting?'
    'I started acting in my early teens.'

11 'What _____ your first film?'
    'My first film was *Critters 3*.'

12 'What _____ your name?'
    'My name is ... (*Can you guess?*)'

Photocopiable   **19**

2 Place Overview

This unit is about places, and the emphasis is on ways to describe them. There is also grammar work on countable and uncountable nouns, asking questions about what people and places are like and questions about quantity.

Students begin by discussing photographs of four places from around the world and finding common features in the pictures. They listen to people who live in the four places describing them and what it is like to live there. This leads into language work on asking and answering *What's it like?* questions and some practise in identifying and using countable and uncountable nouns.

The emphasis on description continues in the next section where students re-write a letter describing a holiday destination, changing it from a very negative description to a positive one. They then do some work on country and nationality words and the correct stress on each.

Next, students look at a competition to win a dream holiday. They produce their own entries to the competition by answering some general knowledge questions about places around the world and writing a short paragraph on a holiday destination they would like to go to.

Next they look at how to talk about quantity; this is linked to the work they did earlier with countable and uncountable nouns. They practise asking each other questions using *How much?* and *How many?*

Finally they do a communicative activity about cities of the world and end with an Anecdote, an extended speaking activity in which they tell a partner about the best city they have ever visited.

Section	Aims	What the students are doing
Introduction pages 10–11	*Conversation skills*: fluency work	Looking at photos and discussing what it is like to live in these places.
	Lexis: features of cities	Identifying features of places in photographs.
	Listening skills: listening for gist	Listening to people talking and establishing who likes the place where they live.
		Completing sentences from the listening with adjectives.
Close up page 11	*Grammar*: *What's it like?*; countable and uncountable nouns	Matching questions and answers.
		Identifying countable and uncountable nouns and forming their plurals.
		Asking questions with *What's it like? / What are they like?*
First impressions page 12	*Writing skills*: changing negative to positive	Re-writing a letter from a holiday destination to make it positive rather than negative.
	Pronunciation: word stress	Completing a table with countries and nationalities and identifying the correct stress.
	Conversation skills: fluency work	Discussing what is the best in the world.
Dream holiday page 13	*Reading skills*: reading for gist	Reading a competition to win a holiday and ranking the destinations in order.
	Writing skills: a fifty-word paragraph	Completing a competition entry by answering questions and writing about where you would like to go.
Close up page 14	*Grammar*: quantity	Completing a text and talking about what country it might describe.
		Practising using *How much?* and *How many?* correctly.
Cities of the world page 15	*Conversation skills*: fluency work	Identifying capital cities.
		Talking about the location of cities.
		Anecdote: talking about the best city you have ever visited.

Place *Teacher's notes*

Closed books. Whole class. Think of a city that you and your students know well, or which is so famous that they are likely to know about it. Tell them that you are thinking of a city and that they must ask questions to find out where it is. Encourage them to ask about buildings and things in the city as well as which country it is in. A student who identifies the city can then think of a new city and answer questions from the class.

Pairwork. Students look at the photos and check the names of the cities. Students then discuss the questions in their pairs and report back to the class.

Lexis (p 10)

1 Students could mark the letters of the photos in which they find each item in the box. Point out that some of the items may be in more than one photo. Allow them to compare notes in pairs or small groups before checking answers.

> a) Venice: a canal, a church
> b) La Bastide: a fountain, a church(?), a square
> c) Heidelberg: a river, a hill, a bridge, a castle
> d) Rio de Janeiro: high-rise buildings, a hill, a statue, the sea

2 Allow students to discuss the question in pairs or small groups. If none of the items in the box can be found at a reasonable distance from your school, you may like to substitute other items, such as a road, a post office, etc.

Listening (p 11)

1 🔲 07 SB p 133

Go through the instructions with the students. Play the recording and ask them to match the speakers to the photos and then to say who likes living in their city and who doesn't. Encourage students to say what they can remember about the reasons the speakers give.

> 1 d   2 c   3 b   4 a
> 1 and 2 like where they live.
> 3 and 4 don't like where they live.

🔲 **07**

1

(I = Interviewer; P = Paulo)

I: *Do you like your city?*

P: *Oh yes, I feel lucky to be living in a city that's so big and exciting. I love looking out of my apartment window over the high-rise buildings.*

I: *What's the city centre like?*

P: *Some people say it's too noisy and crowded, but I love that. There's always something to see and do. We also have the most famous beach in the world – Copacabana Beach. Then, on the other side of the city, there are beautiful mountains. The highest one is called Corcovado, and it has the famous statue of Christ. If you look down at the city from there, the view is spectacular.*

I: *What's the weather like?*

P: *It's great most of the time. The only time I don't like Rio much is in the summer: it's too hot and humid.*

2

(I = Interviewer; G = Gisela)

I: *Do you like your city?*

G: *Yes, it's wonderful. I think my city has everything.*

I: *What's the architecture like?*

G: *It's a mixture of old and new with plenty of shops for everybody. The castle is the most famous monument, and at night it looks amazing.*

I: *What's the nightlife like?*

G: *It's a young city because of the university, so there are plenty of cheap restaurants and interesting cafés and bars. It's got a great nightlife.*

I: *And what are the people like?*

G: *Well, some people are a bit reserved, but in general they're really friendly.*

3

(I = Interviewer; A = Armelle)

I: *Where do you live?*

A: *Well, I live in a small village with my parents. My grandparents live here too, and my aunts and uncles. In fact, I think I'm related to about fifty per cent of the people in my village.*

I: *What's your village like?*

A: *It's very pretty. The countryside is beautiful, and the air is lovely and clean. But it's too quiet. I find it so dull and boring here – there aren't any discos or cinemas.*

I: *What are the people like?*

A: *Oh, they're lovely, but there aren't many young people. I want to go and live in the city. Soon.*

4

(I = Interviewer; L = Luigi)

I: *What do you think of your city?*

L: *It is a very special place. There is nowhere else in the world like my city – it's so romantic.*

I: *What's the city centre like?*

L: *The buildings are beautiful, and we have San Marco, one of the most famous churches in the world. San Marco Square is wonderful, and during carnival in February Venice is the best place in the world to be.*

I: *Do you like living here?*

L: *No, I really hate living here. It's horrible. There are too many tourists everywhere.*

I: *Oh dear. What are the shops like?*

L: *Well, because of the tourists the shops are too expensive and the canals are dirty and polluted. My city is not big enough for all these people. Why don't they leave us in peace?*

2 Allow students to work in pairs to complete the descriptions if they wish. Point out that they come from the recording, so students should try to complete them in the same way as the speakers. Do not check answers at this stage.

3 Play the recording again for students to check their answers. Then ask them to work individually to use the adjective combinations to describe places in their countries before comparing ideas with a partner. Ask pairs to report back to the class. Encourage them to use more adjective phrases from the listening, such as *the most famous beach in the world, the view is spectacular, great nightlife, the people are really friendly*, etc.

a) exciting   b) crowded   c) humid   d) new
e) clean   f) boring   g) polluted

Close up (p 11)

What's it like?

1 Ask students to answer the question before drawing their attention to the Language reference section on page 15 which has more information about the question *What's it like?*

b)   It's big and exciting.

2 Give students a couple of minutes to think up their three other ways of answering the question, then go round the class getting suggestions.

Possible answers
It's small, boring, dirty, polluted, old, new, great, horrible, etc.

3 Ask students to match the questions and responses. Check each answer by asking one student to ask the question and another to give the appropriate response. You might then ask students to think up their own *What's it like?* questions to ask their classmates.

a 4   b 1   c 2   d 3

Nouns: countable/uncountable (p 11)

1 Establish what we mean by countable and uncountable nouns and ask students for some examples of each. Allow them to work in pairs or small groups to complete the table and remind them that they will find more information about countable and uncountable nouns in the Language reference section on page 15. If your students have problems with these structures, you might like to go through the Language reference section with the class first.

See below.

2 Students use the nouns in the box to continue the table. Check answers with the class.

Nouns	Countable	Uncountable	Singular form	Plural form
a) weather	✗	✔	weather	–
b) architecture	✗	✔	architecture	–
c) people	✔	✗	person	people
d) shops	✔	✗	shop	shops
traffic	✗	✔	traffic	–
restaurant	✔	✗	restaurant	restaurants
nightlife	✗	✔	nightlife	–
public transport	✗	✔	public transport	–
park	✔	✗	park	parks
cinema	✔	✗	cinema	cinemas

3 Pairwork. Establish that nouns with regular plural forms simply add an s to the end of the singular. Ask students for an example of an irregular plural. Students then discuss the questions and report back to the class. Ask them for any further examples of irregular plurals that they know.

a)   person
b)   a man – men; a woman – women;
     a child – children; a foot – feet; a tooth – teeth
c)   Add an s.

4 Pairwork. Students should either choose two places that they both know, or make sure when they start asking questions that the person answering the question is always the one with knowledge of the place being asked about. Demonstrate the activity first with a confident student and point out that we use the plural form of countable nouns when we are talking about things in general. Pairs form questions with nouns from Exercises 1 and 2 and take turns to ask and answer about the places they have chosen.

First impressions (p 12)

Writing

1 Whole class. Students read the letter and say how Rick feels about the place he is describing. Ask them to give some examples of things that he doesn't like about the place. When they give you an example, ask them to give you an opposite opinion of it. So, for example, if they say he doesn't like the weather, they should produce a sentence praising the weather, for example, *The weather is fantastic.* Do this for a couple of examples, to prepare students for the next exercise and to encourage them to think of their own positive sentences for praising something rather than simply substituting the opposite adjective (see below).

> He feels very negative about it.

2 Students have to re-write Rick's letter making it as positive as they can. Substituting the opposite adjective for Rick's negative ones will work most of the time, but not always, so you may need to explain that, for example, *The city centre is really clean and unpolluted* would be a slightly odd thing to say in praise of a city. We don't normally praise something by mentioning the absence of something negative like pollution. *The city centre is lovely and clean* would be more natural. Similarly we would be more likely to say *The sun hasn't stopped shining since I arrived* than *It hasn't rained since I arrived.* Encourage students to take the idea of what is bad in Rick's first letter and think of something natural to say on the same subject in their more positive version. Allow them to work in pairs if they wish and to compare their letters with others before you check answers with the class.

> *Sample answer*
>
> Hi!
>
> I've been here a week, and my first impressions are really good. In fact, they are fantastic. The city is big and exciting. Really exciting! The buildings are old and beautiful, and there are some lovely historic monuments.
>
> The city centre is lovely and clean, and public transport is great / very good. The buses continue all night, and it's easy to get a taxi. This probably explains why the streets are crowded / full of people after six o'clock in the evening and the nightlife is great. There's plenty to do!
>
> The people look cheerful / happy and they're very friendly. I suppose it could be because the weather is lovely / great / good / amazing – it's warm and the sun hasn't stopped shining since I arrived. Seven days of blue sky – can you imagine?

> But the best thing is the food – I love it. And the coffee tastes wonderful. There are plenty of restaurants and they're cheap.
>
> I don't want to come home. I really <u>love</u> it here.
>
> Love, Rick
>
> XXX

Word stress (p 12)

1 08 SB p 12

Allow students to work in pairs or groups to complete the table. When they underline the stressed syllables, encourage them to say the words out loud so that they can get a feel for what sounds right. Then play the recording for them to check their answers. Finally, elicit what happens to the word stress in each set (A, B and C).

Country	Nationality
A	
Cuba	**Cu**ban
Turkey	**Tur**kish
Mo**roc**co	Mo**roc**can
Argen**tin**a	Argen**tin**ian
B	
Egypt	E**gyp**tian
Italy	I**tal**ian
Hungary	Hun**ga**rian
Canada	Ca**na**dian
C	
China	Chi**nese**
Malta	Mal**tese**
Portugal	Portu**guese**
Ja**pan**	Japa**nese**

> In group A the stress pattern is the same.
>
> In group B the first syllable is stressed in the country and the second syllable is stressed in the nationality.
>
> In group C -ese is always stressed at the end of the nationality adjective.

2 Pairwork. Students work individually to choose their three countries, write them down with the nationality and mark the correct stress. They then take turns to tell their partner where they would like to go and why.

Discussion (p 12)

1 Groupwork. In small groups, students discuss the two sentences and report back to the class.

2 Still in their groups, students use the topics in the box, and any others they can think of, together with the nationalities they have learnt to make as many new sentences as possible.

3 Groups look at their sentences and decide which ones they all agree on. Try to keep the discussion in English as much as possible. They then compare their results with other groups.

Dream holiday (p 13)

Books closed. Whole class. Brainstorm different kinds of holidays and things that you can do on holiday and write suggestions up on the board. For example, skiing holiday, beach holiday, adventure holiday, working holiday, learning to play golf, tennis or some other sport, visiting archaeological sights, sailing, cruise, walking, climbing, safari. Find out which students have done, which they like best and which they would really like to do.

1 Students work individually to read through the holiday destinations in the competition and put them in the order according to which they would like best. They then explain their choices in pairs. Encourage them to give full reasons for their choices, with reference to the information in the competition and their own preferences.

2 Pairs work together to try to win the holiday. They have to answer the questions in Part A and in Part B write a fifty-word explanation of why they would like to go to their chosen destination. Obviously you can't offer a holiday to the winner, but if you want to add an element of fun and real competition to this activity, you might provide a small prize (preferably something holiday-related) to spur them on. If you decide to do this and there is enthusiasm for the idea, you could ask the winners to compose a postcard to send back to the rest of the class telling them where they are and what they are doing.

3 Students can check their answers to Part A on page 124. They should compare their summaries with others. If you are having a real competition, you can either take the summaries in and judge them yourself or display them in the classroom and ask students to vote for the best.

> Part A: 1 a 2 b 3 a 4 c 5 b 6 c

Close up (p 14)

Quantity

1 The aim of this exercise is to practise ways of talking about quantity. There is more information about this in the Language reference section on page 15, but you might want to concentrate on the fun aspects of the activity first and do some closer study of the language later.

Students could work individually or in pairs to complete the text. Do not check answers at this stage, but if all your students come from the same country, ask for various suggestions for which country this could be and why it could or could not be their own country. If you have a multinational group, ask individual students from different places to say which country they think it is and why it could or could not be a description of their country.

2 🔲 09 SB p 14

Play the recording for students to check their answers.

> 1 meat 2 cigarettes 3 coffee 4 wine 5 hours
> 6 sleep 7 people 8 cars 9 noise

3 Remind students of the work they have already done on countable and uncountable nouns. If necessary, go through the section on this in the Language reference section on page 15 and ask them to say which of the words in the box in Exercise 1 are countable and which uncountable.

Focus attention on the table and ask students to refer back to the text to help them choose a suitable heading for each category. Check answers with the class.

> A: Use with countable nouns
>
> B: Use with uncountable nouns
>
> C: Use with countable and uncountable nouns

4 Allow students to work in pairs or to compare their answers with others before checking with the class.

> a) much b) lots of c) far too much
> d) enough e) a lot of f) enough

5 Students work individually to decide which of the sentences are true for them. They re-write any that are not true and compare sentences with a partner. Ask pairs to report back to the class on their eating and drinking habits.

6 Pairwork. Demonstrate the activity with a confident student first, asking and answering questions about daily habits using the question frame. Encourage them to use their own nouns and verbs to extend the activity beyond the ideas given on the page. Go round checking that they are using *How much* and *How many* correctly.

> *Possible questions*
>
> How much *chocolate / sleep / money / wine / coffee / meat* etc.?
>
> How many *e-mails / bad TV programmes / friends / people* etc.?

Cities of the world (p 15)

1 Pairwork. Students discuss and identify the six capitals. Do not check answers at this stage.

> The capitals are Tokyo (Japan), Seoul (South Korea), Reykjavik (Iceland), Berlin (Germany), Cairo (Egypt), Prague (Czech Republic)

2 Students turn to their respective pages and follow the instructions, telling each other the locations of the cities marked on their maps. After the students have checked their answers with each other, find out if anyone has visited any of the cities. If so, encourage them to tell the rest of the class about their visit.

> *Possible answers*
>
> Student A
>
> a) Tokyo is in the centre of Japan.
>
> b) Nice is in the south-east of France.
>
> c) Seoul is in the north-west of South Korea.
>
> d) Reykjavik is in the south-west of Iceland.
>
> e) Berlin is in the north-east of Germany.
>
> Student B
>
> f) Barcelona is in the north-east of Spain.
>
> g) Los Angeles is in the south-west of the USA.
>
> h) Cairo is in the north-east of Egypt.
>
> i) Melbourne is in the south-east of Australia.
>
> j) Prague is in the centre of the Czech Republic.

3 Pairwork. Students choose cities they would like to live in and take turns to tell each other their reasons. Go round offering help and encouragement and then get some pairs to report back to the class on their discussions.

Anecdote (p 15)

See the Introduction on page 4 for more ideas on how to set up, monitor and repeat Anecdotes.

Pairwork. Give students plenty of time to decide which city they are going to talk about and to read the questions. They then take turns to talk about their city to their partner.

Test

> Scoring: one point per correct answer unless otherwise indicated.
>
> **1** 1 churches 2 countries 3 children 4 feet
> 5 people 6 women 7 men 8 teeth
>
> **2** (½ point per correct answer)
> 1 U 2 U 3 C 4 U 5 C 6 U 7 U 8 U 9 U
> 10 C 11 U 12 C
>
> **3** 1 bridge 2 high-rise 3 castle
> 4 squares, statues 5 fountain
>
> **4** (½ point per correct word and ½ point per correct stress)
> 1 Bra<u>zil</u>ian 2 <u>Ca</u>nada 3 Chi<u>nese</u> 4 <u>I</u>taly
> 5 Japa<u>nese</u>
>
> **5** 1 a few 2 a little 3 a few 4 many 5 a few
> 6 much 7 lots of 8 a little 9 much 10 a little

2 Place Test

Name: **Total:** ____ /40

1 Plurals *8 points*

Write the plural of each word.

1 church _____

2 country _____

3 child _____

4 foot _____

5 person _____

6 woman _____

7 man _____

8 tooth _____

2 Countable & uncountable nouns *6 points*

Are these nouns countable (*C*) or uncountable (*U*)?

1 love _____   7 traffic _____

2 food _____   8 architecture _____

3 restaurant _____   9 work _____

4 music _____   10 shop _____

5 park _____   11 nightlife _____

6 weather _____   12 car _____

3 Vocabulary – describing places *6 points*

Add the missing vowels (*a, e, i, o, u*) to complete the sentences about some famous cities.

1 'Pont Neuf' is the oldest br__dg__ in Paris.

2 Kiev is a city of two halves. One half is very old and the other half, over the river, is full of modern h__gh-r__s__ buildings.

3 In Edinburgh, you can see the c__stl__ on the hill from almost anywhere in the city.

4 Kathmandu is a fascinating ancient city. It has dozens of sq__ __r__s to walk around and thousands of st__t__ __s of the Hindu gods.

5 People throw money into the 'Trevi F__ __nt__ __n' in Rome to guarantee that they will return to the city.

4 Vocabulary & pronunciation – countries & nationalities *10 points*

Complete the table. <u>Underline</u> the stressed syllable in the words you write.

Country	Nationality
Arg<u>en</u>tina	Argen<u>ti</u>nian
Bra<u>zil</u>	1 _____
2 _____	Ca<u>na</u>dian
<u>Chi</u>na	3 _____
4 _____	I<u>ta</u>lian
Ja<u>pan</u>	5 _____

5 Expressing quantity *10 points*

<u>Underline</u> the correct alternative.

Hi. We arrived in Thailand (1) **a few / a little** days ago. We're going to spend (2) **a few / a little** time in Bangkok and then go to one of the islands for (3) **a few / a little** weeks. There are (4) **many / much** things to do and see in Bangkok. Yesterday, we visited (5) **a few / a little** places (some temples and the zoo), but we are spending far too (6) **many / much** time in cafés and bars! There are (7) **lots of / much** wonderful shops here, and I've already bought (8) **a few / a little** jewellery. I think I've spent too (9) **lots of / much** money already! The monsoon starts soon. There was even (10) **a few / a little** rain this morning. Love, Katy xxx

3 Couples *Overview*

The topic of this unit is relationships, particularly romantic ones.

Students start by looking at information about famous Hollywood couples who are no longer together. They answer questions about them and then discuss some statements about relationships.

In the next section, students practise using more language to talk about relationships. They look at cartoons of a failed love affair and write the story. They then do some work on past simple and past participle forms of irregular verbs.

A television game show forms the basis for the next section. Students listen to a couple being asked the same questions about their first meeting. They score points for every answer they give that is the same.

Students then do some grammar work on past tense forms, choosing between the past simple and the past continuous before reading some more stories of true love.

The unit ends with the song, *Suspicious Minds*. Students complete gaps in the song lyrics and discuss the meaning of the lyrics.

Section	Aims	What the students are doing
Introduction pages 16–17	*Reading skills*: reading for specific information	Reading information about famous couples and answering questions.
	Lexis: vocabulary of relationships	Completing sentences with words from the reading text.
	Conversation skills: discussion	Discussing whether or not they agree with statements about relationships.
Ross & Jane page 17	*Writing skills*: writing a story	Writing the story of a relationship.
	Pronunciation: irregular verbs	Completing a table with the past simple and past participle forms of irregular verbs and looking at the sound groups.
Let's get personal page 18	*Listening skills*: listening for specific information	Listening to part of a game show and determining how many points the contestants score.
Close up page 19	*Grammar*: past tense forms – past simple and past continuous	Practising using regular and irregular verbs in the past simple.
		Choosing between the past simple and the past continuous.
		Listening to sound effects and using the past simple and past continuous to describe what they hear.
True love page 20	*Reading skills*: reading for specific information	Reading a text about some real-life romances and answering questions on it.
		Discussing romantic and sad love stories.
Suspicious Minds page 21	*Listening skills*: listening for specific information	Completing gaps in the lyrics of the song, *Suspicious Minds*.
	Conversation skills: fluency work	Discussing the meaning of song lyrics and relating them to their lives.

3 Couples Teacher's notes

Closed books. Whole class. Prepare a number of labels, each with the name of one member of a famous couple that the students are likely to know, eg: Romeo and Juliet, Bonnie and Clyde, Minnie and Mickey Mouse, Samson and Delilah, Napoleon and Josephine, etc. The couples don't have to be romantically linked, and you can use ones from the students' own culture(s) to ensure that they are well-known. You can even get the students to prepare the labels themselves. Pin the labels to the back of the students' clothing so they cannot see them. Students have to mill around asking questions to find out who they are – the only questions they can't ask are *Who am I?* or *What is my name?* They then have to find their other half. Pairs then report back to the class on what they know about their famous couple.

Reading (p 16)

1   Direct students' attention to the photos and find out which of the couples are well known to them. You might like to ask them if they can name some of the films that they have appeared in. (Cindy Crawford is famous mainly as a model. Lyle Lovett is famous mainly as a singer.)

2   Pairwork. Students work together to find the answers to the questions and report back to the class. To encourage them to scan the text for only the information that they need to answer the questions, you might like to impose a time limit or set the activity up as a race between the pairs to see who can find the information first.

> Richard Gere and Cindy Crawford: 3 years. She wanted to have children and he refused.
>
> Lyle Lovett and Julia Roberts: 2 years. The big difference in age became a problem.
>
> Nicole Kidman and Tom Cruise: 10 years. They both wanted to pursue their own careers.
>
> Bruce Willis and Demi Moore: 11 years. It was a stormy relationship, and there were rumours of affairs on both sides.

3   Students read the information more carefully and answer the questions. Check answers with the class.

> a)   Bruce Willis and Demi Moore.
> b)   Nicole Kidman and Tom Cruise.
> c)   Bruce Willis and Demi Moore: 11 years.
> d)   Lyle Lovett and Julia Roberts: 2 years.
> e)   Nicole Kidman and Tom Cruise.
> f)   Richard Gere and Cindy Crawford.

Lexis (p 17)

1   Encourage students to try to complete the sentences without looking at the text to see how many they can manage on their own. They can then look at the text and compare their answers in pairs or small groups to find any they have missed. Check answers with the class.

> a) get   b) difference   c) pursue   d) out
> e) stormy   f) split   g) have

2   Groupwork. Students discuss the sentences in Exercise 1 and decide whether or not they agree with them. In a general feedback session, find out how much consensus there is within the class.

Ross & Jane (p 17)

Writing

1   The pictures tell the story of a relationship. They are in the correct order; students match the pictures with the items in the box. Allow students to discuss the pictures and do the activity in pairs. Check answers with the class. You might like to ask students to make sentences about the pictures using the words from the box and ask them if they think this is typical in the course of a relationship.

> a) fancy   b) chat up   c) move in   d) have a row

2   Students work individually to put the stages of the relationship in the order that seems right to them. Encourage them to add any stages that they think are necessary. They can then compare ideas with a partner and discuss any differences.

> *Possible order (in Britain)*
> d, b, c, k, i, l, e, h, a, f, g, j

Optional activity

When the students are working out the best order for the stages of a relationship, you might like to give them different criteria, such as:

*   the order you think is normal in your country
*   the order you think women would prefer
*   the order you think men would prefer
*   the order you think your parents would prefer
*   the order you personally would prefer

3 Pairwork. Students work in pairs to write the story. Remind them that they can use sentences from Exercise 2 and any that they wrote for themselves as well as expressions from the Language toolbox. Encourage them to use adverbs of time to structure their stories properly. Students can swap stories with other pairs, but you might like to display all the finished stories in the classroom and make time for everyone to read them before asking students to vote on the best one.

Possible story

One evening Ross met Jane at a disco. They fancied each other. To begin with they rang each other up. After that they went out together to a restaurant. They kissed. After a while they fell in love. A few weeks later they moved in together in a flat in Oxford. Next they met each other's parents. Finally they got married in Oxford. After that they had children – Tom and Alice. Then they had a (terrible) row. In the end they split up.

Irregular verb sound groups (p 17)

1 Allow students to work together to complete the table. If they are slow starting, do a couple with the class as an example. Check answers with the class and elicit what the forms in each table have in common.

A

Infinitive	Past simple	Past participle
meet	met	met
keep	kept	kept
mean	meant	meant
sleep	slept	slept

B

Infinitive	Past simple	Past participle
ring	rang	rung
begin	began	begun
drink	drank	drunk
sing	sang	sung

C

Infinitive	Past simple	Past participle
buy	bought	bought
bring	brought	brought
catch	caught	caught
fight	fought	fought

Table A: The past simple and past participle forms all have the sound /e/.

Table B: The vowel sound in the past simple is /æ/ and in the past participle /ʌ/.

Table C: The vowel sound in both the past simple and the past participle is /ɔː/.

2 🖭 10 SB p 17

Play the recording for students to listen, check their answers and repeat. Ask students to add three other verbs to the tables. Encourage them to refer to the list of irregular verbs on page 132 if they need to.

Let's get personal (p 18)

Books closed. Whole class. Ask students to give you the names of some popular game shows that they watch on television. Ask them then to explain how each one works and which one they like best.

Listening (p 18)

1 🖭 11 SB p 134

Focus attention on the main photo and ask students to say what kind of person they think the man is. Tell them that it is a picture of the host of a game show. Go through the statements with them and then play the recording for them to decide whether they are true or false. Allow students to compare notes before checking answers.

---

a)   False. It's called *Get Personal*.

b)   True.

c)   False. They have to answer the same questions.

d)   True.

e)   False. They are in different studios.

f)   True.

🖭 11

(I = Introducer; BB = Bobby Brown; R = Rosie; D = David)

I: *It's time for our popular competition, 'Get Personal', with your host, Bobby Brown.*

BB: *Good evening and welcome to this week's 'Get Personal'. Let's meet our first couple, Rosie and David.*

Now you'll remember the way the game works. We want to find out just how much they remember about when they first met. So, Rosie and David are going to answer the same questions, and they'll get one point each time they give the same answer.

As you know, Rosie and David are in separate studios – Rosie can't hear David, and David has no idea what Rosie is saying. But they can both hear me. Okay, are you ready to play 'Get Personal'?

R&D: *Yes, Bobby.*

---

2 🖭 12 SB p 134

Students use the cues to write out the questions in full. Play the recording for students to check their answers and then check with the class.

1 When did you meet David?
2 How did you first meet?
3 What time of day was it?
4 What was the weather like?
5 What were you both wearing?
6 Who spoke first and what did they say?

🎞 12

(BB = Bobby Brown; R = Rosie)

BB: *Okay, ladies first, so we'll start with you, Rosie. Tell me, when did you meet David?*

R: *Um, it was exactly three years, four and a half months ago.*

BB: *All right! Now Rosie, how did you first meet?*

R: *Well, I was working as a nurse, and David came into the hospital for an operation.*

BB: *Okay, Rosie. I want you to think about the moment when you first met. What time of day was it?*

R: *Um, it was getting dark, and I was working nights that week. So early evening.*

BB: *And what was the weather like?*

R: *Oh dear, I think it was raining. Yes, I remember now – it was definitely raining when I arrived at work.*

BB: *What were you both wearing when you saw one another for the first time?*

R: *That's easy. I was wearing my nurse's uniform, and he was wearing pyjamas.*

BB: *What colour were the pyjamas?*

R: *Um, blue. Or were they green? No, they were blue.*

BB: *Is that your final answer?*

R: *Yes, blue.*

BB: *Finally, who spoke first and what did they say?*

R: *David spoke first. In fact he shouted at me. He said, 'Nurse, I'm going to be sick.'*

BB: *Oh well, that's very romantic! Thank you, Rosie.*

3 Play the recording again for students to underline Rosie's answers. Check answers with the class.

Answers for 3 and 4	
Rosie	**David**
1 a) Nearly three and a half years ago.	✔
2 a) She was a nurse. He was a patient.	✔
3 c) Early evening.	✖
4 b) It was raining.	✖
5 HER b) A nurse's uniform.	
HIM a) Blue pyjamas.	✖
6 b) He said, 'I'm going to be sick.'	✖

4 🎞 13 SB p 134

Make sure everyone is clear what they have to do. Explain that they are going to hear David answering the same questions. They should circle the tick if he gives the same answer as Rosie and circle the cross if his answer is different.

Play the recording and allow students to compare their answers in pairs before checking with the class.

🎞 13

(BB = Bobby Brown; D = David)

BB: *Now, David, it's your turn. When did you meet Rosie?*

D: *Oh, nearly three and a half years ago.*

BB: *Okay. Second question. Where and how did you first meet?*

D: *Ah, well, I went into hospital for an operation, and Rosie was working there as a nurse.*

BB: *What time of day was it?*

D: *Oh, I don't know. Lunchtime?*

BB: *What was the weather like?*

D: *Oh dear. It was summer, so I suppose the sun was shining.*

BB: *What were you both wearing when you saw one another for the first time?*

D: *Ah, Rosie was wearing her nurse's uniform, and, and she was also wearing lovely perfume. I was wearing my favourite green pyjamas.*

BB: *Finally, David, who spoke first and what did they say?*

D: *Ah, Rosie spoke first. She said, 'How are you feeling?' And I think I said, um, 'I feel terrible.'*

5 Remind students (or elicit from them) that Rosie and David get one point for every answer they give that is the same. Ask students to say how many points they think Rosie and David have scored.

Two points.

6 Pairwork. Students discuss how well they think they would do on *Get Personal* with someone important to them.

Close up (p 19)

Past simple

1 Pairwork. Students look at the verbs in the box and answer the questions. Check answers with the class. The Language reference box at the bottom of the page has more information about the use of the past simple. You can also refer students to the Verb structures section on page 129 and the list of irregular verbs on page 132.

a) *buy, fall* and *go*

b) Add *ed*.

c) Verbs that end in *e* – add *d*. Verbs that end in a consonant + *y* – drop the *y* and add *ied*.

d) Do (did): *I didn't stay up. Did you stay up ...?*

2 Encourage students to work individually, but allow them to compare their answers in pairs or small groups before checking with the class.

a) Yesterday I bought / didn't buy a CD.

b) Last Saturday I stayed up / didn't stay up all night.

c) In January I started / didn't start a new diet.

d) Today I hurried / didn't hurry to my English lesson.

e) This morning I received / didn't receive an e-mail.

f) Last night I fell / didn't fall asleep watching TV.

g) Last year I went / didn't go on holiday abroad.

3 Ask students to read their sentences again and tick the ones that are true for them. Students compare and discuss their sentences with a partner.

Past continuous (p 19)

1 Students make their choice by underlining the correct form. They should be able to see fairly easily that the correct choice is the past continuous and the other verbs in the sentences are all in the past simple. The Language reference box at the bottom of the page has more information about the use of the past continuous.

a) was   b) was   c) were

The other verbs are in the past simple.

2 Elicit the answers to the questions from the class and encourage them to make some example sentences of their own. For example: *I was doing my homework when the phone rang. I met my best friend in 1998.*

Past continuous. Past simple.

3 ▭ **14 SB**
Explain that they are going to listen to some sounds and they have to describe what they hear using the past continuous and the past simple. You could pause the recording after each sound for students to write down their answers, or encourage them to call out sentences.

Possible answers

a) He was having a shower when his mobile phone rang.

b) She was talking to her friend when he asked her to dance.

c) They were having dinner when he asked her to marry him.

d) They were having a row when her mum arrived.

e) They were sleeping when the baby started crying.

4 Pairwork. Students work individually to write their three true and one false sentences. They then work in pairs to ask and answer questions and try to guess which answer is false.

True love (p 20)

Books closed. Whole class. Ask students to give suggestions for the most romantic couple in the world (real or fictional) and the most tragic.

Reading

1 Pairwork. Students work together to look at the photographs and decide their answers to the questions. Tell them not to read the article at this stage. Allow them to compare notes with other pairs.

2 Students read the article and check their answers.

a) Charles.

b) Shah Jahan.

c) The Duke of Windsor / King Edward VIII.

d) Joe DiMaggio.

e) Paul and Linda McCartney.

3 Pairwork. Students turn to their respective pages and follow the instructions.

There are other possible questions but these are the ones expected:

Student A

a) When did Linda McCartney die?

b) When did Shah Jahan build the Taj Mahal?

c) How long did it take to build the Taj Mahal?

d) Where did Charles meet Camilla?

Student B

a) When did King Edward VIII become King of England?

b) When did Paul McCartney leave the Beatles?

c) How long did Marilyn Monroe and Joe DiMaggio's marriage last?

d) How long was Shah Jahan married?

4 Groupwork. Students discuss the questions in groups and report back to the class.

Suspicious Minds (p 21)

Song

Books closed. Whole class. Find out how much students know about Elvis Presley. Perhaps divide the class into teams and award points for every fact they can produce and two points for titles of his songs.

If your students have no interest at all in Elvis Presley, find out who they think the most romantic singer at the moment is. Ask them to tell you everything they know about this singer.

1 Ask students to decide whether *a* or *b* best describes someone with a suspicious mind.

> b)   doesn't believe what you tell them

2 Allow students to work in pairs to discuss and complete the song lyrics with words from the box.

> 1 trap   2 word   3 dreams   4 hello   5 again
> 6 dreams   7 tears   8 never

3 **15 SB p 21**
Play the recording for students to check their answers. Then play it again for them just to listen and enjoy. Some students may like to sing along with the recording. Find out how many students already knew the song.

> **15**
>
> *Suspicious Minds*
>
> *We're caught in a trap.*
> *I can't walk out*
> *Because I love you too much, baby.*
>
> *Why can't you see*
> *What you're doing to me*
> *When you don't believe a word I say?*
>
> *We can't go on together*
> *With suspicious minds.*
> *And we can't build our dreams*
> *On suspicious minds.*
>
> *So, if an old friend I know*
> *Drops by to say hello,*
> *Would I still see suspicion in your eyes?*
>
> *Here we go again,*
> *Asking where I've been.*
> *You can't see the tears are real*
> *I'm crying.*
>
> *We can't go on together*
> *With suspicious minds.*
> *And we can't build our dreams*
> *On suspicious minds.*

> *Oh, let our love survive,*
> *Or dry the tears from your eyes.*
> *Let's not let a good thing die*
> *When, honey, you know*
> *I've never lied to you.*
> *Mmm, yeah, yeah.*

4 Allow students to discuss their answers in pairs or small groups. Check answers with the class.

> a) doesn't want b) unhappy c) thinks
> d) never lies

5 Check answers by asking individual students to read out the sentences with the words from the song in place.

> a) walk out   b) a word   c) go on   d) drops by
> e) dry the tears from your eyes

6 Allow students to work in pairs and to compare answers with others before you check with the class.

> The singer said *a, c* and *e.*
> The suspicious lover said *b* and *c.*

7 Pairwork. Give students plenty of time to think about what they are going to say. You might like to set this preparation for homework. Go round offering help and encouragement and ask confident students to tell their stories to the class.

Test

> Scoring: one point per correct answer unless otherwise indicated.
> **1** 1 met 2 rang 3 didn't have, was
>   4 sent, Did you get
> **2** 1 was waiting   2 were having   3 wasn't using
>   4 were you doing   5 was reading
>   6 was dreaming
> **3** 1   was working, met
>   2   didn't say
>   3   saw, were coming
>   4   was waiting
> **4** 1 met 2 kept 3 mean 4 slept 5 rang
>   6 begin 7 drank 8 sung 9 bought 10 bring
>   11 caught 12 fought
> **5** 1 up 2 date 3 love 4 married 5 age
>   6 children 7 career 8 relationship 9 row
>   10 up

3 Couples Test

Name: _____   **Total:** _____ /40

1 Past simple *6 points*

Complete the sentences with the verbs in the box in the past simple.

| be   get   not have   meet   ring   send |

1 We _____ the new boss for the first time today.

2 I _____ you on your mobile before lunch.

3 I _____ lunch today. I _____ too busy.

4 I _____ you an e-mail. _____ you _____ it?

2 Past continuous *6 points*

Complete the sentences with the verbs in the box in the past continuous.

| do   dream   have   read   not use   wait |

1 I _____ for the taxi when you saw me.

2 We _____ a meeting when you phoned me.

3 I _____ the computer when it crashed.

4 What _____ you _____ at 7 o'clock?

5 I fell asleep while I _____ my book last night.

6 I _____ about work when my alarm clock rang this morning.

3 Past simple & past continuous *6 points*

Put the verbs into the correct tenses: past simple or past continuous.

1 My wife _____ (work) as a waitress when I first _____ (meet) her.

2 Sorry I _____ (not say) hello to you at the party last night.

3 I _____ (see) you last night – you _____ (come) out of that new café.

4 I _____ (wait) for the bus at the time of the accident.

4 Irregular verbs *12 points*

Complete the table.

Infinitive	Past simple	Past participle
meet	met	1 _____
keep	2 _____	kept
3 _____	meant	meant
sleep	slept	4 _____
ring	5 _____	rung
6 _____	began	begun
drink	7 _____	drunk
sing	sang	8 _____
buy	9 _____	bought
10 _____	brought	brought
catch	11 _____	caught
fight	fought	12 _____

5 Vocabulary – marriage & relationship *10 points*

Complete the sentences with the words in the box.

| date   relationship   up   career   married   children up   row   age   love |

1 She started to chat me _____ .

2 She asked me out on a _____ .

3 We immediately fell in _____ .

4 After six weeks, we decided to get _____ .

5 There was a big difference in _____ .

6 She didn't want to have _____ .

7 We both wanted to pursue a _____ .

8 It was a very stormy _____ .

9 Every day, we had a terrible _____ .

10 One year after we met, we split _____ .

Photocopiable

4 *Fit* Overview

The topic of this unit is fitness, with a focus on sporting activity. Students begin by completing a chart with names of sports personalities and words for sports, participants and the places where the sports take place. They then go on to listen to a discussion about using a sports personality to advertise a new drink. They do some work on describing people using comparatives and discuss who they would choose for the advert. The following section has more work on the form and use of comparatives, and students use statistics to make comparisons between sports personalities. Students then identify and practise the schwa (/ə/) sound in common English expressions.

A degree of personalisation is introduced next as students answer a questionnaire and discuss their own fitness and the amount of physical activity they do or would like to do. They then study some collocations to do with sport and talk about the frequency with which they do certain activities.

Talking about sports often involves statistics, and the next few exercises give students training in talking about fractions, decimals, percentages, speeds and large numbers.

These numbers are useful for the next section which looks at the career of Tiger Woods, the famous golfer. Students complete a text about him with statistics, and then they listen to someone who is a big fan of Tiger Woods talking about her feelings for him. They then discuss whether they themselves are mad about anything or anyone.

In the final section, students look at the form and use of superlatives and use them to ask and answer questions. They finish with an Anecdote about their experiences of sport at school.

Section	Aims	What the students are doing
Introduction pages 22–23	*Lexis*: sporting terms	Identifying sports personalities and completing a table with names and sporting terms.
	Listening skills: listening for gist	Listening to a discussion about using a sports personality to advertise a new drink. Deciding who they would choose.
	Conversation skills: fluency work	Practising using comparatives and superlatives to talk about people.
Close up pages 23–24	*Grammar*: comparatives	Making sentences using comparative adjectives.
	Pronunciation: the schwa /ə/	Completing similes and identifying which words have the schwa sound.
Fitness test pages 24–25	*Reading skills*: questionnaire	Answering a questionnaire about fitness.
	Lexis: sport; numbers	Looking at some common collocations to do with sport and using them to talk about students' own experiences.
		Practising using numbers, including fractions, decimals and percentages.
Tiger Woods page 26	*Reading skills*: reading for specific information	Completing a text about Tiger Woods with numbers and dates.
	Listening skills: listening for specific information	Listening to a fan of Tiger Woods talking about her hero and doing some preparatory work on superlatives.
	Conversation skills: fluency work	Describing someone or something you are mad about.
Close up page 27	*Grammar*: superlatives	Writing the superlative forms of adjectives. Using superlatives in questions and answers.
	Conversation skills: fluency work	Anecdote: talking about sports you did at school.

4 *Fit* Teacher's notes

Closed books. Whole class. Write the word *Sport* in the middle of the board and see how many words and expressions students can come up with that have a connection with it. They should be able to name a number of sports, but try to widen the lexical field by prompting them to think of other aspects of sport such as health and fitness. Write all their suggestions on the board in a spidergram, grouping them according to subject (all the sports together; words to do with health together; etc.)

Lexis (p 22)

Pairwork. Students look at the photos of sports personalities and discuss and complete the table. Discourage them from looking up the answers until they have done as much as they can. Then let them turn to page 125 and see which pair scored the most points.

You might like to award extra points for students who can think of words for a fifth column headed *Equipment/Kit*. You could also use this to give students who finish faster than the others something to do.

Examples:
Athletics: *running shoes, shorts, shirt*
Football: *ball, goalposts, boots, shorts, socks, shirt, corner flag, net*
Basketball: *ball, basket, shorts, trainers, hoop, backboard*
Motor racing: *car, helmet, new tyres, suit*
Swimming: *costume, trunks, goggles, cap*
Tennis: *balls, net, racket*

Listening (p 23)

1   16 SB p 134

Establish that a marketing director is responsible for finding the best ways to sell a company's product. An advertising executive works for an agency that makes advertisements for companies and is responsible for thinking up new ideas for advertising campaigns. Isotonic drinks are popular with sports people because they quickly replace the fluids and minerals lost during energetic physical activity.

Play the recording and ask students to say which of the sports personalities on page 22 they choose.

Cathy Freeman.

16

(MD = marketing director; AE = advertising executive)

MD: *OK. Who have you got for me?*

AE: *Well, we now have a short list of six people. I'm sure you'll love all of them.*

MD: *Go ahead then.*

AE: *Well, first of all, we've got Raúl.*

MD: *Who? Never heard of him. Who's next? Someone better, I hope.*

AE: *No, Raúl's really famous. He plays football for Spain.*

MD: *Well, he's no good to me.*

AE: *OK, next, we've got Shaquille O'Neal.*

MD: *Who? I don't know him either.*

AE: *He's massive! Mega-rich, mega-talented, massively famous.*

MD: *He's not famous with people like me. And he's not as good-looking as that other boy, what did you call him, Raúl? We need someone who is attractive. I don't care how good he is at basketball.*

AE: *OK, what about Michael Schumacher? Maybe we could get him. He's more successful than all of them.*

MD: *It doesn't matter. I want someone attractive.*

AE: *Oh right, I get it. You really don't want a man. Oh, fine. Well, what about, hm, I don't know, what about a swimmer? There's that Dutch one, Inge, Inge something. She won a few gold medals and she looks good.*

MD: *Yes, that's the idea. But not swimming – I want something more, you know, erm, more, erm, tennis, for example, tennis is a bit more interesting than swimming.*

AE: *What about someone like Venus Williams, or her sister, what's she called? Or number six on my list, Cathy Freeman, the Australian Olympic 400 metre champion? Venus Williams looks great and is probably more famous than Cathy Freeman, but Cathy is more, well, I mean, she's lovely, isn't she? Such a beautiful smile. But some people may think athletics isn't as interesting as tennis ...*

MD: *Maybe. Come on. Let's decide. Who do you think is sexier? This runner or that football player, Raúl?*

AE: *Oh, Raúl. No question.*

MD: *Well, I disagree. I think this Cathy Freeman is sexier than all of them. See if you can get her.*

AE: *Are you sure? Is that your final decision? I think she's a very interesting choice.*

MD: *Yup, let's go for it. When can you contact her?*

2 Play the recording again for students to listen and complete the sentences. Check answers with the class.

> a) Shaquille O'Neal isn't as good-looking as Raúl.
>
> b) Michael Schumacher is more successful than all of them.
>
> c) Tennis is a bit more interesting than swimming.
>
> d) Venus Williams is more famous than Cathy Freeman.
>
> e) Athletics isn't as interesting as tennis.
>
> f) Cathy Freeman is sexier than all of them.

3 Students work individually to change the sentences so that they reflect their own opinions. They then compare their answers with a partner. In a general feedback session find out how much consensus there is in the class.

4 Groupwork. Students discuss who they would choose to advertise an isotonic drink. Make it clear that they are not limited to the six personalities discussed so far. Encourage them to give their reasons.

Optional activity

Ask students to find a photograph of the sports personality they have chosen and to make their advertisements. They will need to think of a slogan for their advert. Display the finished adverts on the classroom walls for everyone to see. Encourage discussion of the adverts using comparative and superlative adjectives.

Close up (p 23)

Comparatives

1 Students complete the columns with adjectives from the box in their comparative form. Allow them to compare answers with a partner before checking with the class. You might like to ask them to think of one more example of their own for each column. There is more information on comparatives in the Language reference section on page 27.

+ -er / -r	double letter + -er	y + -ier
kind – kinder than	thin – thinner than	sexy – sexier than
strong – stronger than	sad – sadder than	happy – happier than
nice – nicer than	wet – wetter than	lucky – luckier than

irregular	more + adjective
good – better than	famous – more famous than
bad – worse than	successful – more successful than
far – further than	interesting – more interesting than

2 Students use the table of statistics to form sentences about the sports personalities using comparative adjectives and *than*. Allow them to work in pairs or to compare answers before checking with the class.

> a) Shaquille O'Neal is taller than Raúl.
>
> b) Venus Williams is heavier than Michael Schumacher.
>
> c) Inge de Bruijn is younger than Cathy Freeman.
>
> d) Raúl is older than Venus Williams.
>
> e) Cathy Freeman is lighter than Inge de Bruijn.
>
> f) Venus Williams is shorter than Shaquille O'Neal.

3 Establish that *much* and *a bit* are used to modify comparatives to make them a little more precise. *Much* is used when there is a big difference between the two things being compared. When the difference is small, we use *a bit* or *a little*.

Students modify the sentences in 2. Check answers with the class.

> a) Shaquille O'Neal is much taller than Raúl.
>
> b) Venus Williams is a bit heavier than Michael Schumacher.
>
> c) Inge de Bruijn is a bit younger than Cathy Freeman.
>
> d) Raúl is a bit older than Venus Williams.
>
> e) Cathy Freeman is a bit lighter than Inge de Bruijn.
>
> f) Venus Williams is much shorter than Shaquille O'Neal.

4 Students work individually or in pairs to produce their five sentences. They may need to ask each other questions such as *How tall are you?* and *How much do you weigh?* in order to find out the correct information. They can then compare their sentences in groups.

5 Allow students to discuss their answers in small groups before checking on page 125.

The schwa /ə/ (p 24)

1 🔊 **17 SB p 24**

Students complete the expressions and then listen and check their answers.

> a) bird   b) picture   c) fiddle   d) cucumber
> e) feather   f) bat

Optional activity

You might like to point out that expressions such as those in Exercise 1 with *as ... as* are known as similes and that the English language is full of them. Many are traditional, but it is interesting that new ones are being created all the time. One example that has become popular in recent years is *as sick as a parrot*, commonly used by football players to say how they feel after missing a goal or losing a match. No one knows why a parrot should be regarded as a creature prone to sickness; many of these similes have very obscure origins. Although they are used more in daily conversation these days than proverbs are, students should be careful not to overuse them. However, they may be interested to know a few more. You might like to give them this matching exercise to try and ask them how appropriate they think the similes are.

1	as strong as	a)	a pancake
2	as brave as	b)	ice
3	as green as	c)	grass
4	as cold as	d)	hell
5	as hot as	e)	an ox
6	as flat as	f)	a lion

> 1 e 2 f 3 c 4 b 5 d 6 a

2 Elicit what the schwa sound /ə/ is and ask for some examples of words that contain it (eg *mother*, *brother*, etc). Then ask students to say which words in 1 contain the sound. Play the recording for them to check and practise saying the expressions. You might like to ask them how appropriate they think the comparisons in these expressions are, as well as whether or not there are equivalent expressions in their language(s)

> The schwa sounds are underlined.
> a) She's <u>a</u>s free <u>as a</u> bird.
> b) She's <u>a</u>s pretty <u>as a</u> pict<u>u</u>re.
> c) He's <u>a</u>s fit <u>as a</u> fiddle.
> d) She's <u>a</u>s cool <u>as a</u> cucumb<u>e</u>r.
> e) It's <u>a</u>s light <u>as a</u> feath<u>e</u>r.
> f) He's <u>a</u>s blind <u>as a</u> bat.

Fitness test (p 24)

Reading

Students work individually to complete the questionnaire for themselves They then compare answers with a partner.

Lexis: sport (p 25)

1 Allow students to work in pairs or small groups to make their choices. Check answers by asking students to read the sentences aloud so that they hear the forms in context rather than focusing on them in isolation.

> a) do b) play c) go d) did, went e) played
> f) doing

2 Students decide how many of the sentences are true for them and then discuss this with a partner.

3 Pairwork. Explain that collocations are words that always or frequently occur together. For example, we always say *do exercise*, never *play exercise*. Students complete the collocation lists and then add one more sport to each list. Check answers and go round the class asking for the students' additions to the lists.

> a) go b) do c) play

4 Students now use the collocations from Exercise 3 to write sentences about their own experiences of sport. Make sure they understand the sentence beginnings and use a variety of them in their sentences. They then compare with a partner. Check answers by asking individual students to read their sentences aloud.

Lexis: numbers (p 25)

1 ▭ 18 SB p 134
Allow students to discuss this in pairs first. Encourage them to read the numbers aloud to get a feel for what sounds right. Then play the recording for them to check and to repeat the numbers.

> ▭ 18
> *Three quarters.*
> *Nought point two five.*
> *Nought point three three.*
> *One and a half.*
> *An eighth.*
> *A quarter.*
> *One point five.*
> *Nought point one two five.*
> *A third.*
> *Nought point seven five.*

2 ▭ 19 SB p 134

Pairwork. Students work together to match the fractions with the decimals. Go through the example with the class to ensure that they are clear what they have to do. Play the recording for them to check their answers.

> ▭ 19
> *Three quarters is the same as nought point seven five.*
> *Nought point two five is the same as a quarter.*
> *Nought point three three is the same as a third.*
> *One and a half is the same as one point five.*
> *An eighth is the same as nought point one two five.*

3 ▭ **20 SB p 135**

Encourage students to try saying these aloud to get a feel for what sounds right. Allow them to discuss this in pairs before playing the recording for them to listen and repeat.

> ▭ **20**
>
> a) *A speed*
>   *Two hundred and five kilometres an hour.*
>   *One hundred and twenty-eight kilometres an hour.*
> b) *A sum of money*
>   *Fifty-nine million dollars*
>   *Seventeen million dollars*
> c) *A big number*
>   *Ninety-seven million, two thousand, four hundred and forty*
>   *Six hundred and twenty-four million, one hundred and twelve thousand, three hundred and fifty*
> d) *A percentage*
>   *Eight point two per cent*
>   *Twenty-six point seven per cent*
> e) *A distance*
>   *Fifty-one point two five kilometres*
>   *Forty-two point one nine five kilometres*
> f) *A football score*
>   *Four one*
>   *Three nil*

4 Pairwork. Students discuss the questions and try to match them with the numbers from Exercise 3. Allow pairs to compare their ideas with other pairs, but do not check answers at this stage.

> a) Two hundred and five kilometres an hour.
> b) Fifty-nine million dollars.
> c) Six hundred and twenty-four million, one hundred and twelve thousand, three hundred and fifty.
> d) Eight point two per cent.
> e) Forty-two point one nine five kilometres.
> f) Three nil.

5 ▭ **21 SB p 135**

Play the recording for students to check their answers. Find out if any pair got them all correct.

> ▭ **21**
>
> a) *Venus Williams' tennis serve has been recorded at two hundred and five kilometres an hour. It's actually the fastest service in women's tennis.*
> b) *Michael Schumacher earned fifty-nine million dollars in 2000: more than any other sports person.*

c) *The British have a very sweet tooth. They eat a total of six hundred and twenty-four million, one hundred and twelve thousand, three hundred and fifty Mars bars every year.*
d) *Only eight point two per cent of the UK population trust the government.*
e) *The official distance for a marathon, established in 1910, is forty-two point one nine five kilometres.*
f) *France beat Brazil three nil in the 1998 final and became world champions for the first time.*

6 Pairwork. Students turn to their respective pages and follow the instructions. After students have asked and answered their questions, discuss with them which they think are the most interesting pieces of trivia.

> Student A: a) 30 km/h b) $43.2 m c) 7,120
>   d) 20% e) 40,075.16 kms f) 194–0
> Student B: a) 105 km/h b) $38.5 m c) 2,175
>   d) 2% e) 4,203 km f) 32–0

Tiger Woods (p 26)

Books closed. Whole class. Ask students if they have a sporting hero. Encourage them to talk about their heroes, giving as much information about them as they can.

Reading & listening (p 26)

1 Groupwork. Students pool their knowledge about Tiger Woods and note down at least three facts about him, preferably with their books closed. If they show interest in the subject, you might have a competition to see which groups can come up with the most information.

> Tiger Woods is the most famous golfer in the world and possibly the greatest golfer of all time. Students may also know that he was the first golfer to win all four majors in the same year, that he started playing golf as a very small child, and that he is sponsored by Nike.

2 The preparatory work on numbers in the previous section should make this relatively easy for the students. Allow them to work in pairs if they wish. You might like to check that the students have written out the full forms of the numbers correctly, but do not check whether they have placed them correctly in the text at this stage.

> a) 30th December 1975 b) first c) sixteen
> d) a quarter e) 8th April 2001 f) one and a half
> g) 50 million h) an eighth

3 🔲 **22 SB p 135**

Play the recording for students to listen, read and check their answers. Refer them to the tapescript on page 135 to check spellings. You might like to use this text for a shadowing exercise in which students read the text at the same time as they listen, trying to match the speed and intonation of the speaker.

> 1 30th December 1975   2 a quarter   3 an eighth
> 4 one and a half   5 sixteen   6 8th April 2001
> 7 first   8 50 million

🔲 **22**

Golfing genius

Tiger Woods was born on 30th December 1975 in California, USA, of mixed heritage: he describes himself as a quarter black, a quarter Thai, a quarter Chinese, an eighth white and an eighth American Indian. His father, Earl Woods, named him Tiger after a friend who saved his life in the Vietnam war.

He was only nine months old when he started to play golf and he played his first game at one and a half years old. His father was his first teacher.

At the age of eight, he won a tournament and five more before he was sixteen. On 8 April 2001 Tiger Woods made golfing history. He became the first golfer to win all four majors – the most important tournaments – within the same year.

He is helping to make golf more popular with all ages and levels, and most people agree that he is probably the greatest golfer of all time. Certainly, he is already one of the richest.

He now earns more than $50 million a year. He has a $100 million deal with Nike and also has deals with American Express, Buick, Rolex and Wheaties.

What advice would he give prospective parents of golf champions? 'Don't force your kids into sports. It has to be fun.'

The best advice he ever got? From his dad: 'Always be yourself.'

Listening (p 26)

1 🔲 **23 SB p 135**

Go through the items with the class before you play the recording so that they know exactly what they are listening for. You might also ask them to say which ones they think it is likely that Pauline tells the interviewer.

> She tells him a, b, d, f, g.

🔲 **23**

(I = Interviewer; P = Pauline)

I: *And here on Radio Five Live we have a winner in this week's big competition. The prize, the prize this week is a trip to beautiful Augusta for the Masters and the chance to meet Tiger Woods! The winner is Pauline Perkins, and she's on the line right now. Pauline, congratulations. I hear that you're mad about Tiger Woods – you're his biggest fan. Is that right?*

P: *Oh yes. I think he's the most wonderful person in the world and I know absolutely everything about him. I have a website all about him and I write to him every day.*

I: *Really? What do you like most about him?*

P: *He's the greatest golfer of all time and he's gorgeous. So young, too. In fact, he's the youngest player to win four major golf tournaments in one year.*

I: *Oh really? How old is he?*

P: *He was born on 30th December 1975. I always have a party on 30th December and I put pictures of Tiger all round the house.*

I: *Oh, how nice. Pauline, I hear Tiger Woods is one of the richest sportsmen on the planet. Does he live like a typical superstar?*

P: *No, he's different from other superstars. He's the only real superstar. He's just so, ooh, different.*

I: *What do you mean?*

P: *He likes staying at home, playing computer games and table tennis. Oh, and eating his favourite food. He's a perfect man. He's so good.*

I: *What's his favourite food?*

P: *Pizza or cheeseburger and strawberry milkshake. I like the same things.*

I: *And is it true that Michael Jordan is one of his best friends?*

P: *Oh yes. Michael Jordan is like a big brother to Tiger.*

I: *I see. And can I just ask you one last question?*

P: *Sure.*

I: *What are you going to say to Tiger when you meet him?*

P: *I'm going to tell him that I ...*

2 Play the recording again for students to listen and complete the sentences. Check answers with the class. Remind them of their work on comparatives earlier in the unit where they compared two things. Ask them what is being compared here and what the difference is. (Tiger Woods is being compared to more than one other person and superlative forms of adjectives are used. There is more work on superlatives in the next section.)

You might like to ask students what they think the interviewer's attitude to Pauline is. (He thinks her obsession with Tiger Woods is a bit weird/unhealthy. This can be picked up from his intonation.)

> a) most b) the c) youngest d) one e) of

3 Pairwork. Students discuss anyone or anything that they are mad about. Encourage them to say if they would ever take things as far as Pauline Perkins and what they think about her attitude to Tiger Woods.

Close up (p 27)

Superlatives

1 Pairwork. Remind students of the superlatives used by Pauline Perkins in the last section. Ask them to work with a partner to answer the questions. Check answers with the class. You might also ask them to produce a few sentences using some of these superlatives.

> 1 the oldest / the richest / <u>the most exciting</u> / the greatest
>
> 2 <u>the most valuable</u> / the biggest / the hottest / the thinnest
>
> 3 the funniest / <u>the most interesting</u> / the sexiest / the happiest
>
> 4 the worst / the furthest / the best / <u>the most talented</u>

2 Elicit from the class when we use *most* to form a superlative adjective. There is more information on superlatives in the Grammar reference section at the bottom of page 27.

> When the adjective has two or more syllables.

3 Pairwork. Students work together to complete the questions. Make sure that both partners keep a copy of their final questions as they will both need one for the next exercise. Point out that they can use their own ideas as well as the adjectives in 1. This will produce more varied and interesting questions around the class.

4 Pairwork. Students swap partners and take turns asking and answering their questions. They discuss their answers. You might like to get them to take notes of the answers they get and compare them with those received by their original partners.

Anecdote (p 27)

See the Introduction on page 4 for more ideas on how to set up, monitor and repeat Anecdotes.

Pairwork. Give students plenty of time to read the questions and decide what they are going to talk about. They then take turns to talk to their partner about the sports they did at secondary school.

Test

> Scoring: one point per correct answer unless otherwise indicated.
>
> **1** 1 athletics
>   2 basketball player
>   3 football player / footballer
>   4 pitch
>   5 motor racing
>   6 swimmer
>   7 tennis player
>   8 court
>
> **2** 1 go 2 play 3 go 4 play 5 do 6 play
>
> **3** 1 He's <u>as</u> free <u>as a</u> bird.
>   2 She's not <u>as</u> tall <u>as</u> me.
>   3 I'm just <u>as</u> good <u>as</u> you are.
>
> **4** 1 ninety-nine per cent
>   2 one hundred and twenty-five kilometres an hour
>   3 two hundred and fifty thousand dollars
>   4 two nil
>
> **5** 1 bigger 2 more expensive 3 longer 4 sunnier
>
> **6** 1 The tallest
>   2 the oldest
>   3 The most poisonous
>   4 The worst
>   5 the most successful
>   6 The furthest
>
> **7** 1 Snowboarding is much more exciting ~~as~~ <u>than</u> skiing.
>   2 Rugby is not <u>as</u> interesting as football.
>   3 Carl Lewis is the ~~most~~ <u>fastest</u> athlete ever.
>   4 Fishing is <u>the</u> most popular sport in the world.

4 Fit Test

Name: _____ Total: _____ /40

1 Vocabulary – sport (1) 8 points
Complete the table.

Sport	Person	Place
1 _____	athlete	track
basketball	2 _____	court
	_____	
football	3 _____	4 _____
	_____	
5 _____	racing driver	race track
_____		
swimming	6 _____	swimming pool
tennis	7 _____	8 _____
	_____	

2 Vocabulary – sport (2) 6 points
Add the correct verb: do, go or play.

1 Let's _____ swimming this afternoon.
2 How often do you _____ golf?
3 Do you ever _____ fishing?
4 I can't _____ tennis very well.
5 Did you _____ athletics at school?
6 I don't know how to _____ volleyball.

3 Pronunciation – schwa /ə/ 8 points
Underline the schwas in each sentence. The number in brackets shows you how many there are in the sentence.

1 He's as free as a bird. (3)
2 She's not as tall as me. (2)
3 I'm just as good as you are. (2)

4 Vocabulary – numbers 4 points
Write exactly how you say these numbers.

1 99% _____
2 125 km/h _____
3 $250,000 _____
4 2–0 (football score) _____

5 Comparatives 4 points
Put the adjective into the correct form.

1 Canada is _____ (big) than the USA.
2 Tokyo is _____ (expensive) than Delhi.
3 The Nile is _____ (long) than the Amazon.
4 Saudi Arabia is _____ (sunny) than London.

6 Superlatives 6 points
Put the adjective into the correct form.

1 _____ (tall) person ever is Robert Wadlow. He was 2.74 metres when he died.
2 Jeanne Calmet is _____ (old) person ever. She died in 1997, aged 122 years and 164 days.
3 _____ (poisonous) animal in the world is a frog. It lives in the forests of Colombia.
4 _____ (bad) earthquake in history was in China in 1556 when 830,000 people died.
5 Brazil's Pelé is _____ (successful) goal scorer of all time. He scored 1,281 goals in his career.
6 _____ (far) we can see into space without a telescope is 21,000,000,000,000,000,000 km.

7 Comparatives & superlatives 4 points
Correct the grammar mistakes in the sentences.

1 Snowboarding is much more exciting as skiing.
2 Rugby is not interesting as football.
3 Carl Lewis is the most fast athlete ever.
4 Fishing is most popular sport in the world.

5

Review 1 Teacher's notes

Sophie & Paul (p 28)

Questions

Focus students' attention on the definition in the margin of a blind date. Ask students whether they have ever been on a blind date and to tell the class what happened. Be aware that this may be a sensitive subject for your students, so don't force them to talk about personal experience if they are uncomfortable with this. Other possible questions might be to ask them if they know of anyone who has been on a blind date or if they know how their parents first met. They may also be aware of (and able to talk about) the popular UK TV programme *Blind Date* or its equivalent in their own countries.

1 You might like to extend this activity by putting students in pairs with someone they know well and asking each student to write a brief description of the person they would choose to fix up a blind date for their partner. They then swap descriptions and say how suitable they think the person chosen for them would be.

2 Pairwork. Give students time to prepare a list of questions and then to compare them with other students. Go round checking how accurately pairs are forming their questions and deal with any problems in a class feedback session.

3 Pairwork. Students look at the photos of Sophie and Paul and talk about them. Encourage them to describe their appearance and also to say what kind of people they think they are, what their interests might be, etc. They should then decide whether or not their blind date will be successful. Keep a record of each pair's decision and keep students in the same pairs for the next three exercises.

4 Pairwork. Students work individually to write out their questions and then compare them and discuss any differences.

Possible questions

1 What's your name?
2 How old are you?
3 What do you do?
4 What's your star sign?
5 How tall are you?
6 What are you like? / What sort of person are you?
7 What sort / kind of films do you like?
8 Who is your favourite actor / actress?
9 What sort of clothes do you usually wear? / What sort of clothes do you like wearing?
10 What do you do in your free time?
11 What is your worst fault?
12 What is your dream weekend?

5 Pairwork. Students ask each other questions about Sophie and Paul, using the answers on the questionnaires. Student A should look at page 127 only. Student B should look at page 28 only.

6 Pairwork. Students look back at the predictions they made in Exercise 3 about whether or not Sophie and Paul's date would be successful and discuss whether the new information they have learnt about them has altered their views.

Reading (p 29)

Pairwork. Students read their respective reports on the blind date and answer the questions. They then tell each other what they read and compare answers to the questions. Go round the class and see how many pairs think that Sophie and Paul will see each other again.

Paul's report

1 He couldn't believe his eyes. She was amazing. She looked like a model. He fancied her.

2 He said she was quite serious, difficult to get to know, not very talkative, not the same sense of humour.

3 He thought it went very well.

Sophie's report

1 She thought he was wearing unusual clothes. He looked kind and friendly and had a nice smile. She didn't fancy him.

2 She said he was very talkative. He laughed at his own jokes and his sense of humour irritated her. He was too macho.

3 She thought it was miserable.

Writing (p 29)

Books closed. Whole class. Find some examples of lonely hearts ads from English magazines and newspapers. (If these are not available, you could get them from publications in the students' own language and ask them to translate them into English.) Photocopy them and distribute them to students to look at and discuss. You might like to ask them what they think the following abbreviations, which are often used in these adverts, mean:

GSOH = good sense of humour
WLTM = would like to meet

1 Look at Paul's advert with the class and discuss how accurately it describes him. Elicit from the students the kinds of things people put in adverts of this sort – physical appearance, age, interests, job, personality, etc. Students then work individually to write their own lonely hearts adverts. Encourage them to be imaginative so that they don't all write the same things.

2 Collect in all the papers and shuffle them. Redistribute them around the class for student to read and guess who wrote them.

Vinnie & Tanya (p 30)

Listening

1 Pairwork. Students look at the photograph and describe the man using the four sentence beginnings given and the ideas in the box. Allow them to compare their results with other pairs. Let students make any decisions they wish about what the man looks like and do not tell them anything about him at this stage. If anyone recognises him, discourage them from telling the others.

2 Go round the class eliciting other ways of completing the four sentences.

3 📼 **24 SB p 135**
Tell students that they are going to listen to an American radio programme about the man in the photograph. They should just listen and decide in what ways the impressions they expressed in 1 and 2 were correct and in what ways they were wrong. (Tell students that in American English *football* is called *soccer* and *a hard man* is called *a tough guy*.)

📼 **24**

(I = American radio interviewer; B = Brenda)

I: *We've been hearing a lot over here in the States about the actor, Vinnie Jones. Over in Britain he's really well-known, isn't that right?*

B: *Well, yeah, he's much better-known in Britain than he is over here.*

I: *So, what's the big deal? What's so special about Vinnie Jones?*

B: *Well, before he became an actor, he was already well-known as a soccer player. In fact, I'd say he's still more famous for his soccer skills than as an actor.*

I: *And which team did he play for? Manchester United?*

B: *No, no, actually, for much of his career, he played for Wimbledon.*

I: *Wimbledon?*

B: *Yes, they're not as successful as Manchester United, but while he was playing for them they beat Liverpool and won the Cup. But it wasn't really for his soccer skills that Vinnie became famous. He was well-known in Britain for being the toughest guy on the pitch.*

I: *The toughest guy on the pitch? In what way?*

B: *He was always in trouble with the referee. Basically, he was a good player, but he was violent.*

I: *Is there anything special about that?*

B: *Not really, no, but Vinnie was much more violent than other soccer players.*

I: *Jeez. What exactly did he do?*

B: *Well, for example, on one occasion, he told another player he would tear his ear off.*

I: *Ugh!*

B: *And on another occasion he tried to bite the nose of a sports journalist.*

I: *Wow. He sounds like a very unpleasant person.*

B: *Well, believe it or not, there is another side to him. If you met him, you'd probably like him – he's a lot nicer than many people think.*

I: *From what you say, he doesn't sound exactly, erm, nice!*

B: *He's a happily married family man, married to a girl he met when he was twelve, devoted to his son and step-daughter, and he's one of the most generous people I've ever met.*

I: *No kidding.*

B: *No, I'm serious.*

I: *OK, so how did he get into acting?*

B: *In 1997, at the age of 33, Vinnie's soccer career was coming to an end. He got a job as a chat show host with Sky TV, and then one thing led to another. He got a phone call from Guy Ritchie, Madonna's boyfriend – now her husband – asking him to take the part of a gangster in the film that he was making. The film, 'Lock, Stock and Two Smoking Barrels', was extremely successful in Britain.*

I: *So that was the start.*

B: *Yup, that was the start, and in the last few years he has acted with John Travolta, Brad Pitt and Nicholas Cage.*

I: *Well, it's a great story – soccer tough guy becomes Hollywood star!*

B: *Yes, that's right. Obviously, he's not as good-looking as Brad Pitt, but he's a great character actor.*

I: *OK, Brenda, thanks for that. Now, it's back to ...*

---

4 Students listen to the recording again and complete the sentences. Check answers with the class and remind them of the work they did on comparison structures in Unit 4.

---

a) much better-known

b) more famous

c) not as successful as

d) toughest

e) much more violent than

f) a lot nicer than

g) one of the most generous

h) not as good-looking as

---

5 Elicit opinions around the class as to whether or not students would like to meet Vinnie Jones. Encourage them always to give reasons for their answers.

Comparison structures (p 30)

1 Allow students to compare their answers in pairs before checking with the class.

> tall, taller, tallest
>
> emotional, more emotional, most emotional
>
> good-looking, better-looking, best-looking
>
> talented, more talented, most talented
>
> sexy, sexier, sexiest
>
> punctual, more punctual, most punctual
>
> optimistic, more optimistic, most optimistic
>
> lucky, luckier, luckiest
>
> young, younger, youngest
>
> generous, more generous, most generous
>
> flexible, more flexible, most flexible
>
> ambitious, more ambitious, most ambitious

2 Students work individually to complete the sentences about themselves using the comparative and superlative forms of the words in Exercise 1. Look at the example with the class first. Make sure students understand that they should write one false sentence and four true ones and that they should hide the false one amongst the true ones. They can then swap sentences with a partner and try to identify their partner's false sentence.

Reading (p 31)

Books closed. Whole class. Write *Love at first sight* on the board and ask students what it means and whether they believe in it.

1 Tell students that Tanya is Vinnie Jones' wife. Ask them what information they can remember about her from the listening. (She is happily married to Vinnie Jones. Vinnie met her when he was twelve. She has a daughter from another relationship.) Students then read the article and decide if it was love at first sight for Vinnie and Tanya.

> No, it wasn't 'love at first sight'.

2 Students read the article again and choose the correct verb alternative. Allow them to compare answers in pairs and remind them of the work they did on the past simple and past continuous in Unit 3 and quantity expressions in Unit 2. Do not check answers with the class at this stage.

> 1 A few   2 took   3 some   4 didn't work out
> 5 got married   6 Many   7 was standing
> 8 got up   9 a few   10 spent

3 📼 **25 SB p 31**
Play the recording for students to listen and check their answers.

4 Pairwork. Students discuss the question in pairs and then form small groups to compare their answers.

Anecdote (p 31)

See the Introduction on page 4 for more ideas on how to set up, monitor and repeat Anecdotes.

Pairwork. Give students plenty of time to decide which film character they are going to talk about and to read the questions. They then take turns to talk about their film character to their partner.

Neighbours (p 32)

Books closed. Whole class. Tell students that you are going to find out how good they are at gossiping (you might want to go through the definition of *gossip* on page 32 with the class first). Ask them to stand up and form a circle. Make up two pieces of gossip. These could be about someone famous the students will know or about someone closer to home, so long as it will not cause offence. Whisper one piece of gossip to one of the students and ask them to whisper it to the person on their left and so on. Then whisper the other piece of gossip to another student who has to whisper it to the person on their right. You should then have two pieces of gossip travelling around the circle in different directions. Students must pass on exactly what they have heard. They cannot ask for clarification and if they miss something, or misunderstand something, they must pass on what they think they heard. When the gossip has gone full circle ask the last student to write what they have heard on the board. See how much the gossip has changed.

1 Groupwork. Students discuss the questions in groups of four. Encourage them to report back to the class any interesting information they learn.

2 Pairwork. Students look at the pictures and discuss with a partner how different they are from their own street and neighbours. Again, encourage students to report interesting information back to the class.

3 📼 **26 SB p 33**
Make sure students realise that they can read the sketch (*Gossip*) as they listen. Read the question first so they know what they are listening for. Play the recording, then put students in pairs to discuss how to explain the confusion between Mrs Jones' cat and Mrs Jones' husband.

4 Groupwork. Students work in groups of four to perform the sketch. Give them time to assign roles and practise their parts. If students are enthusiastic about this, you might allow them to prepare to perform their sketches in the next lesson and to use costumes and props. If facilities permit, students generally enjoy seeing their performances on video afterwards. Students might like to do Exercise 5, in which they prepare a final scene, at the same time and perform the whole play together.

5 Groupwork. In groups of four, students write a final scene for the sketch and perform it for the class.

Test

1 1 What's your

2 How, are you

3 What do you

4 What are your

5 What are your

6 What do you do

7 What's your

8 What, do you want

2 1 younger

2 the, most common

3 the biggest

4 The oldest

5 more popular

6 The busiest

3 1 much 2 a little 3 a few 4 many

5 a few 6 much

4 1 became 2 was already programming 3 started

4 was 5 founded 6 was studying

7 didn't finish 8 became (Bill Gates)

5 1 began 2 bought 3 catch 4 drank 5 fought

6 kept 7 meant 8 met 9 rang 10 sang

6 1 I'm not <u>as</u> old <u>as</u> she is.

2 He can't see <u>a</u> thing – he's <u>as</u> blind <u>as</u> <u>a</u> bat!

3 I may be seventy-five, but I'm <u>as</u> fit <u>as</u> <u>a</u> fiddle.

7 1 A<u>meri</u>ca, C<u>ana</u>dian

2 <u>Ja</u>pan, Japa<u>nese</u>

3 Portu<u>guese</u>, Bra<u>zil</u>

8 (Answers 1 to 6 in any order.)

1 crowded 2 fountain 3 nightlife 4 polluted

5 statue 6 square

(Answers 7 to 10 in any order.)

7 date 8 fancy 9 go out with 10 split up

(Answers 11 to 15 in any order.)

11 fit 12 nil 13 pitch 14 practise 15 track

9 1 calls 2 after 3 ex-wife 4 look 5 making

6 high-rise 7 up 8 in 9 stormy 10 up

11 court 12 go 13 cool 14 per 15 per cent

5 Review 1 Test

Name: _____   Total: _____ /80

1 Questions 8 points

Complete the questions.

1 '_____ name?'
   'Paul Pearce.'

2 '_____ old _____ ?'
   '23.'

3 '_____ do?'
   'I'm a drummer.'

4 '_____ best characteristics?'
   'I'm friendly, funny and romantic.'

5 '_____ worst characteristics?'
   'I'm always late for everything.'

6 '_____ in your free time?'
   'I go clubbing, to parties and listen to music.'

7 '_____ favourite item of clothing?'
   'An old pair of jeans.'

8 '_____ kind of person _____ to
   meet?'
   'I want to meet someone who's fun, rich and likes
   music.'

2 Comparatives & superlatives 6 points

Put the adjective into the correct form to complete these
facts about the internet.

1 Half of all users are _____ than 25. (young)

2 Japanese is _____ second
   _____ language used on the internet.
   (common)

3 Hotmail is _____ free e-mail provider.
   (big)

4 _____ Internet Service Provider is
   Compuserve. (old)

5 The internet is _____ with males than with
   females. (popular)

6 _____ website ever was when Sir Paul
   McCartney received three million questions in thirty
   minutes. He was promoting his album *Flaming Pie* in
   1997. (busy)

3 Countable & uncountable nouns 6 points

Complete the dialogues using *much, many, a little* or
a few.

A: How (1) _____ money have you got left?

B: Only (2) _____ , I'm afraid. Just (3) _____
    dollars.

                    *   *   *

C: Were there (4) _____ people at the party?

D: No, just (5) _____ .

                    *   *   *

E: What's the matter?

F: I think I ate too (6) _____ for lunch.

4 Past simple & past continuous 8 points

Underline the correct tense to complete this profile of a
famous person.

He first (1) **became / was becoming** interested in

computers at an early age and he (2) **already

programmed / was already programming** computers

by the time he was twelve years old. He (3) **started /

was starting** his first company when he (4) **was / was

being** at school and he (5) **founded / was founding**

Microsoft in 1975 while he (6) **studied / was studying**

at university. He (7) **didn't finish / wasn't finishing**

his studies. He (8) **became / was becoming** a

billionaire at thirty-one.

(*Who is he?* _____)

5 Irregular verbs *10 points*

Add the missing verb form: infinitive, past simple or past participle.

1 begin, _____ , begun

2 buy, bought, _____

3 _____ , caught, caught

4 drink, _____ , drunk

5 fight, _____ , fought

6 keep, _____ , kept

7 mean, _____ , meant

8 meet, met, _____

9 ring, _____ , rung

10 sing, _____ , sung

6 Pronunciation – schwa /ə/ *6 points*

<u>Underline</u> the schwas in these sentences. The number in brackets shows you how many there are in the sentence.

1 I'm not as old as she is. (2)

2 He can't see a thing – he's as blind as a bat! (4)

3 I may be seventy-five, but I'm as fit as a fiddle. (3)

7 Pronunciation – word stress *6 points*

<u>Underline</u> the most stressed syllable in each of the countries, nationalities and languages.

1 'Are you from **America**?'

'No, I'm **Canadian**, actually.'

2 'I really want to go to **Japan**.'

'You should speak to Yuki, my **Japanese** friend.'

3 'You speak **Portuguese**!'

'Yes, I lived in **Brazil** for two years.'

8 Vocabulary – general (1) *15 points*

Put the words in the box into the correct category.

> crowded date fancy fit fountain go out with
> nightlife nil pitch polluted practise split up
> statue square track

In the city	Relationships	Sport
1 _____	7 _____	11 _____
2 _____	8 _____	12 _____
3 _____	9 _____	13 _____
4 _____	10 _____	14 _____
5 _____		15 _____
6 _____		

9 Vocabulary – general (2) *15 points*

<u>Underline</u> the correct alternative.

1 My name's James, but everyone **calls / names** me Jim.

2 I was named **after / from** my grandfather.

3 I met your **past-wife / ex-wife** yesterday.

4 You **look / look like** tired. You should go to bed.

5 I hate **taking / making** decisions.

6 The city is full of **tall-rise / high-rise** buildings.

7 Someone chatted me **up / down** in the club last night.

8 His problem is that he's always falling **for / in** love.

9 They have a very **windy / stormy** relationship.

10 Did you hear? Tom and Jo split **apart / up** last week.

11 Fred's new house has got a tennis **court / pitch**.

12 Do you want to **go / do** swimming this afternoon?

13 She always stays as **calm / cool** as a cucumber.

14 We always drove at 180 kilometres **per / for** hour.

15 I got ninety **per cents / per cent** in my English test!

6 Shop *Overview*

This unit is about shopping, particularly shopping for presents for other people, and the differences in attitude between men and women when it comes to shopping and giving gifts. The grammatical focus is on verbs with two objects, present and past simple with adverbs of frequency and verbs + -*ing* form.

Students begin by discussing the giving of presents and exploring the difference in attitudes to presents of men and women. This leads on to looking at common collocations. They then do some grammar work on verbs with two objects and practise using them to talk about presents they have been given. They also tell each other Anecdotes about the last time they went shopping to buy a present for someone. They then go on to look at adverbs of frequency, find examples in the previous reading text and make up their own sentences using them.

The next section is about the price of clothes. Some famous women are pictured together with a breakdown of how much each item of clothing cost them. Students discuss their own clothes shopping habits before going on to do some work on verbs + -*ing* form and comparing the attitudes to shopping of two different men.

They then listen to two conversations in shops, discuss how typical the shoppers are and write their own shop dialogues to perform to the class.

Section	Aims	What the students are doing
Introduction pages 34–35	*Conversation skills*: fluency work	Discussing giving and receiving presents.
	Reading skills: reading for gist	Reading a woman's account of what men and women want as presents.
	Lexis: collocation	Matching words to make collocations and discussing common and unusual presents.
Close up pages 35–36	*Grammar*: verbs with two objects	Re-writing sentences where verbs have two objects.
		Identifying word order in sentences where the verbs have two objects and writing more sentences.
	Conversation skills: fluency work	Anecdote: talking about buying a present.
Close up page 36	*Grammar*: adverbs of frequency	Identifying adverbs of frequency in a reading text.
		Writing sentences with adverbs of frequency about a partner and checking if they are true.
		Comparing your life as a child and now.
How much is she wearing? page 37	*Reading skills*: reading for specific information	Identifying famous women and matching photos to texts.
		Identifying the most expensive items.
		Covering photos and remembering what is in them.
	Conversation skills: fluency work	Discussing clothes shopping.
◉ **Close up** page 38	*Grammar*: verbs + -*ing* form	Completing statements about the attitude of men and women to shopping.
		Identifying verbs that take the -*ing* form.
		Reading and correcting two interviews.
		Discussing attitudes to shopping.
◉ **I'll take it** page 39	*Listening skills*: listening for gist	Identifying who says what in a shopping dialogue.
		Reading, completing and listening to a second shopping dialogue. Discussing how typical the people are.
	Writing skills: dialogue	Writing a shopping dialogue.

Shop Teacher's notes

Books closed. Whole class. Bring to class several objects wrapped up in paper to make interesting-looking parcels. If possible, disguise the shapes a little. Ask students to pass them around, feel them, shake them, smell them and talk about what they think is inside. Ask which one they would most like to receive as a present. Finally, allow them to open the parcels to reveal the contents.

Groupwork. Students discuss the questions and report back to the class.

Reading (p 34)

1 If you want your students to learn to scan a text only for specific information, go through the questions with them first and then set up the activity as a race. The first student to find all the answers is the winner.

> a) A woman (reference to 'my husband').
> b) No.
> c) No.
> d) According to her, men want gadgets, and women want jewellery.

2 Encourage students to try to form the sentences without looking them up in the article. Then let them read the article again to find the sentences and check their answers.

> a) A real present is something you can keep.
> b) Books are a waste of time.
> c) Most women are not interested in gadgets.
> d) Women are sensitive and intuitive.
> e) Men don't usually want brightly coloured ties or silly socks.
> f) Men like anything digital or electronic.

3 Pairwork. Students discuss whether or not they agree with the sentences.

Lexis: collocation (p 35)

1 Students match items in column A with those in column B to make common collocations. When checking answers, encourage students to say the expressions aloud rather than just matching the numbers with the correct letters. This will help them to memorise the collocations and recognise them when they encounter them next.

> a 4   b 6   c 1   d 3   e 2   f 5

2 Pairwork. Students discuss whether the items in Exercise 1 would be common or unusual presents in their countries. If you have students of different nationalities, encourage them to give mini-presentations on what the gift-giving customs are in their countries and whether there are any things that would definitely not be given as presents there.

Close up (p 35)

Verbs with two objects

1 Focus attention on the table and the first sentence: *Men buy gadgets for women*. Practise using the terms for the different parts of a sentence by asking individual students to change the part of the first sentence that you call out. For example:

You: Subject
Student A: Children buy gadgets for women.

You: Direct object
Student B: Men buy perfume for women.

You: Indirect object
Student C: Men buy gadgets for themselves.

Then elicit what has changed in the example sentence (the indirect object has been placed after the verb and *for* has been left out).

Students change the other sentences in the same way. Ask them to check their answers in the article on page 34. There is more information on verbs with two objects in the Language reference section at the bottom of page 35.

> a) My husband bought me a gadget.
> b) He got me one of those things.
> c) I gave my husband a small torch.

2 Allow students to discuss this in pairs or groups. If you have a multilingual class, allow them to form pairs or groups with students who speak the same language to do the exercise and then report back to the class on how their language functions.

3 Look at the example with the class and make sure students realise that they are not limited to the expressions in the boxes alone, but must include each of the specified parts of a sentence. Students then work individually to construct their four sentences. Make sure they hide their false sentences amongst the true ones. They then exchange papers with a partner and try to identify their partner's false sentence.

Anecdote (p 36)

See the Introduction on page 4 for more ideas on how to set up, monitor and repeat Anecdotes.

Pairwork. Give students plenty of time to decide what they are going to talk about and to read the questions. They then take turns to talk about their present to their partner.

Close up (p 36)

Adverbs of frequency

1 Encourage students to complete the sentence without looking it up in the article on page 34. Then allow them to check their answers in the article.

> I *always* look for the diamond ring hidden in the flowers, but it's *never* there.

2 You could set this activity up as a race with the first student or pair to find all the adverbs of frequency as the winner. They should find eleven adverbs: *usually* (x3), *always* (x5), *hardly ever, never* and *normally*. There is more information about adverbs of frequency in the Language reference section at the bottom of page 36.

> Adverbs of frequency come before main verbs.
> Adverbs of frequency come after *be*.

3 Make sure students realise that the order they have to put the adverbs in is the order of frequency, with *always* at one end and *never* at the other. Allow them to compare in pairs before checking with the class.

> always, usually, normally, often, sometimes,
> occasionally, rarely, hardly ever, never

4 Students work individually to complete the sentences about the person sitting next to them. Make sure they do this in silence without conferring.

> a) He/She [adverb] spends more than £25 on a present.
> b) He/She is [adverb] positive about life.
> c) He/She [adverb] goes out at the weekend.
> d) He/She is [adverb] on time.
> e) He/She [adverb] has lunch at home during the week.
> f) He/She [adverb] goes to bed before 10.00 pm.

5 Students show their sentences to their partners to see how many are true. They then decide how similar or different they are and report back to the class.

6 Pairwork. Students make sentences about their lives as children. Go round offering help and encouragement and ensure that they are using an adverb of frequency in each one. They then discuss the changes in their lives with their partners.

How much is she wearing? (p 37)

Books closed. Whole class. Write the title of this section on the board and ask students to speculate on what it will be about. Accept all suggestions but do not confirm or deny any.

Reading

1 Students look at the photographs and say which women they recognise and whose clothes they like best. They then match the photos with the texts. All the women are actresses, though Kylie Minogue is more famous as a pop star.

> a 2   b 4   c 1   d 3

2 Students work individually to work out who is wearing the most expensive items and then check their answers in pairs.

> a) dress: Catherine Zeta Jones (£7,500)
> b) trousers: Gwyneth Paltrow (£500)
> c) top: Gwyneth Paltrow (£2,500)
> d) shoes: Gwyneth Paltrow (£2,000)
> e) ring: Catherine Zeta Jones (£180,000)
> f) earrings: Jennifer Aniston (£10,000)

3 Make sure students cover the photos before deciding whether the statements are true or false. They then uncover the photos to check their answers and correct the false information. Find out who has the best memory in the class.

> a) False: Jennifer Aniston is wearing a red evening dress.
> b) True.
> c) True.
> d) False: Catherine Zeta Jones is wearing a black silk wrap.
> e) True.
> f) False: Kylie Minogue is wearing a plain top.
> g) False: Gwyneth Paltrow is wearing trousers.
> h) False: Kylie Minogue's coat is brown and her top is dark blue.

4 Pairwork. Remind students that they can find useful language in the Language toolbox in the margin. They discuss the issues in pairs and report any interesting information to the class.

Close up (p 38)

Verbs + -ing form

1 Pairwork. Students discuss the statements and complete them as they think appropriate. Find out how much difference there is between the answers given by male and female students. Having same sex pairs for this exercise may make this easier.

2 Students read the statement again and underline the verbs and verb phrases followed by the -ing form. There is more information on this in the Language reference section at the bottom of page 38.

Ask students to practise these forms by producing sentences of their own using them.

> a) can't stand shopping
>
> b) don't mind spending
>
> c) spend ... going, comparing ...
>
> d) don't bother looking
>
> e) don't waste time shopping
>
> f) prefer going ... going shopping.

3 Allow students to work in pairs if they wish. They should find twelve mistakes. Do not check answers at this stage.

4 🔊 **27 SB p 136**

Play the recording for students to listen and check their answers. Then ask them if they know any men with similar attitudes to shopping or whether their own attitudes correspond to either those of Russell or Billy.

> 1 Do you mind going   I don't mind going   shopping   I prefer watching
>
> 2 ... do you like going into   I love listening
>
> 3 ... you hate going into   I don't bother going   I can't stand going
>
> 4 Do you enjoy buying   I don't waste time   shopping   I like having   I don't enjoy trying

> 🔊 **27**
>
> (I = Interviewer; R = Russell; B = Billy)
>
> I: *Right, okay. Question one. Do you mind going round the shops?*
>
> R: *Not really. But after about an hour I want to go home.*
>
> B: *It depends. I don't mind going shopping, but on Saturdays I prefer watching football on TV.*
>
> I: *Right, okay. Um, let's see. Question two. What kind of shops do you like going into?*
>
> R: *Book shops. I could spend a whole day in a book shop.*
>
> B: *I love listening to music, so music shops are my favourite.*

> I: *Right, okay. Question three. Are there any kinds of shops you hate going into?*
>
> R: *I hate supermarkets so I don't bother going into them any more. I do my shopping on the internet.*
>
> B: *I can't stand going into shoe shops with my girlfriend. She tries on ten pairs and then buys the first pair.*
>
> I: *Right, okay. Last question. Question four. Do you enjoy buying clothes for yourself?*
>
> R: *Not really. I don't waste time shopping for clothes unless I really need something.*
>
> B: *I like having new clothes, but I don't enjoy trying them on.*
>
> I: *Right, thanks.*

5 Pairwork. Students take turns asking and answering the questions in Exercise 3. They then report back to the class.

I'll take it (p 39)

Closed books. Whole class. Ask students what most shops are like in their countries. Are they like supermarkets where you take the things you want off a shelf, put them in a basket and have no contact with shop staff until you get to the checkout, or are they more friendly with assistants who help you to make your choice? Ask also whether they prefer shops with assistants or prefer to be left alone to make their own choices.

Listening

1 Remind students that Russell is one of the men interviewed in the last section. Students read the extracts from his conversation with a shop assistant and decide who says what. Allow them to compare answers in pairs but do not check answers at this stage.

2 🔊 **28 SB p 136**

Play the recording for students to check their answers.

> a) Can I help you? (SA)
>
> b) I'm just looking, thanks. (R)
>
> c) What sort of thing are you looking for? (SA)
>
> d) What colours have you got? (R)
>
> e) Purple suits people with green eyes. (SA)
>
> f) What size is she? (SA)
>
> g) I'll take it. (R)
>
> h) How would you like to pay? (SA)
>
> i) Here's your receipt. (SA)
>
> j) Can she exchange it if it doesn't fit? (R)

28

(SA = Shop assistant; R = Russell)

SA: *Can I help you?*

R: *Oh, I'm just looking, thanks. Well, actually, I'm looking for something for my girlfriend.*

SA: *And what sort of thing are you looking for?*

R: *I don't really know. A top?*

SA: *Right. What colour would you like?*

R: *Um, what colours have you got?*

SA: *We've got any colour you want, sir. What colour does your girlfriend usually wear?*

R: *Oh dear ...*

SA: *Okay, what colour are her eyes?*

R: *Green.*

SA: *Right, purple suits people with green eyes.*

R: *Oh great. Yes, purple's fine.*

SA: *Now, what size is she?*

R: *Um, well, sort of, she isn't very big, but she's not particularly small.*

SA: *That'll be medium then.*

R: *Yes, good, medium.*

SA: *Well, we have this rather nice silk evening top here ...*

R: *Good, I'll take it.*

SA: *Are you sure you don't want to see any more ...?*

R: *No, that's great. I'll take it. Thank you. How much is it?*

SA: *That's £70, sir. How would you like to pay?*

R: *Seventy?! By credit card, please.*

SA: *Fine. If you could just sign ...*

R: *Here you are. Goodbye.*

SA: *Just a minute, sir. Here's your receipt.*

R: *Oh yes, er ... can she exchange it if it doesn't fit?*

SA: *Yes, but she needs to keep the receipt.*

3 Discuss these questions with the class and elicit various opinions.

> *Possible answers*
> embarrassed, nervous, self-conscious, no enjoyment

4 Pairwork. You may like to point out to students that Roz is a woman and ask them to say what similarities and differences they can find between her conversation with the shop assistant and Russell's.

Students read the conversation and complete it with appropriate words. Allow them to compare with other students, but don't check answers at this stage.

5 **29** SB p 136

Play the recording for students to listen and check their answers.

> 1 help   2 looking   3 sort   4 What   5 suit
> 6 suit   7 suit   8 take   9 like   10 receipt

29

(SA = Shop assistant; R = Roz)

SA: *Can I help you?*

R: *Yes, I'm looking for a mobile phone.*

SA: *And what sort of mobile phone are you looking for, madam?*

R: *Um – what do you mean?*

SA: *Well, what do you want to do with your mobile phone – do you want to access the internet, send text messages, play games ...?*

R: *No, no. I just want to make telephone calls.*

SA: *Right. Something like this perhaps? This model comes with a Call Register facility which keeps track of the calls you have received, missed and dialled – also, if you take our pre-pay option, you can find out how much credit you still have.*

R: *No, no, I'm not interested in all that. I just want to make telephone calls.*

SA: *Fine. How about this basic model? It's very easy to use.*

R: *Yes ... What colours have you got?*

SA: *Well, we have this rather nice red one.*

R: *Red doesn't suit me.*

SA: *Red doesn't suit you??*

R: *That's right. I wear a lot of pink.*

SA: *I see. Um, well, we haven't got pink but we have this one in blue. Does blue suit you?*

R: *Yes, I like blue. I'll take it.*

SA: *Fine. I don't suppose you're interested in the clock function ...*

R: *No.*

SA: *... or voice and speed dialling ...*

R: *No. I just want to pay!*

SA: *Okay, that'll be £60. How would you like to pay, madam?*

R: *In cash. Here you are.*

SA: *Thank you, madam. Here's your receipt. Oh, and don't forget this catalogue that tells you all about our mobile phone accessories. I'm sure you'll ...*

6 Pairwork. Students discuss whether they think Russell and Roz are a typical man and woman.

7 Pairwork. Students work together to produce a shopping dialogue. Remind them that there are useful expressions they can use in Exercise 1 and in the dialogue in Exercise 4. Ensure they know that they must use at least six of the words in the box. Go round offering help and encouragement.

Allow time for pairs to practise and perform their dialogues. If facilities permit, you might like to record or video them.

Test

Scoring: one point per correct answer unless otherwise indicated.

1   1 pair   2 bunch   3 packet   4 box   5 bottle
       6 piece

2   1   I lent a hundred pounds <u>to</u> my brother.
           Or I lent <u>my brother a hundred pounds</u>.

       2   Tom bought ~~for~~ me a CD for my birthday.
           Or Tom bought <u>a CD for me</u> for my birthday.

       3   Amy's making <u>us</u> coffee ~~us~~ at the moment.
           Or Amy's making coffee <u>for</u> us at the moment.

       4   The shop assistant explained the problem <u>to</u> us.

3   1   I didn't send an e-mail to anyone today.

       2   His parents bought him his first car.

       3   She is making a pizza for us.

       4   Did Steve show you his holiday photos?

4   1   I normally do my shopping at the weekend.

       2   We hardly ever eat in restaurants.

       3   He is often late for work.

       4   She often works at weekends.

       5   She is always looking for a good bargain.

       6   He doesn't usually drink white wine.

5   1 help, looking   2 suits, size
       3 exchange, fit, receipt, pay

6   1 ✔   2 to go   3 buying   4 ✔   5 ✔   6 trying

7   1 going   2 walking   3 being able   4 queuing
       5 shopping   6 waiting

6 Shop Test

Name:

Total: _____ /40

1 Vocabulary – collocations *6 points*
Complete the sentences with words from the box.

bottle box bunch packet pair piece

1 I need to buy a new _____ of jeans.

2 He got me a _____ of flowers to say sorry.

3 How much is a _____ of cigarettes here?

4 He ate the whole _____ of chocolates!

5 We must buy a _____ of wine for the party.

6 Would you like another _____ of cake?

2 Verbs with two objects (1) *4 points*
Correct the mistakes in these sentences.

1 I lent a hundred pounds my brother.

2 Tom bought for me a CD for my birthday.

3 Amy's making coffee us at the moment.

4 The shop assistant explained the problem us.

3 Verbs with two objects (2) *4 points*
Reorder the words in *italics*.

1 I didn't *anyone an e-mail to send today* .

   _____

2 His parents *his first car him bought* .

   _____

3 She *for is making us a pizza* .

   _____

4 Did Steve *his holiday photos you show* ?

   _____

4 Adverbs of frequency *6 points*
Put the adverb into the correct position in the sentence.

1 I do my shopping at the weekend. (normally)

2 We eat in restaurants. (hardly ever)

3 He is late for work. (often)

4 She works at weekends. (often)

5 She is looking for a good bargain. (always)

6 He doesn't drink white wine. (usually)

5 Vocabulary – shopping *8 points*
Add the missing vowels (*a, e, i, o, u*) to complete the dialogues.

1 'Can I h__lp you?'

   'It's okay, I'm just l__ __k__ng, thanks.'

2 'The shirt really s__ __ts you.'

   'Yes, I like it, but it's a little big. Have you got a
   smaller s__z__ ?'

3 'Can I __xch__ng__ it if it doesn't f__t?

   'Of course, as long as you keep the r__c__ __pt. How
   would you like to p__y?'

6 Verbs + -*ing* form (1) *6 points*
Are the **bold** verbs in the correct form or not? Tick (✔)
the correct forms and correct the incorrect forms.

A: I never bother (1) **going** _____ shopping with my
   boyfriend. He always wants (2) **going** _____
   home after half an hour.

B: I really enjoy (3) **to buy** _____ presents for other
   people.

C: It's important to spend time (4) **looking** _____ in
   different shops, comparing prices and quality.

D: I can't stand (5) **going** _____ shopping with my
   girlfriend – she always wastes time (6) **to try**
   _____ on the same clothes again and again.

7 Verbs + -*ing* form (2) *6 points*
Complete the sentences with the -*ing* form of the verbs
in the box.

be able go shop wait walk queue

I don't bother (1) _____ into supermarkets any
more. You waste too much time (2) _____ up and
down the aisles, and I hate not (3) _____ to find
what I want. And I can't stand (4) _____ at the
checkout. I prefer (5) _____ on the internet these
days. If you don't mind (6) _____ a day or so for
your food to arrive, it's the perfect way to shop.

7 Job *Overview*

The topic of this unit is employment, and the grammar focus is on the present perfect simple tense. The lexical focus is on employment words and expressions with *hand*.

Students start by discussing what you can tell about a person's job by looking at their hands, and they listen to three people, whose hands are illustrated, talking about their work. They then study some common expressions which use the word *hand*.

The unit continues with a reading about nightmare jobs. Students first predict the sorts of bad experiences people might have in certain jobs and then read what three people say about their worst jobs. They then discuss what they think the worst job in the world would be.

The next section gives students the opportunity to do some structured work on the form and use of the present perfect simple tense. They then go on to ask each other questions about their own past experiences.

The focus then turns to the question of age and employment. Students hear about an interesting company where nobody is forced to retire and over half the staff are over sixty-five. Students examine some key employment vocabulary and then they have the opportunity to talk about a retired person they know, using the Anecdote procedure to structure what they say.

In the final section, students learn how to write a letter of application for a job and look at ways of doing an oral self-introduction.

Section	Aims	What the students are doing
Introduction pages 40–41	*Conversation skills*: fluency	Talking about people's hands.
	Listening skills: listening for gist and specific information	Listening to three people talking about their work, matching them to jobs and answering questions.
	Lexis: expressions with *hand*	Studying and using expressions with *hand*.
	Reading skills: reading for detail	Reading a text about nightmare jobs to see how students' ideas about the jobs match the experiences in the text.
	Conversation skills: fluency work	Discussing bad working conditions.
Close up pages 42–43	*Grammar*: present perfect simple; time expressions	Studying extracts from the previous reading to see how the present perfect simple works.
		Completing sentences with appropriate time expressions.
		Examining the past participle forms of irregular verbs.
Class experience page 43	*Conversation skills*: fluency work	Using the present perfect simple tense in a questionnaire to ask each other about past experiences.
Youth versus experience page 44	*Listening skills*: listening for detail	Predicting the answers to questions about an unusual company from a photograph, then listening to check.
		Listening to determine whether statements are true or false and correcting the false ones.
	Lexis: employment	Using words and expressions from the interview to complete sentences about employment.
	Conversations skills: fluency work	Anecdote: talking about a retired person students know well.
Presentation page 45	*Reading skills*: reading for detail	Improving a job application letter by adding more suitable formal expressions.
	Writing skills: letter of application	Writing an application letter for a dream job.
	Conversation skills: fluency work	Preparing and making an oral self-introduction, concentrating on pausing, correct stress and highlighting important or difficult words.

7 *Job* Teacher's notes

Closed books. Whole class. Before students open their books, ask them how easy it is to decide what someone's job is just by looking at them. Ask them what things can give them a clue (e.g. someone's clothes, their voice, whether or not they have a suntan, etc.). Encourage students to tell the class of any times they have correctly or incorrectly guessed someone else's job and what the consequences were, if any.

If anyone suggests that someone's hands can give a clue, tell them to open their books and look at the photographs on page 40. If not, suggest it yourself and then have them look at the photographs.

Pairwork. Students look at the photographs of hands and discuss the questions. Direct their attention to the Language toolbox for some useful expressions for speculating about people and go round offering help and encouragement where necessary.

In a feedback session with the whole class, see how much agreement there is on what the photographs tell them about the people and their lives. You might also like to find out if students don't notice people's hands when they meet them, what feature it is that they do notice first.

Listening (p 40)

1 **30 SB p 136**

Go through the instructions with the class and make sure that everyone understands *midwife, farmer* and *guitarist*. Ask students to predict which hands belong to which person. Then play the recording and ask them to say which speaker is which.

> A guitarist   B midwife   C farmer

30

A

Yeah, right, it all started when we were at school. We wanted to, like, start a band. I got this second-hand guitar for my sixteenth birthday, and my friend was really good at singing. That's how it started really, you know what I mean? We found a drummer and started doing gigs. And suddenly the band got really big – we started having hit records and making loads of money. So I dropped out of school and really concentrated on the music. I've got fifteen guitars now, but my favourite is still the one I got for my sixteenth birthday, you know what I mean?

B

I work in the maternity department of a large hospital and I've delivered 649 babies so far. It's a great job because it brings happiness to people's lives. When I hand the new baby to the parents, I know that it's one of the happiest moments of their lives. On the other hand, it's a very stressful job. I usually work nights and I work long hours, so I haven't had time to have a baby of my own yet!

C

I couldn't live in a city – I love the outdoor life. It's a hard life, but I've never missed a single day's work through illness and I'm sixty-nine years old. With the new tractor, I have a bit more time on my hands, but I still get up at five o'clock every morning and feed the animals before breakfast. My eldest son gives me a hand at weekends, but I still do most of the work myself – you know you're living when you're outdoors.

2 Go through *a* to *h* with the class and explain any unknown vocabulary. Students may not know *dropped out of school* (= gave up school early, without finishing a course) and *loads of* (= a lot of).

Play the recording again. Students match *a* to *h* to the speakers. Check answers with the class.

> a B   b C   c B   d A   e C   f A   g C   h B

3 Read the example with the class to ensure they know what to do. Then allow students time to complete the sentences individually with the names of people they know before they compare answers with a partner. Encourage them to expand the sentences with further details as in the example.

Lexis: expressions with *hand* (p 40)

1 Allow students to work in pairs or small groups to replace the underlined words with the expressions from the box. Check answers with the class and ask if students know any more expressions with *hand*. There are many of these in English, eg: *lend a helping hand, give someone a big hand* (= clap), *to have your hands full* (= to be very busy), *to be in good hands* (= to be looked after by someone who can be trusted). Find out if such expressions exist in the students' own language(s).

> a) second-hand   b) time on my hands   c) hands
> d) On the other hand   e) gives a hand

2 Pairwork. Students discuss with a partner whether any of the sentences are true for them. Encourage them to add further details if they are and to report back to the class anything interesting they learn.

Optional activity

English has a number of expressions which include the names of body parts. Encourage students to keep a look out for these and to keep a record of them. They could do this in their vocabulary notebooks or on a wall chart. You might like to draw the outline of a body on a large piece of paper and encourage students to add expressions in appropriate places as they encounter them. Here are a few to start you off.

to be a bit long in the tooth (= to be rather old)
to keep an eye on something (= to watch something very carefully)
bone idle (= very lazy)
headstrong (= determined to do what they want)
to have a finger in every pie (= to be involved in everything)

Reading (p 41)

Closed books. The next section is about unpleasant jobs and bad working conditions. Before starting this work, you might like to ask students what kind of things would make a job their 'dream job'. List these on the board and see how much agreement there is about what would make a job ideal. Is it just a question of salary or are working conditions more important to them?

1 Groupwork. Students look the jobs up in a dictionary and discuss the possible bad experiences you could have in these jobs.

Go round offering help with vocabulary and encouragement where necessary and get groups to report back to the class on their discussions.

You might like to ask the class to vote on which of the jobs they would least like to do.

2 Students read the article to see how closely it matches their own ideas. Give them plenty of time to do this and answer any question they may have on difficult vocabulary.

3 Allow students to work in pairs or small groups to read the article again and find the words to complete the sentences. Make sure they understand that the sentences themselves are not from the article. They have to find words from the article that fit the context of the sentences. The initial letters are given to help them.

Check answers with the class, asking students to read out their completed sentences.

> a) nasty b) off c) break d) permission e) noisy
> f) disgusting

4 Pairwork. Students discuss the questions with a partner. In a feedback session with the whole class, encourage them to provide as much detail as possible. See how much agreement there is in the class about what the worst job in the world would be.

Close up (p 42)

Present perfect simple

1 Pairwork. Students read the two sentences from the article and discuss the questions. Refer them to the Language reference section on page 43 for help in identifying the tenses and the forms. You can also refer them to the Verb structures section on page 129. The time lines given on page 43 may help them to visualise and understand the difference between 'finished time' and 'time up to now' and hence the difference between the past simple and the present perfect simple.

Check answers with the class.

> a) Sentence 1. Past simple
> b) Sentence 2. Present perfect simple
> c) I've done. I haven't done. Have I done?

2 Allow students to work in pairs to decide whether the expressions in the box are 'finished time' or 'time up to now'. Check answers by writing these headings on the board and encouraging individual students to come up and write the time expressions under the correct headings. Then elicit and write up under the appropriate headings the new time expressions the students have thought of.

'Finished' time	Time 'up to now'
when I was a student	over the years
a few years ago	recently
last week	today
yesterday	never
in 1999	this week

3 Students work individually to complete the sentences with time expressions. Make sure they understand they can use their own expressions as well as those in 2 in order to make the sentences true for them. They then compare their sentences with a partner.

Check answers by eliciting sentences from individual students around the class.

4 Establish that the verbs in 3 are all irregular (they do not follow the usual grammatical pattern). Look at the verbs in the two groups with the class and ensure students understand the difference between Group A (where the past participle and past simple forms are the same) and Group B (where they are different). Check that they understand by eliciting another verb for each group.

You may need to explain that *gone* is also a past participle form of *go*, and that there is a difference in meaning between *been* and *gone*. *He has gone to Tokyo* implies that he is still in Tokyo. *He has been to Tokyo* implies that he went there and has now returned. *Been* is the form used in the present perfect simple to talk about completed action in 'time up to now'.

Students then work individually to put the verbs from 3 into the correct groups. Allow them to compare their answers in pairs or small groups before checking with the class.

If you are confident that your students have understood the principles here, you could allow them to do 5 before checking answers.

5 Students add the verbs from the box to the correct groups. Point out that their completed table after 4 and 5 should have eight verbs in Group A and twelve in Group B. Check answers with the class.

Group A

Infinitive	Past simple	Past participle
meet	met	met
buy	bought	bought
spend	spent	spent
feed	fed	fed
hear	heard	heard
sell	sold	sold
sleep	slept	slept
stick	stuck	stuck

Group B

Infinitive	Past simple	Past participle
go	went	been
see	saw	seen
do	did	done
bite	bit	bitten
choose	chose	chosen
drive	drove	driven
eat	ate	eaten
give	gave	given
hide	hid	hidden
take	took	taken
wear	wore	worn
write	wrote	written

6 Pairwork. Students make questions from the prompts. Check answers before going on to 7.

a) What's the best / worst holiday you've ever been on?

b) What's the best / worst meal you've ever eaten?

c) What's the best / worst joke you've ever heard?

d) What's the best / worst car you've ever been in?

e) What's the best / worst T-shirt you've ever worn?

f) What's the best / worst party you've ever been to?

g) What's the best / worst bed you've ever slept in?

7 Pairwork. Students take turns asking and answering their three chosen questions. Encourage them to ask follow-up questions in order to elicit as much detail as possible and to report back to the class on what they have found out.

Class experience (p 43)

1 Students work individually to complete the sentences with the names of people in the class. Make sure they understand that they should try to match people with things they really think there is a good chance that they will have done, but that they may not consult other students as they do this. If there are more than eleven students in your class, they will need to write more sentences in order to use each name once. Go round checking that they are forming questions using the present perfect simple correctly. It would be a good idea to fill in some of the sentences yourself with students' names for use as an example in the next exercise.

2 Demonstrate the activity by reading the example questions in the book with the class and then using your own list of sentences to check whether any of your predictions about students are correct.

Students then mill around asking questions to find out if their sentences are true or not. Suggest that they tick those sentences that are true so that they have a record for the subsequent feedback session.

3 Have a feedback session with the whole class to find out who had the largest number of true sentences.

4 Whole class. Find out who has done the largest number of things on the list in 1.

Youth versus experience (p 44)

Listening

Closed books. Establish the meaning of *retire* (= to stop work at the end of your working life). Ask students at what age people in their culture(s) retire. Is it a different age for men and women? Do they think this age has changed over the last hundred years? At what age do they think people ought to retire? Do they think people should be forced to retire at a certain age?

1 Pairwork. Students look at the photograph of Mr Reynold and discuss possible answers to the questions. Emphasise that you do not expect them to get the answers right but would like them to speculate based on what they can see. Remind them of the expressions in the Language toolbox on page 40 which they used to speculate about the hands.

2 🔲 **31 SB p 136**
Play the recording for students to check their answers.

a) A department store.

b) In 1948.

c) He is 85 (nearly 86).

(P = Presenter; I = Interviewer; Mr R = Mr Reynold)

P: *... And this week, in our regular report from over there in little old England, our interviewer, Gloria Sacks, walked into a department store with a difference ...*

I: *Mr Reynold, can you tell us what is so special about your department store?*

Mr R: *Well, yes, it is special. Reynold's is a large department store and you can find everything you want for the home here. Oh, and it stays open late on Thursdays and Saturdays.*

I: *Yes, that's right, but isn't there something special about the staff – you know – has anybody retired recently?*

Mr R: *Ah, oh I see. No. Nobody has retired recently, and we never force anybody to retire here.*

I: *How old is your oldest employee?*

Mr R: *Well, that would be Arthur. Arthur is our cleaner, and he's 87.*

I: *87! And he cleans the store every day?*

Mr R: *Well, not alone, no. He works with two other cleaners. They're not so old – Mabel's 70 and Ivy's 75 – no 76. That's right, she's just had her birthday.*

I: *And they don't want to retire?*

Mr R: *No, I think they enjoy the work, and it keeps them young. Also, we pay a decent salary, and they get four weeks' paid holiday a year.*

I: *So how many workers do you have who are over retirement age?*

Mr R: *Well, we employ a staff of a hundred and five, and I'd say that maybe half of those are over 65. The young ones work in the office – we've got computers now, you know.*

I: *Really? Has the store changed much over the years?*

Mr R: *No, not really. I started working here in 1948 and I've only had two secretaries in all that time. Edith, my first secretary, handed in her notice when she was 72.*

I: *Oh, why did she leave Reynold's so young?*

Mr R: *Well, she was getting married to someone who lived in another town.*

I: *Jeez! That's amazing. Tell me, have you ever fired anybody?*

Mr R: *No, not yet. I can't see any reason to fire somebody, unless they're dishonest. That's not a problem we have with the older employees.*

I: *And do you think you will ever retire, Mr Reynold?*

Mr R: *Oh yes. I'm nearly 86! My son's going to take over the business next year. It'll be good to have a younger man in charge. He's, er, only 64.*

3 Give the students time to read the statements before you play the recording again. Ask them to mark each one true or false as they listen. Allow them to compare with a partner before checking answers with the class.

> a) True. Mr Reynold never forces anybody to retire.
> b) False. The oldest employee at Reynold's is 87.
> c) True.
> d) False. Employees get four weeks' paid holiday.
> e) False. About half the staff are over the retirement age.
> f) True.
> g) True.
> h) False. Mr Reynold's son is going to run the business from next year.

Lexis: employment (p 44)

1 Students work individually to use the underlined expressions from Exercise 3 in the previous section to complete the sentences. Allow them to compare with a partner before checking answers with the class.

> a) weeks' paid holiday   b) a decent salary
> c) retirement age   d) to retire   e) run

2 Groupwork. Students discuss the statements and decide whether they agree or disagree with them. In a feedback session encourage them to change any of the statements that they disagree with to ones that they would agree with.

Anecdote (p 44)

See the Introduction on page 4 for more ideas on how to set up, monitor and repeat Anecdotes.

Pairwork. Give students plenty of time to decide who they are going to talk about and to read the questions. They then take turns to talk about their retired person to their partner.

Presentation (p 45)

Letter of application

1 Go through the instructions and read the words and expressions in the box with the whole class. Then give students time to read the application letter individually and to decide where to put the words. Allow them to compare answers in pairs before checking with the whole class.

Establish why the words in the box improve the letter (mostly it is a question of register: using the correct degree of formality for a business letter):

1 *Dear Sir or Madam* is the correct greeting for a letter to someone whose name you don't know.

2 *would like to apply for* is more polite and formal than *want*.

3 (*enclosed*) is a shorter and more formal way of saying the same thing and is more suitable for a business letter.

4 *reached retirement age* is a more formal expression than *got too old*.

5 *a new challenge* is a more formal and businesslike expression than *new things*.

6 *look forward to hearing* is more formal and appropriate for a business letter than *can't wait to hear*, which would be more suitable for a letter to a friend.

1	Sir or Madam
2	would like to apply
3	(enclosed)
4	reached retirement age
5	a new challenge
6	look forward to hearing

2 This could be set for homework if you have no time in class. Students will need plenty of time to decide what their dream job is and to prepare the letter.

If the letters are done in class, go round offering help and suggestions. If they are done at home, collect them in for comments and corrections.

Make sure students use the correct register for their letters and point out the difference between formal and informal language wherever possible. Using the correct register is one of the hardest things for students of English to learn. You could encourage them to keep lists of formal expressions and their informal equivalents in two columns in their vocabulary notebooks.

Presenting yourself (p 45)

1 Go through the instructions with the class and then give students time to read the self-introduction and to decide how they would introduce themselves on a training course.

2 Pairwork. Go through the instructions carefully with the whole class before allowing students to work in pairs. Establish that they don't have to change the wording of the self-introduction, just to re-write it so that it is easier to say. Point out that stressed words in a sentence are generally the most important words, those that carry the most meaning, and that when talking to strangers for the first time, it is a good idea to say new or unusual words, such as your name, particularly clearly. Check answers with the class, putting the rewritten text on the board.

Good <u>mor</u>ning. //
Let me intro<u>duce</u> myself. //
My name's <u>Lourdes</u> / <u>Rivas</u> //
and I <u>work</u> for British <u>Air</u>ways. //
As you probably <u>know</u> //
we are a <u>ma</u>jor / inter<u>na</u>tional / <u>air</u>line. //
I'm <u>based</u> at <u>Son</u>dika / airport in Bil<u>bao</u> //
where I'm in <u>charge</u> of <u>sales</u> and pro<u>mo</u>tion. //
I'm looking <u>for</u>ward to doing this <u>course</u>.

3 📼 **32 SB p 137**
Play the recording first for the students just to listen. Then ask them to repeat it as you play it for the second time.

4 Give students plenty of time to prepare their own self-introductions. Remind them that they can invent one if they wish (shy students or those with little to say may prefer this option). They should write their self-introductions out using the techniques in 2 and then.take turns in introducing themselves to the class.

Here is some useful language that you might want to put on the board to help them:
I'm a banker / an artist.
I work at head office / from home.
I work in the marketing department / accounts.
I'm responsible for export sales / computer software.
My job involves dealing with complaints / a lot of travel.

Test

Scoring: one point per correct answer unless otherwise indicated.
1 1 second-hand 2 a hand 3 hands 4 hand
2 1 went 2 recently 3 this year. 4 Did you talk
   5 haven't seen 6 today 7 met
   8 have ever eaten
3 1 Have, worked 2 worked 3 was
   4 've never been 5 've been 6 was
4 1 chosen 2 drove 3 eaten 4 gave 5 go
   6 gone 7 heard 8 sold 9 wrote 10 written
5 (Two points per correct answer.)
   1 Dear Sir or Madam
   2 would like to apply for the job.
   3 curriculum vitae (enclosed) for more details.
   4 look forward to hearing from you.
6 1 salary 2 employees 3 retire 4 paid

7 Job Test

Name: **Total:** _____ /40

1 Vocabulary – expressions with *hand*   *4 points*

Complete the sentences with the words in the box.

> hands   hand   second-hand   a hand

1 It's not new. It's _____ .

2 That looks heavy. Let me give you _____ .

3 Since I left my job, I've had a lot of time on my
_____ .

4 I love my job. The pay is terrible, on the other
_____ .

2 Present perfect simple (1)   *8 points*

Underline the correct alternative.

1 I **went / have been** to New York a few years ago.

2 I've spoken to him **recently / last year**.

3 We haven't been on holiday **this year / last year**.

4 **Did you talk / Have you talked** to Sam last night?

5 I **didn't see / haven't seen** any good films recently.

6 She's e-mailed me twice **today / yesterday**.

7 We **met / have met** them when we were in Spain.

8 This is the worst meal I **ever ate / have ever eaten**.

3 Present perfect simple (2)   *6 points*

Put the verb into the correct form: present perfect or past simple.

A: (1) _____ you ever

_____ (work) in a shop?

B: Yes, I (2) _____ (work) in

a supermarket one summer when I

(3) _____ (be) a student.

         *   *   *

C: I'm really excited about going to India.

I (4) _____ (never go) there before.

D: Lucky you! It's amazing. I (5) _____

(go) there twice actually. The last time

(6) _____ (be) two years ago.

4 Irregular verbs   *10 points*

Complete the table.

Infinitive	Past simple	Past participle
choose	chose	1 _____
drive	2 _____	driven
eat	ate	3 _____
give	4 _____	given
5 _____	went	6 _____
hear	heard	7 _____
sell	sold	8 _____
write	9 _____	10 _____

5 Letter of application   *8 points*

Reorder the words in *italics* in this letter of application.

(1) *or Madam Dear Sir* _____ ,

I recently saw your advertisement for a tour guide in
Paris and I (2) *apply like for the job would to.*

_____ .

I am an experienced tour guide and I speak fluent
English, French and Spanish. Please see my (3) *more
(enclosed) curriculum vitae details for* _____
_____ . I would
be available for an interview at any time. I (4) *forward
hearing you from look to* _____
_____ .

Yours faithfully, Steve Tyler

6 Vocabulary – employment   *4 points*

Complete the questions with words from the box.

> employees   paid   retire   salary

1 What's the average _____ in your country?

2 How many _____ does your company have?

3 When do you think you will _____ ?

4 How many week's _____ holiday do you get?

8 Rich *Overview*

The topic of this unit is wealth. The grammar focus is on future forms: *going to* and the present continuous.

Students begin by looking at the song, *Money*, which was a hit for the Beatles. Students complete the lyrics, talk about the attitude to money presented in the song and examine some common sayings about money. Next they read about three millionaires who have very different ideas about what to do with their money. Students talk about what they would do if they were millionaires and practise using some common money expressions.

The focus then returns to music and students listen to an interview with a pop star, Matt McKay, who made a fortune by the age of twenty and then left his band to pursue a solo career. Students identify his reasons for leaving the band and talk about what he is going to do in the future.

This leads into some grammar work on the use of *going to* for talking about decisions in the future. Students correct some sentences with *going to* and then use the structure to talk about their own future decisions. They then look at a poster for Matt's European tour, listen to another interview with him and identify which concerts he has cancelled. Finally they use some of the words they have heard in the interview to complete sentences about music and concerts.

The next section has grammar work on the use of the present continuous to talk about events in the future which have been arranged. Students practise making and talking about arrangements for the following week.

In the final section, students read about the Prince's Trust, an organisation that helps young people start up businesses and gain the experience and skills necessary to get work. They read three applications for grants and decide which is best before writing their own applications for companies they would like to set up.

Section	Aims	What the students are doing
Money page 46	*Listening skills*: listening for specific information	Completing the lyrics of the song, *Money*, and listening to check.
	Conversation skills: Discussion	Discussing the attitude to money presented in the song.
	Lexis: sayings about money	Talking about money sayings in English and students' own language.
Millionaires page 47	*Reading skills*: reading for gist	Matching adjectives with people in a text.
	Conversation skills: fluency work	Discussing the millionaires in the text and which one they sympathise most with.
	Lexis: money expressions	Finding money expressions in the reading text and using them to complete sentences.
Going solo page 48	*Reading skills*: reading for gist	Reading an extract from a TV guide and identifying what an interview is about.
	Listening skills: listening for detail	Listening to an interview with pop star, Matt McKay, and finding his reasons for leaving a band.
		Predicting what Matt is going to do and listening to check.
Close up pages 49–50	*Grammar*: (be) going to	Practising using *(be) going to* to talk about future decisions.
	Listening skills: listening for detail	Listening to another interview with Matt McKay and identifying which concerts he has cancelled.
		Using words from the interview to complete sentences
Close up page 50	*Grammar*: present continuous	Examining and practising the use of the present continuous to talk about future arrangements.
		Making future arrangements with classmates and talking about them.
Now give me money (that's what I want) page 51	*Reading skills*: reading for detail	Reading a text about the Prince's Trust and identifying how it can help young people.
	Writing skills: an application	Assessing the quality of three applications for grants and writing their own for a company they would like to set up.

8 *Rich* Teacher's notes

Money (p 46)

If your students are interested in the Beatles, you might like to have a competition to see which group of students know the most facts about them or can name the most Beatles songs.

Alternatively you could do a warm-up activity related to money as students are often interested in what money looks like as well as what it can buy. With a multinational class, you could ask students to bring some banknotes from their country to class to show the other students and explain what the designs on them are. You could also bring some banknotes from your own country to show to the students and get them to ask questions about what is pictured on them. European students might like to talk about the design of the euro currency and whether they prefer it to their old national currency.

Song (p 46)

1 Pairwork. Students read the lyrics of *Money*, a hit for the Beatles in 1963. They choose the most appropriate words to complete the lines. Allow them to compare notes with other pairs, but do not check answers at this stage.

2 33 SB p 46

Play the recording for students to listen and check their answers. Then play it again for them just to listen and enjoy or sing along if they wish.

> 1 free 2 bees 3 thrill 4 bills 5 true 6 use

33

Money

The best things in life are free.
But you can keep them for the birds and bees.
Now give me money.
That's what I want.
That's what I want, yeah.
That's what I want.

Your lovin' gives me a thrill.
But your lovin' don't pay my bills.
Now give me money.
That's what I want.
That's what I want, yeah.
That's what I want.

Money don't get everything, it's true
What it don't get, I can't use.
Now give me money.
That's what I want.
That's what I want, yeah.
That's what I want.

Now give me money.
Whole lot of money.
Yeah, I want to be free.
Whole lot of money.
That's what I want.
That's what I want, yeah.

3 Encourage students to quote lines from the song in support of their opinions. You may like to point out that the very opposite of this view of money is presented in other Beatles lyrics such as 'I don't care too much for money; money can't buy me love'.

> c) Money is the most important thing in life

4 Pairwork. Students discuss the questions and report back to the class.

5 Allow students to work in pairs or small groups to discuss what they think the sayings mean. With multilingual classes, encourage students to translate any of the money sayings they know in their language into English for the rest of the class. You might like to give them some more English sayings and expressions to think about, or see if they know any more, eg: *The love of money is the root of all evil; money for old rope; put one's money where one's mouth is;* etc.

> Money talks. = If you're rich, it means you've got power and influence.
>
> Money doesn't grow on trees. = Money isn't free – it has to be earned.
>
> Time is money. = Time is as important a resource as money.

Millionaires (p 47)

Most countries seem to have an equivalent of the UK television show *Who wants to be a millionaire?* Ask students if they have seen this and to talk about what they have seen. Do they think the questions are difficult? Do they think it is possible for a contestant to cheat? If so, how? Would they like to appear on the show? Interested students might like to prepare some questions for a class version of the show. All they need is a series of general knowledge questions with four alternative answers, only one of which is correct. You can act as question master, or get a confident student to do it. Encourage tension by repeatedly asking the answering student if they are absolutely sure of their answers. You could also include the 'ask the audience' or 'phone a friend' options. Students are only allowed to do this once.

Reading (p 47)

1 Groupwork. First establish that a millionaire is someone who has a million pounds (or dollars). Obviously because of exchange rates these are different amounts of money, and with other currencies, a million may not amount to very much at all. Explain that the term has come to mean someone who is extremely wealthy.

Students discuss the questions in small groups. In a feedback session, see how long a list the class can produce for ways of becoming a millionaire.

2 Elicit the meaning of *generous* from the class (someone who is generous with money is happy to give money to other people, but the word can be applied to other things and can simply mean kindhearted). Ask them to read the article and match the adjectives to the people. Note that answers here are subjective. Students may not feel that Brian Williamson's attitude to money is necessarily bad. By not leaving his money to his children, he may be preventing them from having life too easy and being spoilt.

> *Probable answers*
>
> Brian Williamson: bad.
>
> Eric Miller: extremely generous.
>
> Mike and Kathy Dawson: good.

3 Pairwork. Students discuss which of the millionaires they most sympathise with.

Lexis: money expressions (p 47)

1 Students read the article again and underline all the money expressions. Check answers with the class.

> *Possible answers*
>
> Introductory paragraph: money; yachts, limousines and luxury homes; millionaire; rich people
>
> Paragraph about Williamson: one of Britain's richest men; spent £40 million on; palace; make his money by investing it; inherit any of his fortune
>
> Paragraph about Miller: he sold his business and made a very large profit; he donated the house; the poor
>
> Paragraph about the Dawsons: earn; give away; large house; expensive cars; save some money; doubled their salary; charities

2 Students should work individually to complete the sentences, but allow them to compare with a partner before checking answers with the class.

> a) spent b) make c) made d) earn, earn
>
> e) save f) give

3 Pairwork. Students ask and answer the questions in Exercise 2. Encourage them to report back to the class on any interesting information they find out.

Going solo (p 48)

Reading & listening

1 Pairwork. Students discuss the questions. In a multinational class you could ask them to give small presentations to the class on the bands they have been talking about.

2 Go through the questions with the class first so they know what information they are looking for. They then read the extract from the TV guide. Check answers with the class.

> He is a pop singer and he is talking about why he left a successful band called *Ozone*.

3 **34 SB p 137**

Go through the possible reasons with the class first and make sure they understand them all. You might like to ask them to predict which ones Matt will give in the interview. Then play the recording and ask them to tick the reasons they hear. Allow them to compare notes in pairs before checking answers with the class.

> *b, d,* and *f* are correct.

34

(I = Interviewer; M = Matt)

I: *Matt, 'Ozone' was a very successful band. Why did you decide to leave?*

M: *I was very young when I joined the band. At first, all the money and fame and success was very exciting, and I enjoyed the attention. But after a while, I started to lose my identity.*

I: *What do you mean?*

M: *Well, we had no freedom at all. Our manager told us how to dress, how to sing and what to sing, how to dance, what to say to the press, where to go and where not to go.*

I: *But your manager turned you into a chart-topping band.*

M: *Yes, but we worked very hard and never went out. It wasn't a normal life for a teenager. We weren't even allowed to have relationships.*

I: *But you were making a lot of money.*

M: *Yes, that's true. And at first I enjoyed the money but I wasted it on stupid things. Also, I spent too much time with people who weren't my real friends – people who were only interested in my money. I lost my real friends. Then one morning I woke up and thought, 'I don't know who I am.' It was scary.*

4 Students match the verbs and phrases. Point out that in some cases more than one answer is possible. Check answers with the class and make sure that everyone understands the items.

> **Probable answers**
> a3 b1 c6 d2 e8 f9 g4 h5 i7

5 🔲 **35 SB p 137**
Before playing the recording ask students to discuss the items in Exercise 4 in pairs. They should tick the ones they think Matt will say he is going to do in the second part of the interview and cross the ones they think he will say he isn't going to do. Then play the recording for them to check whether they predicted correctly or not.

> Going to: carry on singing; pursue a solo career; employ a decent manager; spend more time with my family; write my own songs; play the kind of music I like
>
> Not going to: waste money on stupid things; forget my real friends; make the same mistakes again

> 🔲 **35**
> I: *And that's when you decided to leave?*
> M: *Yes, that's right.*
> I: *Matt, that was three months ago. Have you decided what you're going to do next?*
> M: *Yes. I've had time to think about my future. I'm going to carry on singing and pursue a solo career.*
> I: *Do you think you've learnt anything from your experience in 'Ozone'?*
> M: *Oh yes. This time I'm going to employ a decent manager who listens to me and who gives me good financial advice. I'm not going to waste money on stupid things. Also, I'm going to spend more time with my family and I'm definitely not going to forget my real friends.*
> I: *And what kind of music are you going to play?*
> M: *I'm going to write my own songs and play the kind of music I like. I've learnt my lesson and I'm definitely not going to make the same mistakes again.*
> I: *So, another Number 1 hit in the near future?*
> M: *Definitely.*

6 Pairwork. Students discuss the different options with a partner. Go round offering help and encouragement and making sure that students give reasons for their opinion. In a class feedback session, find out how many students chose each option.

Close up (p 49)

(be) going to

You might like to point out that students have encountered *going to* earlier in the unit and ask them what it was used for on page 48 to talk about what Matt is going to do in the future). There is more information on the use of *going to* in the Language reference section on page 50.

1 Allow students to work in pairs to identify the mistakes. Establish that *going to* is used to talk about decisions about the future. Remind them that the Language reference sections throughout the book are there to help them and to give them somewhere to check back on certain structures when reviewing their work. The Language reference section for *going to* is on page 50, and there is more information in the Verbs structures section on page 130. Check answers with the class.

> a) 'I<u>'m</u> going to carry on singing.'
> b) 'I'm definitely not go<u>ing</u> to forget my real friends.
> c) 'What kind of music are you going <u>to</u> play?'

2 Pairwork. Students should complete all the situations, first giving details of what happened to make last time's experience a disaster and then using *going to* to make some decisions about what they are going to do and not going to do next time. Go round the class asking pairs to read out one of their situations.

3 Pairwork. Students use the table to ask and answer as many questions as they can about decisions about the future that they have made. Go round offering help and encouragement and making sure they are using *going to* correctly.

Listening (p 49)

1 🔲 **36 SB p 137**
Focus students' attention on the poster and give them time to read it through. You may like to point out that the mistakes are factual not grammatical. Make sure they know the meaning of *cancelled* (something which has been arranged is now not going to happen).

Play the recording and ask students to write *cancelled* next to the concerts that Matt is not doing. Note that the present continuous is used here to refer to the future. This will be the focus of the next section's grammar work. In this case *not going to do* could also have been used.

Younger students with access to the internet might like to visit the Matt McKay website: *www.mattmckay.com*. They will find further pictures of Matt and some simple language exercises.

> Ireland 8 November
> Luxembourg 14 November
> Croatia 28 November

36

(S = Suzy; M = Matt)

S: *Welcome back to Suzy B on Radio 103. Matt McKay, ex-lead singer of 'Ozone', is sitting here with me in the studio today. Matt, how's life?*

M: *Really good.*

S: *That's great. Now your first solo single is coming out tomorrow. How are you feeling?*

M: *I'm feeling great, really positive. We've worked very hard on the album, and I think we've come up with some really good songs.*

S: *Excellent. And what about gigs? Are you doing any concerts?*

M: *Actually, we're starting a European tour next week. We're doing three nights in London. Then we're flying to Berlin. We're doing gigs in three German cities, then we're going onto Holland, Belgium and Denmark.*

S: *Wow, heavy. That's quite a schedule.*

M: *Oh, that's not all. We're having a short holiday the following week and then we're touring France, Switzerland, Spain and ... I think that's it.*

S: *Phew. You'll need another holiday after that.*

M: *Well, you know, it's important to get out and meet the fans.*

S: *Of course. But enough about work – have you got any plans for your holiday yet?*

M: *Yes. I'm taking my mum and dad to the Canary Islands for some sun.*

S: *Excellent. Matt. Good luck for tomorrow. I've heard the single, and if you ask me, it's going to go straight to the top of the charts.*

M: *Thanks. I hope you're right.*

S: *Okay, let's listen to the single now. Out tomorrow, this is Matt McKay's first solo single, 'I'm the one'.*

2 Students should work individually to complete the sentences, but allow them to compare notes with a partner before playing the recording for them to check their answers. As they have only heard these words and not seen them on the page, they may need to hear the recording several times. As a final check go through the sentences with the class. You may need to explain that gig is a fairly modern word for a pop or jazz concert.

> a) single b) album c) gigs d) tour e) fans
> f) charts

3 Pairwork. Students discuss how many of the sentences are true for them. You may like to extend this to a class discussion of favourite music and concert-going experiences.

Close up (p 50)

Present continuous

This section looks at another way of talking about the future: the present continuous, used for future arrangements. There is more information on both future forms taught in this unit in the Language reference section at the bottom of page 50. You may like to draw students' attention to the note in the Language reference that *going to* can also be used to talk about future arrangements. You may also like to refer students to the Verb structures section on page 130.

1 Give students time to study the example sentences and decide which ones refer to arranged future events and which to a present event. Check answers with the class and elicit or point out that the verbs in all the sentences are in the present continuous. Direct students' attention to the Language reference section at the bottom of the page for more information on the use of the present continuous for talking about the future.

> a, c, and d refer to arranged future events.
> b refers to a present event.

2 Emphasise that students should imagine that they are extremely rich and famous, so their arrangements should reflect this and are unlikely to include such things as doing homework or feeding the cat! They should give the time of each arrangement and there should be at least one for every day of the week.

3 Go through the instructions carefully. Before mingling, students should decide on three times and three activities to do with other students. They then take their diaries with them as they go around the class trying to make appointments with each other. Make sure they are asking questions properly and, if they already have an arrangement at the time someone asks them to do something, that they tell each other what they are already doing at that time using the present continuous. When they have finished, have a class feedback session in which students report on what they are doing and who they are doing it with.

4 Pairwork. Students discuss their real arrangements for next week and compare it with the life they have imagined. Go round making sure they are using the present continuous correctly.

Now give me money (that's what I want) (p 51)

Reading

The Prince's Trust is an organisation set up by Prince Charles in 1983 to help young people start new businesses and acquire the experience and skills that will help them find employment. Many thousands of people have been helped by grants (point out the definition in the margin) from the organisation to start up a wide variety of companies. Young people and those interested in starting up non-traditional businesses often find it difficult to get funding from banks, and the Prince's Trust is somewhere they can go for help, advice and money.

1 Students read the information on the website and find out what the organisation can help applicants to do. Allow them to compare notes in pairs before checking with the class.

> a) get help, get a grant and get into work
> b) improve your skills
> c) do a training course
> d) learn new skills
> e) buy the equipment you need
> f) start your own business

2 Students discuss whether there are similar organisations in their countries to help young people get a start in business.

Writing (p 51)

1 Pairwork. Students work together to decide what kind of business they would like to set up and what they would need to do it.

2 Ask students to read the applications. Then ask for suggestions as to which is the best application and why. Answers here will be subjective but *c* is the expected answer as this application is the one which uses the most formal language, gives the most detail about what the money would be used for and includes a business plan for the future which suggests that the applicant has long-term plans to ensure that the business succeeds. Applicant *a* only appears to want to start a business in order to make some extra money for a holiday. There is no suggestion of a long-term commitment to window cleaning. The language is also too informal for an application. Applicant *b* seems to have a worthy cause, but the group are not really running a business, providing employment for young people, so much as pursuing a hobby that involves some charity work.

> Summary c is the best.

3 Pairwork. In the same pairs as Exercise 1, students plan and write their own summaries of what they want to achieve. You may want to get them to do this on separate sheets of paper so that you can display them in the classroom. This will make Exercise 4 easier to organise.

4 Students read all the applications. Ideally these should be displayed in the classroom and plenty of time allowed for students to read and discuss them. They then say which of the applications they think is most likely to succeed.

Test

Scoring: one point per correct answer unless otherwise indicated.

1 1 earn 2 make 3 spend 4 save 5 made
   6 give

2 1 trees 2 talks

3 1 fan 2 single 3 charts 4 gigs 5 tour
   6 album

4 1 What are you going to do this evening?
   2 I'm going to cook a meal.
   3 I'm going to do my homework.
   4 I'm going to read the newspaper.
   5 I'm not going to do anything else.
   6 When are you going to talk to him?

5 1 'm going to wash
   2 are you going to write
   3 're going to look for
   4 Are you going to invite
   5 is going to cook
   6 'm not going to ask

6 1 's having a meeting
   2 's visiting
   3 's meeting Ali
   4 are arriving
   5 's meeting Kai
   6 're having dinner

7 1 'm meeting, 're going
   2 are you doing
   3 isn't coming, 's taking
   4 Is Ann staying
   5 're getting
   6 is Sonia flying

Name: _____ **Total:** _____ /40

1 Vocabulary – money expressions *6 points*
Complete the missing verbs.

1 I e_____n about £25,000 a year in my job.

2 I want to m_____e a lot of money and then retire.

3 I s_____d most of my money on clothes and CDs.

4 I'm trying to s_____e enough money to buy a car.

5 We m_____e a big profit when we sold our house.

6 I admire people who g_____e money to charity.

2 Vocabulary – money sayings *2 points*
Underline the correct alternative.

1 Money doesn't grow on **trees / flowers**.

2 Money **speaks / talks**.

3 Vocabulary – music *6 points*
Complete the sentences with the words in the box.

album	charts	fan	gigs	single	tour

I'm the pop group Superhead's biggest (1) _____ .
I bought their very first (2) _____ about five years
ago. It was number one in the (3) _____ for ten
weeks. They're brilliant live. In fact, I'm going to one of
their (4) _____ next month. They're in the middle of a
world (5) _____ at the moment to promote their new
(6) _____ .

4 (be) going to (1) *6 points*
Correct the mistakes in these sentences.

1 What you going to do this evening?

2 I'm going cook a meal.

3 I going to do my homework.

4 I'm go to read the newspaper.

5 I'm going not to do anything else.

6 When you are going to talk to him?

5 (be) going to (2) *6 points*
Complete the sentences, using the *(be) going to* form of
the verbs in the box.

not ask	cook	look for	invite	wash	write

1 I _____ the car when it stops raining.

2 When _____ you _____ to your mum?

3 We haven't booked a hotel. We _____
one when we arrive in Rome.

4 _____ you _____ Sara to the party?

5 Mohammed _____ dinner for us tonight.

6 I _____ you again. Tidy your room now!

6 Present continuous (1) *6 points*
Look at Tara's arrangements for tomorrow. Complete the
sentences using the present continuous.

9.00: have meeting	2.30: Kate and Tom arrive
10.30: visit new factory	4.15: meet Kai at the airport
12.30: meet Ali for lunch	8.00: have dinner at Pete's.

1 At 9.00, she _____ .

2 She _____ the new factory at 10.30.

3 At 12.30, she _____ for lunch.

4 Kate and Tom _____ at 2.30.

5 At 4.15, she _____ at the airport.

6 At 8.00, they _____ at Pete's.

7 Present continuous (2) *8 points*
Complete the sentences, putting the verb in the present
continuous.

1 I _____ (meet) Sam at 7.30 and then we
_____ (go) for a meal.

2 What _____ (you do) this evening?

3 He _____ (not come) to the party tonight.
He _____ (take) a client out for dinner.

4 _____ (Ann stay) with us tonight?

5 They _____ (get) married in May.

6 When _____ (Sonia fly) home?

9 Rules *Overview*

The topic of this unit is rules: rules for successful relationships as well as those for education and training. The grammar focus echoes the unit topic and is on the use of *must*, *should* and other modal structures to talk about obligation, advice, permission and necessity.

Students begin by reading an extract from an online bookshop webpage on a self-help book for women which gives rules for winning the heart of their ideal partner. They examine the concept of what makes someone Mr or Ms Right and read some reviews of the book. In the next section there is work on using *must* and *should* to give suggestions and orders, and students get the opportunity to complete sentences giving rules to men for successful dating. There is further work on sentence linking and giving advice.

Students then practise using past modals to talk about obligation and permission. They complete a text about the schooldays of rock star Bill Wyman and write accounts of each other's schooldays saying what they had to and didn't have to do.

The next section takes us to Japan with an article about the rigorous training and rules that a trainee geisha experiences. Students talk about training and professional schools in their own countries and then look at the correct stress on school subject words. Finally, in an Anecdote section, they tell each other about their favourite school subjects.

Section	Aims	What the students are doing
Introduction pages 52–53	*Reading skills*: reading for gist	Reading an extract from an online bookshop about a self-help book and some reviews of the book.
	Conversation skills: fluency work	Discussing the rules outlined in the book and the reviews.
	Lexis: describing character	Finding opposite adjectives describing character and deciding which one they would use about Mr or Ms Right.
Close up pages 53–54	*Grammar*: *must* and *should*	Studying the form and use of *must* and *should*.
		Completing sentences giving men rules for successful dating.
	Conversation skills: fluency work	Discussing what makes a successful date.
	Pronunciation: linking	Practising linking sentences with *must* and *mustn't*.
	Listening skills: listening for gist	Listening to a woman whose relationship broke up because of the self-help book.
		Deciding on good advice to give the woman.
Close up pages 54–55	*Grammar*: past modals – obligation and permission	Matching modal forms with their meanings.
		Completing a text about Bill Wyman's schooldays.
	Conversation skills: discussion	Discussing schooldays with a partner.
	Writing: using past modals	Writing a short account of a partner's schooldays.
Geisha pages 56–57	*Reading skills*: reading for specific information	Predicting whether sentences about a geisha's life are true or false.
	Conversation skills: discussion	Discussing special schools and job training in students' own countries.
	Lexis: education	Using words from the reading text to complete sentences about education.
	Pronunciation: word stress	Practising using the correct stress with school subjects.
	Conversation skills: fluency work	Anecdote: talking about students' favourite school subject.

9 Rules *Teacher's notes*

Books closed. Whole class. Tell students that this unit is about rules. Ask them to brainstorm as many areas of their lives as they can in which there are rules that they have to follow. Put all the ideas on the board and ask for examples of rules in each area.

Reading (p 52)

1 Pairwork. Establish the meaning of *self-help book*, a book designed to help you improve your life, overcome problems yourself, etc. Students then discuss the questions and report back to the class. Find out if self-help books are common in their cultures and what the most popular ones are. You might also like to ask them what kind of people they think read self-help books and whether the majority of them are men or women.

2 Focus attention on the webpage and ask students to read it quickly just to find out who the book is for.

> For women who want to get and keep a man.

3 Pairwork. Students read the extract from the webpage more carefully. They then discuss the questions in pairs and report back to the class. You may want to point out that the expression *Mr Right* is commonly used to refer to a woman's ideal but usually as yet unfound partner. The female equivalent is *Miss* or *Ms Right* and the opposite would be *Mr Wrong*.

Lexis: describing character (p 52)

1 Students look through the website extract again to find the opposites of the adjectives in the table. Allow them to compare notes in pairs, but do not check answers at this stage.

2 🔲 **37 SB p 52**
Play the recording for students to check their answers. Then play it again for them to underline the stressed syllables in each word. They can practise saying them at the same time as the recording or to each other.

a)	<u>chee</u>rful	≠	<u>mi</u>serable
b)	<u>tal</u>kative	≠	<u>quiet</u>
c)	<u>sen</u>sible	≠	<u>si</u>lly
d)	<u>o</u>pen	≠	mys<u>te</u>rious
e)	<u>in</u>teresting	≠	<u>bo</u>ring
f)	hard-<u>wor</u>king	≠	<u>la</u>zy
g)	<u>ho</u>nest	≠	dis<u>ho</u>nest
h)	opti<u>mis</u>tic	≠	pessi<u>mis</u>tic
i)	<u>sen</u>sitive	≠	in<u>sen</u>sitive
j)	<u>con</u>fident	≠	inse<u>cure</u>

3 Students work individually to decide which of the adjectives describe their ideal partner, Mr or Ms Right, and which describe Mr or Ms Wrong. Encourage them to add any other adjectives they think are appropriate.

4 Pairwork. Students share their ideas with a partner.

Reading (p 53)

1 Allow students to work in pairs or small groups to read the reviews and match them to the headings. You may like to highlight the use of the word *sexist*. Someone or something which is sexist displays an unfair or discriminatory attitude towards someone because of their sex. Ask students if they know any more words that have *ist* at the end and relate to unfair treatment of a particular group. Other examples include *racist* and *ageist*, and new coinings of such words often appear in the media. (Note, however, that the ending *ist* does not always imply unfair treatment as in *feminist*, *motorist* and *dentist*!)

Check answers with the class.

> a 4 b 1 c 3 d 2

2 Pairwork. Students discuss which review they agree with most and report back to the class.

Close up (p 53)

must & should

1 Pairwork. Students read the sentences and decide which is advice or a suggestion and which an order or an obligation. Check answers with the class.

> *a* expresses an order or an obligation.
>
> *b* offers advice or a suggestion.

2 Elicit answers from the class and write the negative sentences and questions on the board. Draw students' attention to the use of *must* and *mustn't* in the webpage extract on page 52. There is more information on *must* and *should* in the Language reference section on page 55. Also refer students to the Verb structures section on page 130.

> a) You mustn't follow *The Rules*. Must you follow *The Rules*?
>
> b) You shouldn't follow *The Rules*. Should you follow *The Rules*?

3 Pairwork. Students work together to complete the sentences with *must* and *mustn't*. They then write one more rule of their own using either *must* or *mustn't*. Check answers with the class and ask some pairs to tell the class their new rules.

> a) must b) mustn't c) must d) must
> e) mustn't

Optional activity

Ask the students to discuss whether they think the rules in Exercise 3 were written by a man or a woman.

4 Pairwork. Students discuss whether or not they agree with any of the rules in Exercise 3. *In a class feedback session find out if the sex of the students affects their answers.*

5 Groupwork. Students here have an opportunity to state their own views and prepare some advice for both men and women using *should* and *shouldn't*. They can then compare their lists with other groups.

Linking (p 54)

1 📼 **38 SB p 54**

Play the recording for students to listen and repeat. Then ask them what happens to the pronunciation of the *t* before a vowel and before a consonant. Ask students to practise saying the sentences in pairs and go round checking that they are linking words correctly.

> When the following word starts with a vowel you pronounce the 't' (b, c, e). When it starts with a consonant you don't pronounce the 't' (a, d, f).

2 📼 **39 SB p 54**

Pairwork. Students practise saying the sentences to each other before you play the recording for them to check. With confident students, you might like to ask the class to stand up and then ask a student to read the first sentence aloud. The rest of the class should sit down if they think it was read correctly and remain standing if they think it was wrong. The student then has an opportunity to try again until all students are sitting down. If opinions are divided, you will have to adjudicate. Do this with other students for the remaining sentences.

> Pronounce the 't' in b, c, and f.

3 Pairwork. Students read the sentences in Exercise 2 again and decide who is speaking to whom, what the situation is and what other thing they could say using *must*. They then report back to the class on their ideas.

> *Probable answers*
> a)   A doctor to a patient.
> b)   A parent / grandparent to a child.
> c)   A teacher to a student.
> d)   A girlfriend to a boyfriend? Two lovers?
> e)   An examiner (teacher) to an examinee (student).
> f)   A driving instructor to a learner driver.

Listening (p 54)

1 📼 **40 SB p 137**

Go through the instructions with the students first so they know what information they are listening for.

Play the recording and elicit answers to the questions.

> The relationship ended in disaster when Michael discovered she was reading *The Rules*. Now she is reading *The Joy Of Being Single*.

> 📼 **40**
>
> *I decided to do 'The Rules' because I wanted a proper relationship. My relationships always fail because I'm too soft, and people take advantage of me. Even my best friends sometimes take advantage of me.*
>
> *Before I started doing 'The Rules' I was seeing Michael four or five times a week and talking on the phone several times a day.*
>
> *So it was difficult following 'The Rules' because I couldn't phone him, and when he phoned me, I had to finish the conversation first. I love chatting on the phone but I had to tell him I was busy even when I wasn't.*
>
> *At first, 'The Rules' worked. He became more interested and he even took me to meet his mum.*
>
> *But then he said I was acting strangely. He said I'd changed – at first I was warm and friendly, but I was getting colder and harder. I knew it wasn't the real me, but I couldn't tell him about 'The Rules' – that's one of the rules!*
>
> *The rules are supposed to make you mysterious and fascinating, but he just thought I was behaving like a cow.*
>
> *Then I began to fall in love with him and I wanted to see him more, but I couldn't. I didn't like playing games with him any more. It didn't feel right.*
>
> *And then something awful happened. He saw the book … He was so angry!*
>
> *He told me to go and play games with somebody else and left.*
>
> *Anyway, I threw away my copy of 'The Rules' and now I'm reading a book called 'The Joy Of Being Single'. I've decided that I don't have to find a man and get married to be happy. I'm much happier now.*

2 Play the recording again for students to listen and choose the correct alternatives to complete the sentences. Allow them to compare their answers in pairs before checking with the class.

a 1   b 2   c 1   d 2   e 2   f 1   g 2

3 You could make this a class discussion or put students in pairs or groups.

Close up (p 54)

Past modals: obligation & permission

1 If students have difficulties with modal structures for obligation and permission, you might like to go through the Language reference section on page 55 with them first.

Students complete the sentences with the structures from the box. Check answers with the class.

a) I couldn't   b) I had to

2 Pairwork. Students work together to look at their completed sentences and the remaining items in the box in Exercise 1 and match the modal structures with their meanings. Check answers with the class and ask students to produce one sentence of their own with each of the structures.

a)   I couldn't
b)   I had to
c)   I could
d)   I didn't have to

3 Allow students to work in pairs to complete the text. Do not check answers at this stage.

4 🔊 **41 SB p 55**
Play the recording for students to listen and check their answers. Then check with the class.

1   had to
2   had to
3   couldn't
4   didn't have to
5   had to
6   couldn't

5 Pairwork. Students discuss how their own schooldays compare with Bill Wyman's. Suggest that they take notes of what their partners say as this will help them in the next exercise.

6 Students write short accounts of each other's schooldays. They can use the notes they made of the discussion in Exercise 5, but allow them to ask each other for extra information if necessary. You might like to set this exercise for homework. If you do it in class, go round offering help and encouragement and check that students are including the sentence beginnings given in the instructions.

Geisha (p 56)

Contrary to popular belief, a geisha is not a Japanese prostitute. The word translates into English as 'person of the arts', and geishas are highly trained and skilled performers in dance, music and other traditional Japanese art forms. You may need to clarify this point with students, though the text itself makes it clear that a geisha is a highly reputable professional artist.

Reading (p 56)

1 Most students should have some idea of what a geisha is (but see the note above). If they don't, or have the wrong impression, it would probably be best to explain the term first and then let them look through the questions and make their predictions. You might read the sentences and ask students to put their hands up if they think they are true, but don't reveal the answers at this stage.

2 Students read the article to find out if they were right. Check answers with the class.

a) False   b) True   c) True   d) True   e) False
f) False   g) False

Optional activity

Ask students to make up three comprehension questions on the text. They then exchange questions in pairs and try to answer the ones they have been given.

3 Pairwork. Students discuss the questions in pairs or small groups and then report back to the class on any interesting information they found out.

Lexis: education (p 57)

1 Students look through the geisha text to find suitable words to complete the sentences. Line numbers are given to help them. Allow them to compare their answers in pairs or small groups before checking with the class.

a) training   b) become   c) study   d) costs
e) move   f) take   g) pass   h) role

2 Groupwork. With multinational classes it may be possible to form groups of students from the same country. Each group can discuss the questions and give a small presentation to the class on the situation in their particular country.

Word stress (p 57)

1 Go through the stress patterns with the students first and get them to hum them. Encourage them to read the words in the columns aloud to get a feel for what sounds right. They then match the stress patterns to the correct columns. Check answers with the class.

> a 3   b 5   c 1   d 2   e 4

2 🔲 **42 SB p 57**
Play the recording for students to listen, check and repeat.

3 Pairwork. Students look at the school subjects in Exercise 1 and discuss them. They then report their findings back to the class.

Anecdote (p 57)

See the Introduction on page 4 for more ideas on how to set up, monitor and repeat Anecdotes.

Pairwork. Give students plenty of time to decide what they are going to talk about and to read the questions. They then take turns to talk about their favourite school subject to their partner.

Test

Scoring: one point per correct answer unless otherwise indicated.

1 1 d   2 f   3 e   4 a   5 g   6 b   7 h   8 c

2 1 study   2 train   3 become   4 move into
5 take   6 pass

3 1 Biology   2 Economics   3 History   4 interesting
5 Music   6 mysterious   7 optimistic
8 Philosophy   9 Politics   10 talkative

4 (Two points per correct answer.)
1 should   2 don't have to   3 must   4 can't
5 must   6 could   7 can't   8 must

9 Rules Test

1 Vocabulary – describing character *8 points*

Match the adjectives (*1–8*) with their opposites (*a–h*).

1	cheerful	a)	boring
2	confident	b)	pessimistic
3	hard-working	c)	quiet
4	interesting	d)	miserable
5	open	e)	lazy
6	optimistic	f)	insecure
7	sensible	g)	mysterious
8	talkative	h)	silly

2 Vocabulary – education *6 points*

Complete the sentences with the words in the box.

become	move into	pass	study	take	train

I'm going to (1) _____ English literature at university and after that, I want to (2) _____ to (3) _____ an English teacher. I live at home now, but I hope to (4) _____ student accommodation when I start university. People tell me that the course is difficult, but I think I can (5) _____ my exams again if I don't (6) _____ them the first time!

3 Pronunciation – word stress *10 points*

<u>Underline</u> the most stressed syllable in each word.

<u>mi</u>serable

1 Biology
2 Economics
3 History
4 interesting
5 Music
6 mysterious
7 optimistic
8 Philosophy
9 Politics
10 talkative

4 Obligation & permission *16 points*

Re-write the sentences using *can't, could, should, must* and *don't have to*.

In the United Kingdom ...

1 People usually leave a 10% tip in a restaurant.

You _____ leave a 10% tip in a restaurant.

2 It isn't necessary to carry an identity card with you.

You _____ carry an identity card with you.

3 We drive on the left side of the road.

You _____ drive on the left side of the road.

4 You must be 16 or over to buy cigarettes.

You _____ buy cigarettes if you are under 16.

5 The law requires you to wear a seatbelt in a car.

You _____ wear a seatbelt in a car.

6 But before 1983, it was possible to drive without a seatbelt.

Before 1983, you _____ drive without a seatbelt.

7 You aren't allowed to drive on the roads until you are 17.

You _____ drive on the roads until you are 17.

8 It is necessary to be 18 to drink alcohol in a pub.

You _____ be 18 to drink alcohol in a pub

10 *Review 2* *Teacher's notes*

Fact or fiction? (p 58)

Appropriate language

1 This exercise reviews a variety of structures that the students have learnt in the previous four units. Establish the meaning of *lie* (to say something that is not true) and allow students to compare their answers in pairs before checking with the class.

> a) had to   b) couldn't   c) never
> d) 'm going to give up   e) always keep
> f) 've ever had

2   **43 SB p 138**
Pairwork. Students read the lies again and discuss who is speaking to whom and what the situation is. They then report back to the class on their ideas. Play the recording for them to check their answers.

You might like to ask if anyone has ever used or heard any of these particular lies.

> a)   High-flying wife and suspicious husband.
> b)   Unpunctual schoolboy and resigned teacher.
> c)   Small businessman and supplier.
> d)   Husband and wife.
> e)   Gossipy women.
> f)   Middle-aged couple and hosts

> **43**
>
> **a)**
> W1: *I'm home! Sorry I'm late, darling. I had to work late at the office.*
> M1: *But it's eleven o'clock! And this is the third time this week!*
> W1: *I know. I'm really sorry, but it's an important contract.*
>
> **b)**
> B: *Sorry, sir. Can I come in, please, sir? I couldn't get here earlier – the bus was late. Sorry.*
> T: *Your bus is always late, Ronnie. Why don't you catch the earlier one?*
> B: *Yes, sir. Sorry, sir. Tomorrow I'll catch the earlier bus.*

> **c)**
> M2: *Sir, we sent you the bill on the first Monday of last month.*
> M3: *You sent it last month? I never received it! How much was the bill for?*
> M2: *Twenty-four thousand, three hundred and fifty ...*
>
> **d)**
> W2: *When are you going to stop? I can't stand the smell of your cigarettes in this house. You know it's bad for the children. And for you.*
> M4: *I know, I know. I'm going to give up. Tomorrow. Next week. Soon.*
> W2: *I've heard that before ...*
>
> **e)**
> W3: *I've got some amazing news about Tina and Brian, but you mustn't tell anyone. OK?*
> W4: *Of course not. You can trust me. I always keep a secret. What's going on?*
> W3: *Well, you know Brigitte from number 9. She said that ...*
>
> **f)**
> W5: *Thank you. That was the best meal we've ever had. Wasn't it, Donald?*
> M5: *Oh yes, delicious.*
> W5: *Ah, thank you. We must do it again soon.*

3 Groupwork. Students discuss the questions in small groups. Have a class feedback session and find out whether students think it is ever acceptable to lie.

Listening (p 58)

1 Pairwork. Check that students understand that customs officers are people who work at the borders of a country (and its ports and airports) and check that travellers are not bringing in anything they shouldn't. Ask them what they think the connection is between this job and the subject of lying (customs officers spend their days deciding who is lying about what goods they are bringing into the country and are very adept at telling who is lying and who is not). Students then work together to choose words and phrases from the box that they associate with this job. Check answers and ask them if there are any other words that they can add.

> Probable answer: alcohol, contraband cigarettes, conveyor belt, inside information, legal limit, search

2 📼 **44 SB p 138**

Go through the statements before you play the recording so students have some idea of what they are going to hear and what they should be listening for. You may like to point out that Dover is a seaport on the south coast of England. Many ships come into Dover, including a large number of ferries from France and other European countries.

Play the recording, more than once if necessary. Students listen and mark the sentences *T* or *F*. Allow them to compare answers in pairs or small groups before checking with the class.

---

a F   b T   c F   d F   e F   f T   g T   h F

📼 **44**

(I = Interviewer; K = Gerald Kelly; D = Driver)

Part 1

I: *Welcome to 'Tools of the Trade', our weekly look at professional secrets. This week – the world of the customs officer. We spent a day at the port of Dover with Gerald Kelly, a senior customs officer in the fight against contraband cigarettes. We join Mr Kelly as he interviews a driver passing through customs.*

K: *Good afternoon, sir.*

D: *Afternoon.*

K: *Have you been far, sir?*

D: *No, I haven't been far.*

K: *Could you be more precise, sir? Where exactly have you been?*

D: *I don't know what the place is called – it's a little town on the coast about twenty kilometres from Calais.*

K: *I see, sir. Did you buy any alcohol or cigarettes during the trip?*

D: *Er, no. Well, not much. Erm, my sister's getting married next week, so I just went over to buy her a few bottles of champagne. We're having a party after the wedding. Do you want to come? Erm, only joking!*

K: *Well, if you don't mind, I'm going to have a look in the back of the car. Is it open?*

Part 2

I: *The back of the car contained six cases of champagne – no problems there. But then they found eight thousand cigarettes – the legal limit is eight hundred. The driver was arrested.*
   Mr Kelly, do you search every car that passes through?

K: *No, that would be impossible. Thousands of cars drive through the port every day.*

I: *So how do you know which cars to stop?*

K: *Well, we often have inside information, but this time, I had a feeling.*

I: *Just a feeling!*

K: *Well, perhaps a little more than that. You see a guy on his own, he doesn't look like a businessman, it's the middle of the week ... and you think, 'What is he up to?'*

I: *That's it?*

K: *No – then we ask a few simple questions. We watch their body language, and you can usually tell if they're lying.*

I: *You can see it in their eyes?*

K: *Well, not in the eyes, because they don't usually look at you. They often hide their hands, too. But there are other signs. Have you ever noticed the way people sometimes touch their face a lot when they are lying?*

I: *So, just by looking at them, you can –*

K: *No, you have to listen, too. To begin with, they often say very little, just the minimum. Just 'Morning, officer' or 'Afternoon, sir.' They don't give you precise information like names of places. And then they sometimes start saying too much, saying any old rubbish to fill the silence.*

I: *I've read somewhere that liars usually use more negative verbs. Have you found this?*

K: *Yes, that's right. Also, their voice often goes up, 'Er, no, not much,' and they sound scared.*

I: *Does anyone ever get past you?*

K: *Oh, yeah. We've caught hundreds of the little guys, but we hardly ever catch the big ones, the real professionals.*

I: *Gerald Kelly, thank you very much. With contraband cigarette sales approaching fifty per cent in some parts of England, customs officers have clearly got a difficult job on their hands.*

3 Students rearrange the words to make comments about liars. Play Part 2 of the recording again for them to check their answers.

---

a) They don't usually look at you.

b) They often hide their hands.

c) People sometimes touch their face a lot.

d) They often say very little.

e) They sometimes start saying too much.

f) Liars usually use more negative verbs.

g) Their voice often goes up.

Speaking (p 59)

1 Students work individually to write two answers to each question. Make sure they don't compare notes.

2 Pairwork. Students follow the instructions, taking it in turns to ask questions, give both the true and the false answer and guess which is which. Remind them that they can use the information given by the customs officer to try to detect the lies.

3 In a class feedback session, find out which student in each pair was the most successful liar. You might like to put these students together and try the exercise again until you find the most successful liar in the class.

Numbers (p 59)

1 Pairwork. Students look at the table and discuss what they think should go in the gaps. They should keep a note of their guesses. Allow pairs to compare with other pairs but do not confirm or deny anything at this stage.

2 🔊 **45 SB p 138**

Play the recording for students to listen, note down the correct answers and check how accurate their guesses were. In a class feedback session find out which pair had the most correct guesses.

> a) Spain
> b) 117,000,000
> c) The Czech Republic
> d) 137.7
> e) Norway
> f) 1,305
> g) The USA
> h) 201

> 🔊 **45**
>
> *The top 3 whisky drinkers in bottles consumed per year are:*
>
> *1 Spain: 145,000,000*
>
> *2 France: 137,000,000*
>
> *3 The USA: 117,000,000*
>
> *The top 3 beer drinkers in litres consumed per person per year are:*
>
> *1 The Czech Republic: 160*
>
> *2 Ireland: 141.3*
>
> *3 Germany: 137.7*
>
> *The top 3 coffee drinkers in cups consumed per person per year are:*
>
> *1 Norway: 1,356*
>
> *2 Denmark: 1,305*
>
> *3 Finland: 1,293*

> *The top 3 Coca-Cola drinkers in glasses consumed per person per year are:*
>
> *1 The USA: 343*
>
> *2 Mexico: 322*
>
> *3 Germany: 201*

3 Play the recording again. Students listen and repeat each number. Then ask them which statistic they found the most and the least surprising.

Verbs with two objects (p 59)

1 Remind students of the work they did on verbs with two objects in Unit 6. Ask them to complete the sentences individually, but allow them to compare with a partner before checking with the class.

> a) The last time I went abroad I bought my family lots of presents.
>
> b) The last time I went to dinner with friends I took them a box of chocolates.
>
> c) The last time I went to a wedding I got the couple a very expensive gift.
>
> d) The last time I went on holiday I sent all my friends a postcard.
>
> e) On my last birthday my mother made me a big cake.
>
> f) On Valentine's Day my sweetheart gave me a beautiful bunch of flowers.

2 Pairwork. Students read the sentences again and mark the ones they think are true for their partners. They then ask their partners to find out how accurate their guesses were.

Growing up (p 60)

Books closed. Whole class. Ask students how many generations of their families are still alive today. Does anyone have great grandparents or great aunts and uncles still living? Ask what interesting information or advice they have received from the older generations of their families.

Teach the term *generation gap* which is often used to express misunderstanding between people of different generations because of vastly differing upbringings and experiences. Ask if they have ever experienced this in their own families.

Reading (p 60)

1 Groupwork. Students work in groups of three to decide which member of the three generations of the Bennett family is most likely to have said each thing. Do not check answers at this stage.

> 1 a) S   b) GS   c) GF
>
> 2 a) GS   b) GF   c) S
>
> 3 a) S   b) GS   c) GF
>
> 4 a) GS   b) GF   c) S

2 Students decide who is going to read each text. They are each responsible for checking the answers for their particular person and they then explain to the other members of the group the background behind what was said. Go through the example with the class to make sure they understand this point.

Possible answers

1

a) The son couldn't disturb his father – because he was very tired / worked a lot.

b) The grandson doesn't have to hide anything from his father – because he's more like a best mate.

c) The grandfather had to obey his father without question – because he was a very strict man.

2

a) The grandson didn't have to come home at a certain time – because his parents trusted him.

b) The grandfather had to make his own entertainment – because there was no television.

c) The son could only watch TV at the weekend – because his father made him do his homework.

3

a) The son's parents didn't have to support him financially – because the government gave him a grant to study.

b) The grandson thinks colleges and universities should be free – because they were in his parent's day.

c) The grandfather had to walk to school – because there was no other way of getting there.

4

a) The grandson should get married one day – because his parents (and his girlfriend's parents) want him (and his girlfriend) to.

b) The grandfather couldn't bring girlfriends home – because it wasn't done in those days.

c) The son (and his girlfriend, Louise) had to get married – because Louise found out she was pregnant.

---

3 Students work individually to read the whole text. They note down the differences between the lives of the three generations of the Bennett family and those of the corresponding generations of their own family. They then compare with a partner.

Optional activity

Ask students to discuss how different they think the lives of three generations of women in the Bennett family would have been.

Lexis: *work* or *job*? (p 61)

1 Pairwork. Students complete the questions with *work* or *job* and then take turns asking and answering them. Check answers with the class and ask them to produce some more sentences of their own using *work* and *job* correctly.

---

a) job   b) work   c) job

---

2 Students write down their questions using words from the box to replace the underlined words in Exercise 1. They should work individually to do this.

3 Pairwork. Students take turns asking and answering their questions from Exercise 2. Elicit or point out that they can find out as much information as they can by listening carefully to what is said and asking follow-up questions.

Lexis: work expressions & collocations (p 61)

1 Set a time limit for students to find the jobs in the word snake, or have a race to see who can find all eight of them first.

There are eight: drummer, factory worker, financial adviser, geisha, managing director, shop assistant, telesales person, vet

---

2 Allow students to work in pairs if they wish. They should complete the sentences with words from the box first and then match them with the jobs from Exercise 1. Check answers with the class and as a final check ask students to explain what each of the people in Exercise 1 does.

---

a)   make (a financial adviser)

b)   take (a factory worker)

c)   make (a vet)

d)   spend, make (a telesales person)

e)   have / take (a shop assistant)

f)   run, make (a managing director)

g)   make (a drummer)

h)   make (a geisha)

Discussion (p 61)

1 Whole class. Ask the students to call out jobs for you to write on the board or get them to come up to the board and write them there themselves. Leave the words up for the next exercise.

2 Groupwork. In small groups, students discuss the questions with reference to the jobs on the board. Encourage them to find out any information they don't know about a particular job from the student who has done the job or whose parents or grandparents have done it. Groups report back to the class on their decisions.

The Revision Game (p 62)

Students follow the rules and play the game. All the correct answers with the relevant Language reference pages are given below.

Player 1 (Red)

1 ✔
2 ✔
3 I've got two children: a boy and a girl. (page 15)
4 There are a lot of problems. (page 15)
5 (Speaking task)
6 There's a little wine left but no beer. (page 15)
7 What were you both wearing? (page 19)
8 ✔
9 Raúl is not as tall as Venus Williams. (page 27)
10 (Speaking task)
11 The teacher explained the exercise to us. (page 35)
12 ✔
13 ✔
14 ✔
15 (Speaking task)
16 She called you a few minutes ago. (page 43)
17 ✔

Player 2 (Blue)

1 Why did she get married? (page 8)
2 ✔
3 He's got two mice. (page 15)
4 ✔
5 (Speaking task)
6 There was lots of good food at the party. (page 15)
7 The last time I lost my keys was two weeks ago. (page 19)
8 ✔
9 I gave my husband a small torch. (page 35)
10 (Speaking task)
11 The teacher explained the exercise to us. (page 35)
12 ✔
13 Men don't usually want brightly coloured ties. (page 36)
14 ✔
15 (Speaking task)
16 ✔
17 ✔

Player 3 (Orange)

1 ✔
2 What are the people in your village like? (page 15)
3 I need work. / I need a job. (page 15)
4 ✔
5 (Speaking task)
6 He didn't give me much information. (page 15)
7 ✔
8 ✔
9 ✔
10 (Speaking task)
11 The teacher explained the exercise to us. (page 35)
12 My husband bought me a gadget. / My husband bought a gadget for me. (page 35)
13 I'm normally on a diet. (page 36)
14 ✔
15 (Speaking task)
16 ✔
17 ✔

Player 4 (Green)

1 Who created A.L.I.C.E.? (page 8)
2 It's beautiful weather. (page 15)
3 ✔
4 We want advice. (page 15)
5 (Speaking task)
6 My son found them this morning. (page 19)
7 ✔
8 ✔
9 Venus Williams is a bit heavier than Michael Schumacher. (page 27)
10 (Speaking task)
11 The teacher explained the exercise to us. (page 35)
12 ✔
13 My husband bought a gadget for me. / My husband bought me a gadget. (page 35)
14 ✔
15 (Speaking task)
16 I didn't go to the beach last summer. (page 43)
17 ✔

Test

1 1 He gave *me* a book for my birthday.

2 Petra is making some lunch *for us* now.

3 Have they shown *you* their photos yet?

4 I need to take this report *to Eva*.

2 1 saw

2 Did, buy

3 got

4 Have, heard

5 heard

6 Have, seen

7 haven't seen

8 haven't been

3 1 chosen 2 driven 3 eaten 4 fed 5 hidden
6 sold 7 taken 8 worn

4 1 I hardly ever go to a club these days.

2 I am always tidying up after my children.

3 I am usually in bed by midnight.

4 I often go shopping on Saturdays.

5 1 to go 2 living 3 teaching 4 to continue
5 meeting 6 finding out

6 1 had to 2 mustn't 3 shouldn't 4 couldn't
5 don't have to 6 can

7 1 're going to stay

2 'm going to watch

3 Are you going to see

4 'm going to do

8 1 isn't coming

2 's staying

3 Are you doing

4 'm meeting

9 1 Economics 2 English 3 Geography
4 History 5 Music 6 Philosophy 7 Politics
8 Technology

10 1 miserable 2 hard-working 3 mysterious
4 silly 5 talkative 6 insecure

11 1 flowers, keys

2 jeans, scissors

3 crisps, cigarettes

4 furniture, paper

12 1 help 2 looking 3 suits 4 size 5 exchange
6 receipt

13 1 second 2 give 3 salary 4 paid
5 employees 6 album 7 taking 8 train

10 Review 2 Test

Name: _____

1 Verbs with two objects *4 points*

Put the words in brackets into the correct position in the sentence.

1 He gave a book for my birthday. (me)

2 Petra is making some lunch now. (for us)

3 Have they shown their photos yet? (you)

4 I need to take this report. (to Eva)

2 Present perfect simple *8 points*

Complete the dialogue by putting the verb into the correct tense: past simple or present perfect.

A: Hi, Bella. I (1) _____ (see) you in town yesterday. (2) _____ you _____ (buy) anything?

B: I (3) _____ (get) the new Superhead CD. (4) _____ you _____ (hear) it yet?

A: Yes, I (5) _____ (hear) it at a party last weekend. It's pretty good.

B: (6) _____ you ever _____ (see) them live?

A: Yeah, a few times actually, but I (7) _____ (not see) them recently. Not for a couple of years or so.

B: Well, if you fancy going to their gig in London next week, I know someone who's got a spare ticket.

A: Great. I (8) _____ (not go) to a gig for ages.

3 Irregular verbs *8 points*

Add the past participle of each verb.

1 choose, chose, _____   5 hide, hid, _____

2 drive, drove, _____   6 sell, sold, _____

3 eat, ate, _____   7 take, took, _____

4 feed, fed, _____   8 wear, wore, _____

4 Adverbs of frequency *4 points*

Put the adverb into the correct position in the sentence.

1 I go to a club these days. (hardly ever)

2 I am tidying up after my children. (always)

3 I am in bed by midnight. (usually)

4 I go shopping on Saturdays. (often)

5 Verb + *-ing* form *6 points*

Underline the correct alternative.

I first became an English teacher because I wanted (1) **to go / going** travelling around the world. I thought that if I worked, I could spend more time (2) **to live / living** in each country. But I soon discovered that I really loved (3) **to teach / teaching** English so when I came back to the UK, I decided (4) **to continue / continuing** with it. I enjoy (5) **to meet / meeting** people from different countries and I really like (6) **to find out / finding out** about my students' cultures and languages. It really is a great job.

6 Obligation & permission *6 points*

Underline the correct alternative.

1 Sorry I missed dinner. I **had to / must** work late.

2 You **don't have to / mustn't** do that. It's dangerous.

3 You **shouldn't / don't have to** stay up so late. You'll be tired in the morning.

4 I **couldn't / mustn't** watch TV for more then thirty minutes a day when I was a child.

5 You **mustn't / don't have to** arrive early, but it's a good idea to do so.

6 Excuse me, **can / mustn't** I smoke here?

7 (be) going to 4 points

Complete the dialogues, using the (be) going to form of the verbs in the box.

> do   see   stay   watch

A: Have you and Tim got any plans for this evening?

B: I think we (1) _____ in tonight. I

(2) _____ some TV and go to bed

early.

*   *   *

C: The Van Gogh exhibition opens next week.

(3) _____ you _____ it?

D: Yes, on Monday afternoon actually.

*   *   *

E: Have you sent that e-mail to your brother yet?

F: No, but I (4) _____ it when I have

time.

8   Present continuous 4 points

Complete the dialogues, using the present continuous form of the verbs in the box.

> do   meet   not come   stay

A: Where's Paul? We'll be late for lunch!

B: Oh, he (1) _____ with us. He

(2) _____ in the office to do some work.

*   *   *

C: (3) _____ you _____ anything this

weekend?

D: Yeah, I (4) _____ Jo on Saturday for a

drink.

Do you want to come?

9   Pronunciation – word stress 8 points

<u>Underline</u> the most stressed syllable in each word.

1	Economics	5	Music
2	English	6	Philosophy
3	Geography	7	Politics
4	History	8	Technology

10 Vocabulary – describing character 6 points

Complete the pairs of opposite adjectives.

1   cheerful ≠ mis_____able

2   h_____d-wo_____ing ≠ lazy

3   open ≠ my_____ious

4   sensible ≠ s_____y

5   ta_____ive ≠ quiet

6   confident ≠ ins_____re

11 Vocabulary – collocations 8 points

Complete the lists with the words in the box.

> crisps   flowers   furniture   jeans   keys   paper
> scissors   cigarettes

1   a bunch of _____ , _____

2   a pair of _____ , _____

3   a packet of _____ , _____

4   a piece of _____ , _____

12 Vocabulary – shopping 6 points

Add the missing words in these shopping dialogues between a shop assistant (A) and a customer (C).

A: Can I (1) _____ you?

C: It's okay. I'm just (2) _____ .

*   *   *

C: Do you think it (3) _____ me?

A: Yes, it looks great, but I think you need a smaller

(4) _____ .

*   *   *

C: Can I (5) _____ it if it doesn't fit?

A: Yes, but you need to keep the (6) _____ .

13 Vocabulary – general 8 points

Add the missing vowels (a, e, i, o, u) to complete the sentences.

1   It's not new. It's s__c__nd-hand.

2   That looks heavy. Let me g__v__ you a hand.

3   The job has a s__l__ry of £26,000 a year.

4   I get five week's p__ __d holiday in my job.

5   The company has over a thousand empl__y__ __s.

6   All the songs on their new __lb__m are great.

7   I'm t__k__ng an exam tomorrow.

8   I want to tr__ __n to be a dentist.

11 Smile *Overview*

This unit is about smiling, laughter and happiness, focusing both on what causes us to feel happy and how it shows in our faces. There is a strong lexical focus to the unit, covering words to describe facial features, character and personality, verb patterns and phrasal verbs, particularly those associated with relaxation.

The first section looks at what happens to our faces when we smile and this leads into an exploration of different kinds of smiles and what our smiles say about our personality. Students do a personality test and a questionnaire to find out what kind of person they are.

The song, *Don't Worry, Be Happy*, is used to examine some of the causes of worrying and how music can change our moods. This also leads to some work on using imperatives.

A reading text and discussion on ways to avoid and reduce stress gives an opportunity to examine some useful phrasal verbs and the unit ends with a report on laughter and a game in which students try to keep a straight face while their partners try to make them laugh.

Section	Aims	What the students are doing
Introduction pages 64–65	*Conversation skills*: discussion	Discussing how people are encouraged to smile for the camera.
	Lexis: the face	Reading and completing a text about different types of smile.
		Identifying and discussing features of the face.
		Talking about the ideal face.
	Pronunciation: /s/, /z/ or /ɪz/?	Practising pronunciation of plural forms.
	Lexis: describing character	Matching headings to a text about the connection between smiling and character.
		Listening to people talking and identifying character types.
		Using adjectives to describe character.
		Taking a personality test and discussing the results.
What are you like? page 66	*Reading skills*: questionnaire	Answering a questionnaire about personality.
	Lexis: verb patterns	Choosing appropriate structures to complete sentences.
		Discussing the sentences and writing more.
Don't Worry, Be Happy page 67	*Listening skills*: listening for specific information	Completing the lyrics of the song, *Don't Worry, Be Happy*, with rhyming words.
		Identifying three reasons for worrying given in the song.
	Conversation skills: discussion	Discussing the worries that people of different ages might have.
		Talking about what music makes them feel happy.
Close up page 67	*Grammar*: imperatives	Studying imperative forms. Using affirmative and negative verb forms.
		Writing three-line dialogues with imperatives.
Take it easy page 68	*Reading skills*: reading for detail	Reading and discussing an article on avoiding stress.
		Adding three more suggestions to the list.
	Lexis: phrasal verbs	Completing sentences about personal habits with phrasal verbs and discussing them.
Close up page 69	*Grammar*: phrasal verbs	Identifying phrasal verbs which do not take objects and the correct position for the objects with those verbs that do.
		Putting words in the correct order to make answers to questions.
Laughter – the best medicine page 69	*Listening skills*: listening for specific information	Listening to a report on laughter clubs and identifying the benefits of laughter.
		Playing a game in which one student tries to keep a straight face while their partner tries to make them smile or laugh.

11 Smile Teacher's notes

Books closed. Whole class. Write on the board: *What's the longest word in the English language?* Give students a minute or two to come up with suggestions. Then write the word *smiles* on the board and ask why this might be the longest word (because there's a mile between the first and last letters).

Groupwork. Students discuss the questions in groups. You will need to check that they know the answer to the first one (they say this when they want people to smile for a photograph) before they go on to the others. In a multinational class you will get several answers to the question about what they say in their own language. Ask students to write the words up on the board and let them all have a go at saying them. Find out which one produces the best smile.

Lexis: the face (p 64)

1 Go through the instructions, ensuring that students realise they have to decide whether to use a singular or plural form of each word. Allow them to work in pairs to complete the text if they wish. Do not check answers at this stage.

> 1 tooth 2 cheeks 3 mouth 4 eyes 5 wrinkles
> 6 eyebrows 7 dimples

2 📼 **46 SB p 64**

Play the recording for students to listen and check their answers. Establish that four smiles are mentioned and give students time to practise doing all these smiles in pairs.

> Four smiles are mentioned: the listener/response smile; the polite smile; the miserable smile; the genuine smile.

3 Focus attention on the photograph next to the text and ask students if they can see any of the features listed.

> bags under eyes; beautiful teeth; wavy hair

4 Pairwork. You could do the first question with the class, having a show of hands for who likes each of the features on a man or woman. Then give students time to discuss in pairs their ideal face. This could be for someone of their own or the opposite sex.

5 Pairwork. Students look at the three photographs of eyes and decide which of the people they think are smiling (according to the information given in the text). Encourage them to make definite decisions and to say why they made these decisions before turning to page 125 to see the complete photographs.

/s/, /z/ or /ɪz/? (p 65)

1 📼 **47 SB p 65**

Play the recording for students to listen and repeat the nouns. Pause the recording after each set to allow students to underline the nouns in which the final 's' is pronounced differently.

Play the recording again and check answers.

> a) cheeks b) lips c) eyelashes

2 Read the examples to make sure everyone is quite clear about the three different pronunciations. Allow students to work in pairs and encourage them to say the words aloud as they decide which column to put each one in. This will give them a feel for what sounds right. Make sure they also add the words from Exercise 1. Do not check answers at this stage.

3 📼 **48 SB p 65**

Play the recording for students to listen, repeat and check their answers to Exercise 2. Then ask them which of the nouns they would not expect to use in the plural when describing someone.

> + /s/: backs, wrists, stomachs, cheeks, lips
> + /z/: knees, chins, heads, shoulders, beards, ears, eyes, legs, hands, toes, arms, dimples, freckles, wrinkles
> + /ɪz/: noses, moustaches, eyelashes
>
> Words they would probably not use in the plural are: *backs, stomachs, chins, heads, beards, noses, moustaches.*

You may like to give students the following rules for pronunciation of plural endings.

* After /s/, /z/, /ʃ/, /ʒ/, /tʃ/ and /dʒ/, the plural ending *-es* is pronounced /ɪz/.
* After /p/, /f/, /θ/, /t/ and /k/, the plural ending *-(e)s* is pronounced /s/.
* After vowels and /b/, /g/, /v/, /θ/, /d/, /l/, /m/, /n/, /ŋ/, /r/ and /w/, the plural ending *-(e)s* is pronounced /z/.

Lexis: describing character (p 65)

1 Give students time to read the article and match the headings to the paragraphs. Allow them to discuss their answers, but do not confirm anything at this stage.

2 📼 **49 SB p 65**

Play the recording for students to listen and check their

answers. You might like to ask them if they agree with the assessment of the different smiles in the text, and to say if they can identify any of them as their own smile or the smile of someone they know.

> a 3 b 1 c 4 d 2

3 🔲 **50 SB p 139**

Go through the adjectives in the box with the class before you play the recording. You could ask students to give examples of the sort of behaviour or attitude that they would associate with each one.

Play the recording and ask students to choose the most appropriate adjective for each speaker.

> a) sociable b) bossy c) confident d) ambitious
> e) easy-going f) sensitive

> 🔲 **50**
> a) *I'd love to meet your friends – let's make a date now. We could try that new restaurant in town.*
> b) *No, no, don't do it like that. Do it like this. Go on, do it again, and, oh, then get me a cup of tea.*
> c) *No problem – I'm sure I can win. I know I'm faster than the others.*
> d) *I'm working here to get some experience but I'm going to start up my own company soon.*
> e) *Yeah, whatever – I really don't mind. I'll be happy if we go out. I'll be happy if we stay in. Let's do whatever you want to do.*
> f) *Look, are you sure you're okay, because I can stay longer if you want. Anyway, you know where I am if you need me. Take care.*

4 Draw students' attention to the adjectives in the Language toolbox and make sure they understand them. If there are any unknown words, encourage other members of the class to explain them, where possible, by describing the kind of behaviour or attitude the adjective suggests. Ensure that students work alone to write one of the adjectives next to each thing and that they use adjectives from the Language toolbox (or from their own knowledge).

5 Students turn to page 125 for an analysis of what the adjectives they have chosen for each thing say about their personality. Give them time to discuss with their partner whether or not they think this is accurate and to find out what others chose as their adjectives.

What are you like? (p 66)

Books closed. Whole class. Write on one side of the board *What are you like?* and on the other *What do you like?* Invite students to come up and write answers that show the difference between the two questions.

Reading (p 66)

1 Focus attention on the title of the questionnaire and ask students to say what they think the difference between an optimist and a pessimist might be. An optimist is someone with a cheerful, positive personality, or someone who is content with a particular situation. A pessimist is someone who takes a negative view of life and is always complaining (moaning) and never satisfied.

Give students time to read and complete the questionnaire. Encourage them to work alone. They then calculate their scores, look up the meaning on page 127 and compare with a partner.

2 Go round the class and find out who got the highest and lowest scores. You could do this by asking students to arrange themselves in a line with the person with the highest score (the biggest optimist) at one end and the person with the lowest score (the biggest pessimist) at the other end.

Lexis: verb patterns (p 66)

1 Allow students to work in pairs if they wish and to discuss their answers before you check with the class.

> a) to be b) going out c) to get up d) speaking
> e) to spend f) to grow

2 Pairwork. Students can first guess whether or not the sentences are true for their partner and then ask questions to find out if they guessed correctly.

3 Encourage students to work individually to write their six extra sentences and then to compare them with a partner. You could also ask them to say if their partner's sentences are true for them or not.

Don't Worry, Be Happy (p 67)

Books closed. Whole class. Write *Happy* on one side of the board and *Sad* on the other side. Ask students to suggest things that make them feel either happy or sad.

Song (p 67)

1 Elicit an example of two words that rhyme (eg: *cat* and *mat*). Then give students a minute or two to match the rhyming words in the two columns. Make sure that they all understand the meanings. *Litigate* is likely to be a new word for many students. It means to take someone to court. Check answers with the class.

> style – smile   trouble – double   head – bed
> frown – down   late – litigate   wrote – note

2 📼 **51 SB p 67**

Draw students' attention to the information in the margin box. Find out if anyone has heard the song before. Ask them to read the song and complete the lyrics with the rhyming words from Exercise 1. You might like to point out that the first and second lines of each verse rhyme.

Play the song for students to check their answers. Then play it again for them to listen for enjoyment and sing along if they wish.

> 1 wrote 2 note 3 trouble 4 double 5 head
> 6 bed 7 late 8 litigate 9 style 10 smile
> 11 frown 12 down

📼 **51**

Don't Worry, Be Happy

Here's a little song I wrote.
You might want to sing it note for note.
Don't worry, be happy.

In every life we have some trouble.
When you worry you make it double.
Don't worry, be happy.

Ain't got no place to lay your head?
Somebody came and took your bed?
Don't worry, be happy.

The landlord says your rent is late?
He may have to litigate.
Don't worry, be happy.

Ain't got no cash, ain't got no style?
Ain't got no girl to make you smile?
Don't worry, be happy.

'Cos when you worry, your face will frown.
That will bring everybody down.
Don't worry, be happy.

3 Allow students to work in pairs if they wish as they identify at least three of the reasons for worrying that are given in the song. Check answers with the class.

> You have trouble in your life.
> You haven't got a home (place to lay your head).
> Someone took your bed.
> Your rent is late.
> Your landlord may take you to court (litigate).
> You haven't got any money (cash).
> You aren't very fashionable.
> You haven't got a girl.

4 Pairwork. Give students plenty of time to discuss and list the worries they think each of these people might have. Allow them to compare with other pairs and then have a class feedback session to determine how many ideas have been suggested and how much agreement there is.

Pairwork. Ask students to discuss the effect this song has on them. Does it make them feel happy. Would it have that effect if they were worried about something? Ask them to discuss and report back to the class on what music makes them feel happy.

Close up (p 67)

Imperatives

1 Make sure that students understand that an imperative is used to tell someone to do something or not to do something. Direct their attention to the Language reference box at the bottom of the page for some examples. Elicit some more examples of imperatives both telling someone to do something and not to do something. Then ask students to choose the correct alternative for 'Be happy' from the ones given.

> c) Don't be sad.

2 Look at the example with the class and then ask them to write alternatives for each of the imperatives. Allow them to compare notes with a partner before checking answers with the class.

> a) Don't be naughty.   b) Don't be noisy.
> c) Don't be late.   d) Don't be mean.
> e) Don't be rude.   f) Don't be miserable.
> g) Don't be shy.   h) Don't be angry.
> i) Don't be childish.

3 Pairwork. Students choose one imperative from Exercise 2 to write a three-line dialogue. Go through the example with the class first. Check answers by asking pairs to perform their dialogues. Make a note of which imperatives have been chosen to make sure that all the ones from Exercise 2 are used. If they haven't all been used, you might like to ask students to suggest circumstances in which the others might be heard.

Take it easy (p 68)

Books closed. Whole class. Write the word *relax* on the board and ask students to say what they do to help them relax when they feel tense.

Reading (p 68)

1 Establish that 'No-Stress Day' is a day in which you must be completely relaxed and avoid anything that will make you worried, tense or stressed. Find out if students think this is a realistic idea and if they have ever had such a day.

Pairwork. Students read the article and discuss the questions. Ask them to report back to the class on what they discussed. Have a show of hands on what is the best or worst suggestion for avoiding stress.

2 Pairwork. Students add three ideas of their own to the list. Allow them to compare with other pairs.

Lexis: phrasal verbs (p 68)

1 Encourage students to work individually to complete the sentences with phrasal verbs from the box, but allow them to compare notes with a partner before checking answers with the class.

> a) take off   b) switch off   c) put on   d) give up
> e) switch on   f) throw away   g) hang up

2 Pairwork. Students discuss whether or not the sentences in Exercise 1 are true for them.

Close up (p 69)

Phrasal verbs

1 Pairwork. Students study the examples in the box and work together to answer the questions. Check answers with the class. Direct students' attention to the Language reference section which has more information and examples of sentences with phrasal verbs.

> a) sat down   b) took off   c) ran after

2 Elicit answers from the class. Then ask them to produce further examples of sentences with object pronouns and separable and inseparable phrasal verbs.

> a)   Between the verb and the particle.
> b)   After the particle.

3 Allow students to work in pairs or small groups if they wish and to use a dictionary to find out if a verb is separable or inseparable. A good dictionary will give them this information. Check answers with the class.

> a) Throw it away.   b) Clear it up.   c) Deal with it.
> d) Fill it in.   e) Look after it.   f) Call it off.

Laughter – the best medicine (p 69)

Books closed. Whole class. Find out what makes the students laugh. Ask them to try to remember the time they laughed the longest and the loudest and to say what caused their laughter.

1 **[cassette] 52 SB p 139**
Draw students' attention to the photograph and ask them to describe it. Tell them that they are going to listen to a report on the benefits of laughter and that they should try

not to laugh as they listen. Their task is to note down the benefits described in the report. Play the recording and check answers with the class. Ask students what they think about the idea of 'laughter clubs' and whether they would consider joining one.

> Laughter reduces stress, helps the body fight illness and infection, and exercises the lungs.

[cassette] 52

Laughter clubs

Scientific research has proved that laughter reduces the effects of stress and helps the body to fight against illness and infection. In India, the health benefits of laughter are taken very seriously. There is a network of 600 'laughter clubs' where people meet every day just to laugh. They participate in 'social laughter' (quiet tittering), suppressed laughter (sniggering), and the loud, explosive laugh (roaring with laughter), which exercises the lungs.

2 Pairwork. Students challenge each other not to smile or laugh as they take turns saying funny things to each other. Draw students' attention to the useful expression *to keep a straight face*. You could have a class contest with the winner of each pair taking on the winner of another pair and so on until you end up with a class champion. The whole class can then try to make this person laugh. See how long he or she can keep a straight face.

Test

> Scoring: one point per correct answer unless otherwise indicated.
>
> **1**   1 wrinkles   2 eyebrows   3 eyelashes   4 freckles
>   5 dimples   6 moustache   7 cheek   8 beard
>
> **2**   1 b   2 e   3 d   4 c   5 f   6 a
>
> **3**   1 watching   2 to go   3 to travel   4 finishing
>   5 to learn   6 to earn
>
> **4**   1 ✔   4 ✔
>
> **5**   1 Don't be late.   2 Be quiet.   3 Don't be childish.
>   4 Calm down.
>
> **6**   1 off   2 up   3 up   4 away   5 on   6 off
>
> **7**   (One point for ticking and crossing correctly. One point for each of the corrections.)
>   1   ✘ What a mess! Can you clear it up please?
>   2   ✔
>   3   ✔
>   4   ✘ My sister's ill. I need to stay in and look after her.

11

Smile Test

Name: _____   Total: _____ /40

1 Vocabulary – the face 8 points

Add the missing vowels (a, e, i, o, u) to complete the words.

1	wr__nkl__s	5	d__mpl__s
2	__y__br__ws	6	m____st__ch__
3	__y__l__sh__s	7	ch____k
4	fr__ckl__s	8	b____rd

2 Vocabulary – describing character 6 points

Match the sentences with the character adjectives.

1	He's always calm and relaxed.	a)	ambitious
2	She really enjoys being with people.	b)	easy-going
3	She's sure about her own abilities.	c)	cheeky
4	He doesn't show enough respect.	d)	confident
5	She likes to give orders.	e)	sociable
6	He wants to be successful in life.	f)	bossy

3 Vocabulary – verb patterns 6 points

Put the verb into the correct form: infinitive or -ing.

1 I really enjoy _____ (watch) travel programmes.

2 I've always wanted _____ (go) travelling.

3 At last I've decided _____ (travel) around the world.

4 I'm looking forward to _____ (finish) work.

5 I'm going to try _____ (learn) some new languages.

6 I just need _____ (earn) a little more money and then ... I'm away!

4 Imperatives (1) 4 points

Tick (✔) the two correct sentences.

1 Don't worry. ☐

2 Be not worried. ☐

3 Don't worry you. ☐

4 Don't be worried. ☐

5 Imperatives (2) 4 points

Complete sentence b so it has similar meaning to sentence a.

1	a) Be on time!	b)	_____	late!
2	a) Don't be noisy!	b)	_____	quiet!
3	a) Act your age!	b)	_____	childish!
4	a) Don't be angry!	b)	_____	down!

6 Vocabulary – phrasal verbs (1) 6 points

Complete the dialogues with away, off, on and up.

A: Hi. Come in and take your coat (1) _____ .

B: Thanks. Where can I hang it (2) _____ ?

*   *   *

C: I'm going to try to give (3) _____ smoking.

D: Okay, it's easy. Throw that packet of cigarettes (4) _____ and never buy any more. It worked for me.

*   *   *

E: Is it okay if I put the TV (5) _____ to watch the news?

F: Sure. Can you switch it (6) _____ when it's finished?

7 Vocabulary – phrasal verbs (2) 6 points

Two of these sentences contain a mistake. Tick (✔) or cross (✗) the sentences and correct the mistakes.

1 What a mess! Can you clear up it please?

_____

_____

2 If it continues to rain, they'll call the match off.

_____

_____

3 Here's the form. Can you fill it in before you leave?

_____

_____

4 My sister's ill. I need to stay in and look her after.

_____

_____

12 *Rebel* Overview

This unit is about rebellion and covers two different aspects of the subject. The first is political and social protest, and the second, rebellion against the expectations of one's family. In the first section, students read a text about May Day demonstrations against globalisation, and the discussion is widened to include other popular causes. They listen to four protesters talking about why they are taking part in a demonstration and look at some of the words used to talk about your feelings about certain issues. They also study the change in word stress in nouns derived from certain verbs.

The next section focuses on verbs with dynamic and stative meanings. Students examine some excerpts from the listening text to see how verbs can describe actions and states.

A different kind of rebellion is examined in the next section where students read a text about four celebrities who all acted in a rebellious way. This leads into an Anecdote in which students have the opportunity for extended speaking on times they got into trouble as children.

Another grammar focus of the unit is passives, and the use of these in the texts about celebrity rebels is examined. Students then use passives to complete a text about the famous rebel, Che Guevara.

The final section gives students guided practice in report writing, a skill they will find particularly useful if they wish to take exams in English, such as the Cambridge exams, which often require candidates to write a report.

Section	Aims	What the students are doing
May Day page 70	*Reading skills*: reading for specific information	Discussing a photograph of a demonstrator being arrested by the police.
		Identifying true and false statements about an article on May Day protests.
What are you doing here? page 71	*Listening skills*: listening for gist	Matching demonstrators and their causes.
	Lexis: protest	Completing sentences which express feelings about different causes.
	Lexis: word families	Identifying nouns formed from verbs and practising changes in stress patterns.
Close up page 72	*Grammar*: verbs with dynamic and stative meanings	Looking at the difference between verbs with dynamic and stative meanings.
		Completing sentences describing actions and states.
Celebrity rebels page 73	*Reading skills*: reading for specific information	Scanning a text to match people with their acts of rebellion.
		Discussing the text and rebellion in general.
	Conversation skills: fluency work	Anecdote: talking about times when students got into trouble as children.
Close up pages 74–75	*Grammar*: passives	Examining the use of the passive in the previous reading text.
		Writing the story of Patty Hearst using passive forms.
		Completing a text on Che Guevara with past simple passives.
How green is the class? page 75	*Writing*: report writing	Conducting a survey on environmental attitudes in the class.
		Writing a report on the findings of the survey, using a model report as a guide.

12

Rebel Teacher's notes

May Day (p 70)

Books closed. Whole class. Ask students if May Day (1st May) has any particular significance in their countries. In some countries it is when the work of ordinary people is celebrated and recognised and it is often a public holiday. In recent years May Day has become a focus for demonstrations and protest, particularly against capitalism and big business.

Reading (p 70)

1 Pairwork. Students look at the photograph at the bottom of the page and discuss the questions. Encourage them to report back to the class on their discussion.

2 Allow students to work in pairs or small groups if they wish. You may need to explain *globalisation*, the process by which the whole world has become one big marketplace with larger and larger multinational companies controlling the business sector. This has implications for poorer countries, open to exploitation by wealthier nations and big corporations and for pollution and other environmental issues, as these companies are so powerful that it is difficult for individual governments to keep their activities under control.

Check answers with the class. You might like to ask them if these kinds of demonstrations have taken place in their own countries.

> a) True b) False c) True d) False e) True

Optional activity

You might like to ask students to correct those sentences that are false.

b) Dozens of protesters were arrested in Australia. (One dozen is twelve, and dozens is used to suggest a large number.)

d) In Norway, a protester threw an apple-pie at the foreign minister.

3 Ask for opinions around the class as to whether demonstrations are a good way of making a point or not. Encourage students who don't think they are to say what better ways they can suggest.

What are you doing here? (p 71)

Closed books. Whole class. Brainstorm some other issues that people protest about. Find out which issues students feel strongly about and which ones they have no interest in.

Listening (p 71)

1 Read the instructions with the class and then allow them to work in pairs or small groups to match the slogans with the causes. Check answers with the class.

> a 3 b 5 c 1 d 2 e 6 f 4

2 **53 SB p 139**

Focus attention on the photographs and their captions. Ask students to speculate on what the people might be like, what their interests might be and which cause they think they might support.

Then play the recording for them to listen and check their answers.

> Jake: (a) No to multinationals – 3 Against globalisation.
>
> Debbie: (e) Equal work means equal pay – 6 Against unequal pay for women.
>
> Ronny: (d) Ban animal testing – 2 Against cruelty to animals.
>
> Caroline: (f) Free education for all – 4 Against student fees.

53

(I = interviewer; J = Jake; D = Debbie; C = Caroline; R = Ronny)

I: *It's May 1st, and we are in the centre of London in the middle of an enormous demonstration. People are handing out leaflets with information. There are all kinds of people here, but what exactly are they protesting about?*

Jake

I: *Excuse me! Yes, you. What are you doing here?*

J: *I'm protesting against globalisation. Multinational companies cause a lot of pollution. They are polluting the world's rivers and seas, and they don't care – they just want to make as much money as possible. I'm also giving out peaceful protest leaflets and T-shirts. There are some people here who want violence, but most people are here to protest in a peaceful way. Me, I'm a supporter of peaceful action.*

I: *Thank you.*

Debbie

I: *Excuse me. Can you tell me what you're doing here?*

D: *Well, I'm in favour of many of the causes here but I'm here today with a group of women from Manchester. We're demonstrating for equal pay for women. Women still earn less than men in most jobs, and it's time for that to change. I'm not anti-men – I just want a fairer system. Would you like to sign our petition?*

I: *Er, yes, sure, thank you.*

Ronny

I: *Hi there! Can you tell me what you're doing here?*

R: *I'm selling veggie burgers. I'm against cosmetic companies that use animals in their experiments. At home I have three dogs, two cats and a pet mouse called Jerry. They are my friends. I support animal rights and I'm protesting against cruelty to animals. All right?*

I: *Good luck.*

Caroline

I: *Excuse me. What are you doing here?*

C: *I'm having fun with my friends. I don't feel strongly about politics and I don't know much about it. This is my first demonstration. My friends and I are against student fees – we're demanding financial aid from the government. We want the government to pay. I know so many people who don't go to college because they don't want to get into debt. I don't really care about globalisation and stuff, but students are really important. I mean, we're the future of the country, aren't we?*

Lexis: protest (p 71)

1 Encourage students to complete as many sentences as they can, working in pairs if they wish, before you play the recording again for them to check.

> a) supporter of   b) in favour   c) anti-   d) against
> e) support   f) don't feel   g) really care

2 Pairwork. Students discuss which of the statements in Exercise 1 they agree with. In a feedback session, find out how much agreement there is across the class.

3 Pairwork. Students decide which causes they feel most strongly about. They can introduce causes not already mentioned if they wish.

Lexis: word families (p 71)

1 Elicit the noun forms for each of the verbs and write them on the board next to the verbs.

> pollution, globalisation, demonstration, information

2 📼 **54 SB p 71**

Read the example out, demonstrating how the stress pattern changes from verb to noun and let students practise saying the two forms. Then let them work in pairs to decide where in the table the other verb and noun pairs should go. Encourage them to say the words aloud so they can get a feel for what sounds right. When they have completed the table, play the recording for them to listen, repeat and check their answers.

Alternatively, play the recording first and have students complete the table as they listen to the words. You may need to pause the recording after each pair.

> See Exercise 3.

3 📼 **55 SB p 139**

Play the recording for students to listen, repeat and add a further eight verb and noun pairs to the table. You may need to pause the recording to allow them time to write. Check answers with the class and ask which syllable the stress falls on when a noun ends in -*ion*. Elicit any further examples that they can give.

> A: pollute – pollution; produce – production; reduce – reduction
>
> B: inform – information; explain – explanation
>
> C: demonstrate – demonstration; educate – education; legislate – legislation
>
> D: globalise – globalisation; organise – organisation; legalise – legalisation; modernise – modernisation
>
> When a noun ends in -*ion*, the stress is always on the preceding syllable.

> 📼 **55**
>
> *explain, explanation*
> *organise, organisation*
> *produce, production*
> *legalise, legalisation*
> *educate, education*
> *reduce, reduction*
> *modernise, modernisation*
> *legislate, legislation*

Close up (p 72)

Dynamic & stative meanings

1 Pairwork. If necessary, explain the difference between a verb with dynamic meaning (one describing an action, when something happens) and one with stative meaning (one describing a state, not something that happens). Students look at the extracts in the box and discuss the questions. Check answers with the class. There is more information about verbs with dynamic and stative meanings in the Language reference section at the bottom of page 72.

> a) Actions.   b) Present continuous.

2 Students re-write the sentences using the present continuous form of the verbs in brackets. Check answers with the class and draw students' attention to the fact that the *e* of *make* is dropped when the *-ing* ending is added and the *t* of *chat* is doubled.

> a)   A phone is ringing.
> b)   A teacher in another class is talking.
> c)   The traffic is making a lot of noise.
> d)   A clock is ticking.
> e)   A student is laughing.
> f)   People are chatting.

3 Make sure the students are silent before you start counting the fifteen seconds and ask them to tick the things in Exercise 2 that are true. They should also make a note of any other things that are happening that they can hear. In a feedback session, find out if they all agree on which sentences were true and how many other things they noticed.

4 Pairwork. Again, students look at extracts from the radio interviews they heard earlier and discuss the questions. Check answers with the class.

> a) States.   b) Present simple.   c) No.

5 Students look at both sets of extracts and identify the verb that describes both an action and a state and has two different meanings.

> have

6 Pairwork. Students work together to decide whether the verbs describe actions or states and complete the sentences in the appropriate tenses. Check answers with the class.

> a) (state) likes   b) (state) knows   c) (state) has
> d) (action) is having   e) (state) looks
> f) (action) is looking   g) (action) is thinking
> h) (state) thinks

7 You could do this as a mingling activity with students going round the class asking questions until they have found one name to go in each sentence. The first person to complete all the sentences with a name from the class is the winner.

Celebrity rebels (p 73)

Books closed. Whole class. The focus in this section moves away from political protest to rebelling against your family. Establish the meaning of *rebel* – to do something your family (or society in general) disapproves of. (Note that *rebel*, the noun, is stressed on the first syllable, but *rebel*, the verb, is stressed on the second syllable.) Ask students why they think some people, particularly young people rebel and list their reasons on the board. To start them off give them a couple of suggestions, eg: because they are rich and bored; because they are unhappy with their family life.

Reading (p 73)

1 Go through the list of things the rebels did with the class and then give them a few minutes to find out who did each one. To encourage them to scan a text for specific information, rather than trying to read and understand every word, you could have a race, with the first person to match the rebels with what they did as the winner.

Check answers with the class.

> a) Patty Hearst.   b) Patty Hearst.
> c) Macaulay Culkin.   d) Macaulay Culkin.
> e) Princess Stephanie.   f) Princess Stephanie.

2 Students read through the text to identify words that can replace the underlined ones in the list in Exercise 1. Allow them to compare notes in pairs or small groups before checking answers with the class.

> a) became a member of   b) broke the law
> c) took up   d) dyed   e) unsuitable
> f) ran away with

3 Pairwork. Students discuss the questions and report back to the class.

Anecdote (p 73)

See the Introduction on page 4 for more ideas on how to set up, monitor and repeat Anecdotes.

Pairwork. Give students plenty of time to decide what they are going to talk about and to read the questions. They then take turns to talk about a time when they got into trouble as a child.

Close up (p 74)

Passives

1 Pairwork. Students read the question and the two answers and discuss the questions. You may need to point out that both answers are grammatically correct but one is more natural than the other. Check answers with the class. Refer them to the Language reference section on page 75 for more information about passives.

> a)

2 Pairwork. Students look again at the two answers in Exercise 1 and discuss the questions. Check answers with the class.

> a) Past simple. b) Answer 2. c) *be*

3 Allow students to work in pairs or small groups if they wish. Encourage them to decide on the verb forms first and then to put the events of the story in order. They can check their answers in the text on page 73.

> (8) a) She was charged with bank robbery.
>
> (5) b) She was renamed 'Tania'.
>
> (2) c) She was held prisoner for 57 days.
>
> (7) d) She was photographed robbing a bank.
>
> (3) e) She decided to rebel against her family.
>
> (10) f) She was pardoned by President Clinton in 2001.
>
> (9) g) She was released after three years in prison.
>
> (4) h) She became a member of the SLA.
>
> (1) i) She was kidnapped by a political group.
>
> (6) j) She broke the law.

4 Find out if the students know anything about Che Guevara or have seen the famous photograph of him before. Ask them to complete the text with past simple passives. Allow them to compare their answers in pairs or small groups but do not check with the class at this stage.

5 ▭ **56 SB p 74**
Play the recording for students to check their answers to Exercise 4.

> 1 was pinned 2 was taken 3 was sent
>
> 4 was killed 5 were exhibited

> ▭ **56**
>
> *Image of a rebel*
> *It is an image that became a legend of the twentieth century. It is tattooed on Diego Maradona's arm. A Che poster was pinned on Mick Jagger's wall when he was a student, and millions of T-shirts are still decorated with the image today. The picture was taken on 5 March 1960 at a memorial service in Havana, Cuba. Cuban photographer, Alberto Korda was sent by the magazine Revolución to take photographs of the Cuban leader, Fidel Castro.*
>
> *'Che was standing behind Fidel Castro on the platform,' said Korda. 'You couldn't see him. Then suddenly he stepped forward to the edge of the platform. I managed to take a photo. Then he was gone.'*

> *Seven years later, in October 1967, Che Guevara was killed in Bolivia, and Korda's photograph became an icon for revolutionaries everywhere. Korda's photographs were exhibited in Paris in Spring 2001. It was while he was attending the exhibition of his work that Korda died.*

6 Students can discuss these questions in pairs or small groups and then report back to the class.

How green is the class? (p 75)

You might like to discuss the various meanings of *green* before you start this section. In English it can mean new and naive (*He's only recently joined the company and he's very green.*) as well as concerned about protecting the environment, the meaning used in this section.

Report writing (p 75)

1 Groupwork. Report writing is a useful skill and one that features in many of the English exams that students may want to take (for example several of the Cambridge exams). These exercises and the model provided will give them a guided introduction to writing a report.

Students discuss which of the activities listed are good and which are bad for the environment. They then report back to the class. If there is any disagreement, encourage discussion of the reasons behind their choices.

2 Groupwork. Students follow the instructions to prepare and carry out a survey of the class. It is important that they make notes of the answers they receive.

3 Groupwork. Students work together, using their notes and the model report to produce a report on their survey. These can be displayed in the classroom for everyone to read.

Test

> Scoring: one point per correct answer unless otherwise indicated.
>
> **1** 1 of 2 about 3 anti-war 4 of
>
> **2** 1 pollution 2 educate 3 explanation 4 inform
> 5 legalisation 6 reduction
>
> **3** 1 're thinking 2 Do you want 3 don't know
> 4 Do you think 5 are you cooking 6 looks
> 7 hope 8 like 9 are you looking 10 looks
>
> **4** 1 named 2 was built 3 was first used
> 4 were imprisoned 5 spent 6 kept
> 7 were allowed
>
> **5** 1 is said 2 escaped 3 claim(ed) 4 were swept
> 5 were eaten 6 (was) closed down 7 is visited

Rebel Test

Name: _____   **Total:** _____ /40

---

1 Vocabulary – protest *4 points*

Underline the correct alternative.

1 I'm a supporter **for / of** peaceful demonstrations.

2 We should care more **of / about** the environment.

3 I've been on lots of **anti-war / against-war** demonstrations.

4 I'm in favour **of / for** banning smoking in public.

2 Vocabulary – word families *12 points*

First complete the table. Then underline the most stressed syllable in the words you write.

Verb	Noun
pollute	1 _____
2 _____	education
explain	3 _____
4 _____	information
legalise	5 _____
reduce	6 _____

3 Dynamic & stative meanings *10 points*

Put the verb into the correct form: simple or continuous.

A: We (1) _____ (think) of going to Tim's party tonight. (2) _____ you _____ (want) to come?

B: Well, I (3) _____ (not know) Tim very well. (4) _____ you _____ (think) it's okay to come?

*   *   *

C: What (5) _____ you _____ (cook)? It (6) _____ (look) lovely.

D: It's a surprise! I (7) _____ (hope) you (8) _____ (like) it?

*   *   *

E: What (9) _____ you _____ (look) at?

F: One of the models in this magazine. He (10) _____ (look) just like my boyfriend!

4 Passives (1) *7 points*

Underline the correct alternative: passive or active.

Alcatraz – a brief history

The Spanish explorer Juan Manuel de Ayla (1) **named / was named** the island Alcatraz in 1775. A fort (2) **built / was built** on the island in 1853 and this (3) **first used / was first used** as a prison for the United States' most dangerous criminals in 1889. Many famous criminals (4) **imprisoned / were imprisoned** in Alcatraz. The gangster Al Capone (5) **spent / was spent** five years there, and Robert Stroud, 'The Birdman of Alcatraz', was there for seventeen of his thirty years in captivity. Contrary to popular belief, Stroud never actually (6) **kept / was kept** any birds there; prisoners (7) **allowed / were allowed** food, clothing, shelter and medical attention and very little else.

5 Passives (2) *7 points*

Put the verb into the correct tense and form: active or passive.

It (1) _____ (say) that no-one ever successfully (2) _____ (escape) from Alcatraz; the authorities (3) _____ (claim) that all escapees either (4) _____ (sweep) out to sea by the strong currents or they (5) _____ (eat) by sharks. Alcatraz (6) _____ (close down) as a prison on 21st March 1963. Today, Alcatraz (7) _____ (visit) by around a million people every year.

13 Dance Overview

This unit is about dancing, mostly the sort of dancing teenagers and young adults are likely to be interested in, but also ballet through the story of Billy Elliot, from the film of the same name. The grammar focus is on the present perfect simple and continuous and the use of *for, since* and *been* to talk about experiences and their duration.

The unit begins with a questionnaire on dancing, which provides the basis for some lexical work on the prepositions *on* and *at*. The theme continues in the next two sections which are both about Ibiza and its night clubs. Students read and discuss texts about clubbing and listen to a radio programme in which three different people living in Ibiza talk about their experiences. An opportunity for extended speaking is given in the Anecdote section where students tell each other about a place they have been to where people were dancing and having fun. This leads into some work on talking about experiences using *for* and *since* to express duration and the use of the present perfect simple and continuous.

In the final section, students read and listen to a text about Billy Elliot, who has to face his father's anger when he finds out that Billy has been going to ballet classes instead of the boxing lessons he was supposed to be attending.

Section	Aims	What the students are doing
Introduction page 76	*Reading skills*: questionnaire	Answering a questionnaire on dancing and discussing the results.
	Lexis: on and *at*	Practising using the prepositions *on* and *at* correctly.
The clubbing capital of the world page 77	*Conversation skills*: fluency work	Talking about nightlife in students' own countries.
	Reading skills: reading for specific information	Reading the first part of a text about Ibiza to find the answers to questions.
		Reading the rest of the text to match features with specific night clubs
My Ibiza page 78	*Listening skills*: listening for gist	Matching people with what they say about their lives in Ibiza.
	Lexis: informal language	Studying the meanings of some of the informal expressions used in the listening.
	Conversation skills: fluency work	Anecdote: talking about a time recently when students went to a place where people were dancing.
Close up pages 79–80	*Grammar: for* and *since; been*; present perfect simple and continuous	Looking at the use of *for* and *since* to talk about duration.
		Writing sentences about students own experiences and asking a partner about things they have done.
		Writing sentences using the present perfect simple and continuous.
		Conducting a class survey.
Billy Elliot page 81	*Reading skills*: reading for gist	Identifying the problem that Billy Elliott has and predicting what will happen.
	Listening skills: listening for gist	Listening to an extract from Billy Elliot's story and deciding who students sympathise with most.
		Putting the summary of the extract in order.
		Talking about students' own interests at the age of twelve.

13 Dance *Teacher's notes*

Books closed. Divide the class into groups and give them two minutes to write down as many song titles as they can that include the word *dance* (or derivatives of it). The team with the longest list wins.

Reading (p 76)

Elicit or explain that someone who is a 'disco diva' is good at dancing and someone who has 'two left feet' is clumsy and awkward.

Students read the questionnaire and choose their answers individually. They can then see what their scores mean on page 127 and compare with a partner.

Lexis: *on & at* (p 76)

1 Point out where *on* and *at* are used in the questionnaire (question 1). Students then add *on* or *at* to the noun phrases in the box. Allow them to compare their answers with a partner before checking with the class.

> on the phone, at a concert, on holiday, on a plane, at the doctor's, on the internet, on a business trip, at the hairdresser's, at a night club, on a training course

2 Students work individually to write two true and one false sentence about themselves. They then read them to a partner who has to guess which one is false.

The clubbing capital of the world (p 77)

Books closed. Whole class. Establish the meaning of *clubbing* and find out how many students enjoy clubbing. Ask them where they think the 'clubbing capital of the world' might be (= the place with the most/best night clubs).

Groupwork. Students discuss the questions and report back to the class.

Reading (p 77)

1 Find out if anyone has ever been to Ibiza. If so, ask them to tell the class about their trip. Then ask the students to read the first part of the text (*Party island*) and find the answers to the questions. Allow them to compare notes in pairs or small groups before checking with the class.

> a) Tourists, clubbers, DJs.   b) Two million.
> c) Since the sixties.   d) Acid House arrived.
> e) All tastes: dance, trance, techno, garage, pop, rock and funk.

2 Pairwork. Students discuss whether they have ever been to a club with the features listed. If students don't understand *foam parties*, point out the photograph at the bottom of the page which shows one in action. (*Foam* is a mass of small bubbles.)

3 Students read the second part of the article (*The clubs*) which describes two Ibiza clubs, *Amnesia* and *Privilege*. They match them with the features listed in Exercise 2. Check answers with the class. You might like to ask them to vote on which club they would most like to go to.

> a)   'live' music – *Privilege*
> b)   several different dance-floors – *Privilege*
> c)   foam parties – *Amnesia*
> d)   space for 10,000 people – *Privilege*
> e)   a swimming pool – *Privilege*
> f)   trees planted inside – *Privilege*

4 Pairwork. Students discuss why they would or wouldn't like to go to Ibiza. Encourage them to report back to the class on their discussions.

My Ibiza (p 78)

Books closed. Whole class. Tell students that this section is also about Ibiza but will focus more on people who actually live there. Brainstorm ideas for advantages and disadvantages of living in a place which is very popular with tourists, particularly one famous for its nightlife.

Listening (p 78)

1 Pairwork. Students look at the three photographs and guess who said each of the things listed. See how much agreement there is around the class, but do not confirm any answers at this stage.

> a) Saskia.   b) Antonio.   c) Josh.   d) Josh.
> e) Saskia.   f) Josh.

2 🔲 **57 SB p 139**
Play the recording for students to check their answers to Exercise 1. Then elicit suggestions for which person enjoys their life most.

(I = Interviewer; J = Josh; S = Saskia; A = Antonio)

Josh

I: Josh, how are you?

J: Um, to be honest, I'm completely knackered! I've been dancing all night.

I: You're very white. Don't you like sunbathing?

J: Uh, well, I haven't been to the beach yet.

I: How come? How long have you been here?

J: Dunno. Nine, ten days.

I: Well, what have you been doing since you arrived?

J: I've been clubbing every night and sleeping all day. I've met loads of people, especially girls.

I: So, have you had a good time?

J: Oh yeah, definitely. I reckon this is the best holiday I've ever had. The only problem is I'm skint. I've spent all my money and I've still got a few days to go.

I: Oh dear. Well good luck and have a good journey home.

J: Cheers. You couldn't lend me some money, could you?

Saskia

I: Saskia, how long have you been here?

S: Since 1997.

I: Where are you from originally?

S: Holland, but I haven't been home for a couple of years now.

I: What have you been doing here since 1997?

S: Having a great time – I've been working in clubs. I've been a resident DJ at Amnesia for two years. Oh, and I've been building my own house.

I: Really? Do you make a lot of money working in clubs?

S: You can, but I've also married a guy from Ibiza. His father gave us the land to build a house.

I: I see. Do you think you'll ever go back to Holland?

S: No way. I love the lifestyle here: it's so laid back. And anyway, all my friends and family come and visit me here.

Antonio

I: Good morning, Antonio. How are you today?

A: Not bad, not bad. But I've been working all night in my restaurant so I'm going to go to bed soon.

I: Well, thanks for talking to us. How long have you been here in Ibiza?

A: All my life. I was born in the north but I've been living in Ibiza town since 1995. That was when I opened my own restaurant.

I: What's it like living here in Ibiza?

A: Ah, it used to be a wonderful place, but now the tourists have spoilt it.

I: But tourists have been coming to Ibiza since the sixties.

A: That's true, but they've changed. Tourists used to behave much better than they do today. Englishmen used to be gentlemen. Now it's all tattoos and piercings.

I: What sort of people come to your restaurants?

A: Well ... er ... tourists.

Lexis: informal language (p 78)

1 You may need to point out that the words in the box are informal expressions used by Josh. The sentences with the underlined words are not from the interview. Students have to replace the underlined words with the informal expressions. Check answers with the class. If you wish, you could play the recording again to show how Josh uses these words and ask students to raise their hands as soon as they hear them.

a) knackered   b) how come   c) clubbing
d) reckon   e) I'm skint

2 Pairwork. Students discuss the sentences in Exercise 1 and tell each other whether they are true for them.

Anecdote (p 78)

See the Introduction on page 4 for more ideas on how to set up, monitor and repeat Anecdotes.

Pairwork. Give students plenty of time to decide what they are going to talk about and to read the questions. They then take turns to talk about a time when they went to a place where people were dancing and having a good time.

Close up (p 79)

for & since

1 Focus attention on the diagram. If students are familiar with sentences using *for* and *since*, you could ask them to make up two examples, one using *for* and the other *since*. Then ask them to complete the table with correct information. There is more information on the use of *for* and *since*, in the Language reference section on page 80.

2 Students add more examples to the table. Make sure their new examples include items for both the *since* and *for* columns. You might like to ask them to make up sentences using their new examples.

been (p 79)

1 Pairwork. Students read the sentences and discuss the questions. Check answers with the class. Direct students to the Language reference section on page 80 for more information about the use of *been*.

> a) Present perfect.
>
> b) he hasn't been to the beach; she hasn't been home.
>
> c) Josh has been in Ibiza; Saskia has been in Ibiza.

2 Students work individually to write their sentences and then compare with a partner.

3 Pairwork. Give students a minute or two to note down some places. Then ask them to work in pairs and ask questions to find out if their partner knows or has been to these places. Encourage them to ask follow up questions, as in the example, in order to find out as much as possible.

Present perfect simple & continuous (p 80)

1 Focus attention on the table. Ask students to read out the sentences. Then ask them which facts tell us how long an activity has continued.

> Present perfect facts.

2 Pairwork. Students underline the main verbs in column 3 of the table (Present perfect facts) and discuss the questions. Check answers with the class.

> a) be – She's been
>
> b) Present perfect simple.
>
> c) come – They've been coming
>
> d) Present perfect continuous.

3 Students work individually to write a name for each item. They then decide whether the verbs describe states or single/repeated actions. When they have written eight sentences, they compare them with a partner.

> 1
>
> a) state b) state c) state d) action e) action
>
> f) state
>
> g) state (action) – see note in the Language reference section.
>
> h) action (state) – see note in the Language reference section.

4 Whole class. Students choose their facts, decide on the questions they will ask and then mingle to interview the rest of the class. The results could be written up for homework in the form of a report.

Billy Elliot (p 81)

Closed books. Whole class. Find out if anyone is interested in ballet and how many famous ballet dancers the students can name. Write these up on the board, putting the men in one column and the women in the other. If anyone in the class takes ballet classes ask them to explain what they enjoy about it and what the difficulties are, if any.

Reading & listening (p 81)

1 Read the introduction with the class. Elicit ideas as to what the problem is and what they think will happen.

> Billy has been going to ballet lessons not boxing lessons. His dad is going to be angry when he finds him in a ballet class.

2 🔲 58 SB p 81

Play the recording and allow students to read the text at the same time. Then have a whole class discussion on who they sympathise with most. Find out if anyone has ever been in a similar situation.

3 Allow students to work in pairs if they wish to put the lines in the correct order. Check answers by having one pair read out the completed summary.

> 1 e   2 b   3 d   4 a   5 f   6 g   7 c

4 Pairwork. Students discuss the interests they had when they were twelve and what they wanted to be. Encourage them to say what the reaction of their family was and whether they still have those interests and ambitions.

Test

> Scoring: one point per correct answer unless otherwise indicated.
>
> **1** 1 at 2 on 3 on 4 on 5 at 6 on 7 at 8 on
>
> **2** 1 clubbing 2 knackered 3 How come 4 skint
>   5 reckon
>
> **3** 1 since 2 for 3 since 4 since 5 for 6 since
>   7 for 8 for 9 for 10 since
>
> **4** 1 be 2 go 3 be
>   4 be (note, *be on* the beach, *go to* the beach)
>   5 go 6 be
>
> **5** 1 known 2 been waiting 3 had 4 liked
>   5 been learning 6 wanted 7 been raining
>
> **6** 1 been studying 2 had 3 been 4 been doing

13 *Dance* Test

Name: _____ **Total:** _____ /40

---

1 Vocabulary – *on* & *at* *8 points*
Add the missing word, *on* or *at*.

1 We first met _____ a nightclub.

2 Ssssh! I'm _____ the phone.

3 Are you going _____ holiday this year?

4 She's away _____ a business trip at the moment.

5 I saw Anna _____ the hairdresser's yesterday.

6 I found this picture _____ the internet.

7 Do you think Tom will be _____ Sara's party?

8 Did you watch any films _____ the plane?

2 Vocabulary – informal language *5 points*
Complete the dialogue with the words and expressions in the box.

> clubbing   How come   knackered   reckon   skint

A: Do you fancy going (1) _____ tonight?

B: I'd love to, but I'm a bit (2) _____ . I didn't get much sleep last night.

A: (3) _____ ?

B: Oh, I went out and I didn't get home until 4.30 this morning! I spent a fortune and now I'm (4) _____ . I (5) _____ I'd better stay in tonight.

3 *for* & *since* *10 points*
Which of the following words and expressions are used with *for* and which are used with *since*?

1 _____ yesterday   6 _____ April

2 _____ a few days   7 _____ ages

3 _____ 2001   8 _____ years

4 _____ my last birthday 9 _____ six months

5 _____ half and hour   10 _____ I last saw you

4 *been* *6 points*
In these sentences, is *been* the past participle of *be* or *go*?

1 I've been a DJ for nine years. _____

2 Have you ever been to Ibiza? _____

3 She's been here for a month now. _____

4 I've been on the beach all morning. _____

5 We've just been for a swim. _____

6 He's been in bed all afternoon. _____

5 Present perfect simple & continuous (1) *7 points*
Underline the most appropriate alternative.

1 I've **known / been knowing** my best friend for ten years now.

2 At last! I've **waited / been waiting** for you for ages.

3 I've **had / been having** this watch since I was six.

4 He's **liked / been liking** football since he was a boy.

5 I've **learned / been learning** the piano for a year.

6 I've always **wanted / been wanting** to travel around the world.

7 It's **rained / been raining** for over an hour now.

6 Present perfect simple & continuous (2) *4 points*
Put the verb into the correct form of the present perfect: simple or continuous.

1 How long have you _____ (study) in this class?

2 How long have you _____ (have) a mobile?

3 How long have you _____ (be) a student here?

4 How long have you _____ (do) this test?

Photocopiable

14 Call Overview

The topic of this unit is telephoning. Students begin by talking about their own use of phones and anything they dislike about them. They then read a text in which several people make complaints about phones and study some useful vocabulary about telephoning.

In the next section, students listen to several phone calls by a woman with a domestic crisis who asks other people for help. They identify and discuss her problems. This leads into some grammar work on making offers, requests and requests for permission in formal and informal ways.

The following section takes them back to the woman with the crisis, who now telephones her husband for help. This is followed by work on taking down telephone numbers correctly.

Students then read a text written by a man who does not want his young son to have a mobile phone. Students discuss the arguments for and against letting children have phones. They also look at the rules for the use of *say, tell* and *ask*. The next section gives students some short telephone conversations to listen to. They have to identify the speakers, the subject matter and the location for each one. This is followed by work on direct and indirect questions.

Section	Aims	What the students are doing
Introduction pages 82–83	*Conversation skills*: fluency work	Discussing phone use.
	Reading skills: reading for detail	Listing things students dislike about phones and reading a text to see how many are mentioned.
	Lexis: telephones	Completing sentences with phone words from the reading text.
Domestic crisis page 83	*Listening skills*: listening for gist	Identifying the problems a woman mentions on the phone.
		Answering true/false questions on further phone calls.
		Discussing problems and who to call for help.
Close up page 84	*Grammar*: offers and requests	Looking at the language of offers, requests and requests for permission.
		Assessing the formality of requests and offers.
		Writing short phone conversations involving offers and requests.
Telephone talk page 85	*Listening skills*: listening for specific information	Completing a telephone conversation and then listening to it.
		Taking down telephone numbers correctly.
		Taking turns dictating important telephone numbers.
The 'latest thing' page 86	*Reading skills*: reading for specific information	Predicting the content of a text and reading to check.
	Conversation skills: fluency work	Discussing whether children should have mobile phones.
	Lexis: say, tell, ask	Completing a summary of the reading text and establishing rules for the use of *say, tell* and *ask*.
Who? What? Where? page 86	*Listening skills*: listening for gist	Listening to short phone conversations and identifying speakers, subject and location.
		Discussing which of the situations students have been in.
Close up page 87	*Grammar*: indirect questions	Studying and practising the structure and use of indirect questions.

Books closed. Whole class. Ask students to raise their hands if they have a mobile phone. Ask them to put their hands down if they don't have their mobile phone with them at the moment. If any hands are left up, ask them to put them down if their mobile phone is switched off at the moment. If any students are left with their hands in the air, invite them to the front of the class with their phones and give each a task, eg: to talk for one minute about their phone; to try to persuade the rest of the class to buy their phone; to explain why they think it is necessary to have their phone switched on in class, etc.

Groupwork. Students discuss the questions in small groups and report back to the class.

Reading (p 82)

1 Pairwork. Give students a couple of minutes to list the things they dislike about phones. Then ask them to read the article and find out if it mentions any of the things on their lists.

2 Open this question up for class discussion.

Lexis: telephones (p 83)

1 If you wish, you could make this a race with the first student to complete all the gaps and raise their hand as the winner. Check answers with the class.

> a) mobile
> b) switch, off
> c) voice mail
> d) recorded message, options
> e) on hold
> f) through, extension

2 Pairwork. Students choose three questions from Exercise 1 and take turns to ask their partner.

Domestic crisis (p 83)

Whole class. Ask students for examples of things which could be considered a domestic crisis. If necessary, start them off with a couple of ideas such as the washing machine has leaked all over the floor, you have locked yourself out of the house. Find out what the worst domestic crisis they have experienced is and what they did about it.

Listening (p 83)

1 📼 **59 SB p 140**
Go through the list of problems with the class and then ask them to listen to the recording and tick the ones that Lorna mentions. Play the recording a second time if necessary and allow students to compare notes in pairs before checking answers with the class.

> She mentions: a, b, e, g, i.

📼 **59**

(M = Mum; L = Lorna)

M: *Hello.*

L: *Mum! It's me.*

M: *Oh, hello, darling. How are you?*

L: *I can't hear you, Mum. It's a really bad line.*

M: *Sorry, dear. I said how are you?*

L: *Terrible, Mum. My back's killing me, and the house is a mess.*

M: *Don't worry, darling, I'll come and help you clean the house.*

L: *But that's not all – the kids are driving me mad. ELLA PUT HIM DOWN!*

M: *Don't worry, darling. When we've cleaned the house, I'll take the children to the park.*

L: *Oh thanks, Mum. There is something else though. ELLA, I SAID PUT HIM DOWN! Sorry – the thing is, I'm expecting six people for dinner, and the fridge is bare. Do you think you could do some shopping on your way over here?*

M: *No problem, darling. I'll stop at the supermarket and then I'll make a meal your friends will never forget.*

L: *Thanks, Mum. I don't know what I'd do without you. Could you do one more thing for me?*

M: *Of course, darling, what is it?*

L: *Well, I've run out of money. Could you possibly pay for the shopping, and I'll pay you back at the end of the month?*

M: *That's fine. You don't have to pay me back.*

2 Remind students of the problems in Exercise 1 that Lorna mentions. Give them a few minutes to match the words that Lorna uses in the box with the problems and to re-write them. Play the recording again for them to check their answers, then go over them with the class.

a) My back is killing me.

b) The house is a mess.

e) The kids are driving me mad.

g) The fridge is bare.

i) I've run out of money.

3 🔊 **60 SB p 140**

Tell students to listen to the second part of Lorna's conversation and to say who Juliet is and what has happened (Lorna has dialled the wrong number).

Juliet is the real daughter of the mother on the phone.

🔊 **60**

(M = Mum; L = Lorna)

L: *Mum – you're an angel. How's Dad?*

M: *Dad? Darling, you know your father and I divorced when you were thirteen.*

L: *Divorced? Thirteen? Oh no – what number are you on?*

M: *0770 899 490.*

L: *Oh no, I don't believe it. I dialled the wrong number.*

M: *Juliet?*

L: *I'm not Juliet – but please, hold on – does this mean you're not coming over?*

4 🔊 **61 SB p 140**

Go through the sentences with the class before you play the recording so they know what they are listening for. Check answers with the class.

a) T   b) F   c) T   d) F   e) T

🔊 **61**

Conversation 1

(D = Dad; L = Lorna)

D: *Hello.*

L: *Dad?*

D: *Hello, dear. How are you?*

L: *Oh, not too good actually.*

D: *Oh dear, what's the matter?*

L: *PUT THAT DOWN!*

D: *Pardon?!*

L: *No, not, not you, Dad – the children are driving me mad. OH FREDDIE, WHY DID YOU DO THAT?*

D: *Look dear, I'm just going out to play golf. Can I call you back later? Or shall I leave a message for your mother to ring you when she comes in?*

L: *Yes. Please. Could you tell her it's urgent?*

D: *Yes, okay, dear – I think she'll be home ...*

L: *FREDDIE – DON'T TOUCH THAT! Dad, I've got to go.*

D: *Oh – goodbye, dear.*

Conversation 2

(J = Jackie; L = Lorna)

J: *Hello.*

L: *Hello. Is that Jackie?*

J: *Yes. Hold on a minute ... (Turn the music down!)*

L: *Um, Jackie, it's Lorna. Lorna Carr.*

J: *Oh hello, Mrs Carr.*

L: *I was wondering if you could come over and baby-sit for a couple of hours this afternoon.*

J: *This afternoon? Er ... Would you mind hanging on a moment, please? ... (I've got to go and baby-sit.) ... Is it okay if I bring my boyfriend?*

L: *Yes, that's fine. Would you like me to drive over and pick you up?*

J: *It's okay. We'll get the bus.*

L: *NO! Er, no, I need you now actually. I'll be right over.*

5 Pairwork. Students discuss whether they have ever had any of Lorna's problems and if they called anyone for help.

Close up (p 84)

Offers & requests

1 You might like to ask students to try to match the beginnings and endings before you play the recording again. Otherwise, ask them to do it as they listen. Check answers with the class.

a 4   b 7   c 5   d 2   e 6   f 3   g 1

2 Go through the explanations of offers, requests and requests for permission with the class, then ask them to put the opening phrases in Exercise 1 into the three groups. Check answers with the class.

Offers: b, g

Requests: c, d, e

Requests for permission: a, f

3 Students count the words in each of the opening phrases in 1. They then discuss and decide how formal or informal each one is. Elicit the answer to the question from the class. There is more information about offers and requests in the Language reference section at the bottom of page 84.

> Usually, the more words you use, the more polite or formal you sound.

4 Pairwork. Give students time to read the situations and decide who they would phone for each one. They then tell their partners.

5 Pairwork. Students work together to write two short phone conversations for situations in Exercise 4. Go round offering help and encouragement and ensuring that each conversation includes one offer and one request. Invite pairs to perform their conversations for the class.

Telephone talk (p 85)

Whole class. In this section the story of Lorna and her domestic crisis continues. You might like to ask students what they think Lorna will do next and whether they think her problems are serious enough to justify calling other people for help.

Listening (p 85)

1 Allow students to work in pairs to decide on the most appropriate expressions. Encourage them to read the dialogue aloud to get a feel for what sounds right. Do not check answers at this stage.

2 📼 **62 SB p 85**
Play the recording for students to compare with their own versions of the conversation.

> 1   Good morning
> 2   Could I
> 3   Who's speaking?
> 4   Hold on, please
> 5   I'm afraid Mr Carr is not at his desk at the moment.
> 6   Do you know when he'll
> 7   Would you like
> 8   I'm afraid Mr Carr is in a meeting until five o'clock.
> 9   Can I
> 10 Could you tell him

3 Pairwork. Students practise the conversation, taking turns to be Lorna and the receptionist.

Telephone numbers (p 85)

1 📼 **63 SB p 140**
Go through the instructions. Point out that in English people often say 'O' (oh) rather than 'zero' when they are saying telephone numbers. Play the recording. Students correct the numbers. Do not check answers at this stage.

> a)   0870 000 0123
> b)   0845 748 4950
> c)   0870 580 8080
> d)   0800 887766
> e)   020 8846 9000
> f)   192

> 📼 **63**
> ... and here are some useful numbers for travellers in the UK.
> For flight information to and from Heathrow airport, dial O eight seven O ... O double O ... O one two three.
> You can get train times and fare information on O eight four five ... seven four eight ... four nine five O.
> For National Express bus and coach information ring O eight seven O ... five eight O ... eight O eight O.
> If you have problems on the road, the number for the AA 24-hour breakdown service is O eight hundred ... double eight ... double seven... double six.
> The British Tourist Authority can help you find accommodation. Ring O two O ... double eight four six... nine O double O.
> And remember, if you don't know a number, contact Directory Enquiries on one nine two. They will be pleased to help.

2 Pairwork. Students discuss their answers to Exercise 1. They take turns to say what the mistake is and what the correct number should be. Go through the example with them first to establish what they should do and how.

3 Pairwork. Students follow the instructions to practise writing and dictating telephone numbers.

The 'latest thing' (p 86)

Elicit from students what the 'latest thing' (something new that you want because everybody else is getting one) is at the moment. This could be an item of clothing, an electronic gadget, a particular type of car, etc. The details will depend on the age and interests of your students. Ask how important they think it is to have the 'latest thing' and how they feel if they can or can't have it for some reason.

Reading (p 86)

1 Go through the instructions with the class and before they read the text ask them to discuss in pairs all the reasons they can think of why a father might not want his twelve-year-old son to have a mobile phone.

Then ask them to read the article and see if any of their ideas are mentioned. Explain any difficult vocabulary and ask them to give their opinions on what they have read. Ask if the question of mobile phone safety is an issue in their country or not.

2 Groupwork. Focus attention on the cartoon and ask students to explain the joke (*I can't talk now* is what people say on the phone when they are called at an inconvenient time; the baby literally can't talk now because it is too young). Students discuss the questions in small groups and report back to the class.

Lexis: *say, tell, ask* (p 86)

1 Ask students to underline the most appropriate alternative in each sentence of the summary. Allow them to compare answers in pairs or small groups before checking with the class.

> a) asks b) tells c) says d) tells e) asks
> f) says g) tells h) says

2 Students complete the rules with *say, tell* or *ask*. Check answers with the class and elicit some more example sentences.

> a) ask b) tell c) say

Who? What? Where? (p 86)

Books closed. Whole class. Write the word *eavesdrop* on the board and explain that it means to listen in on someone else's private conversation. Ask students to discuss in small groups whether they have ever eavesdropped on a private conversation or phone call and whether they heard anything interesting.

Listening (p 86)

1 📼 **64 SB p 140**
Go through the instructions with the class and the places in the box. Then play the recording. Students make notes on who is speaking, what the situation is and where they are. Check answers with the class.

A   Boy to his dad. He wants a new toy for his birthday. At home.

B   Woman to another woman. She wants the toilets. At a club.

C   Husband and wife or boyfriend and girlfriend. Can't find the car. In a car park.

D   Teenage daughter and her mother. Daughter has arrived home late. At home.

E   Two strangers. Missed the last bus. Bus stop.

F   Two strangers. Person wants to see the lions. At the zoo.

📼 **64**

A

A: *Dad ... Do you think I could have a Zoomatron for my birthday? ... Please?*

B: *What's a Zoomatron?*

A: *It's a kind of space gun. It's really cool.*

B: *Oh no. Not another one ...*

A: *Please.*

B

A: *Could you tell me where the cloakroom is?*

B: *What?*

A: *Do you know where the toilets are?*

B: *Sorry – I can't hear you.*

A: *WHERE'S THE TOILET?*

B: *Over there.*

C

A: *Can you remember where we left it?*

B: *Um, I think it was the second floor.*

A: *Well, this is the second floor, and I can't see it.*

B: *I think we parked next to a white van. ... There it is.*

D

A: *Have you any idea what the time is?*

B: *Dunno.*

A: *Well, it's half past twelve. Where on earth have you been? I've been worried sick. Wait till your father hears about this!*

E

A: *Do you know if the last bus has gone?*

B: *I'm afraid it left a couple of minutes ago.*

A: *Oh no! Do you know where I can get a taxi.*

B: *Try the railway station – there are usually a few taxis there.*

A: *Thanks.*

F

A: *Excuse me – do you know where the lions are?*

B: *They're over there next to the giraffes.*

A: *Oh right. Thank you.*

2 Pairwork. Students discuss which of the situations in Exercise 1 they have been in. Encourage them to give as much detail as possible.

Close up (p 87)

Indirect questions

1 Pairwork. Students look at the table and discuss the questions. Check answers with the class. There is more information on indirect questions in the Language reference section at the bottom of page 87.

> a) The subject goes after the verb (*be*).
> b) The subject goes between the auxiliary and the verb.
> c) The subject goes before the verb.

2 Allow students to do this in pairs if they wish. Play the recording again for them to check their answers. Then check with the class.

Direct questions		Indirect questions
a) Where is *the cloakroom?*	→	Could you tell me where *the cloakroom* is?
b) What is *the time?*	→	Have you any idea what *the time* is?
c) Where are *the lions?*	→	Do you know where *the lions* are?
d) Could *I* have a Zoomatron?	→	Do you think *I* could have a Zoomatron?
e) Where can *I* get a taxi?	→	Do you know where *I* can get a taxi?
f) Where did *we* leave it?	→	Can you remember where *we* left it?

3, 4 Pairwork. Students re-write the indirect questions in the correct order and then take turns to ask them to each other.

> a) Do you know what my address is?
> b) Can you remember who your first English teacher was?
> c) Do you know what your star sign is?
> d) Do you know if your parents were born in this city?
> e) Do you think my English is improving?
> f) Could you tell me how long you have been living in this city?

Test

Scoring: one point per correct answer unless otherwise indicated.

1   1 mobile   2 switched off   3 voice mail
     4 got through   5 recorded message   6 on hold

2   1 morning   2 Can   3 speak   4 Hold   5 put
     6 afraid   7 desk   8 leave   9 Could   10 ask

3   1   Have you any idea what time <u>it is</u>?
     2   Could you tell me where <u>the bathroom is</u>?
     3   Do you know how long ~~does take~~ the job <u>takes</u>?
     4   Can you remember where ~~did~~ I <u>left</u> my pen?
     5   Do you know <u>if</u> Alex <u>is</u> in school today?
     6   Do you think ~~is~~ my English <u>is</u> improving?

4   1   Can you remember what her phone number is?
     2   Do you know where he lives?
     3   Have you any idea if he's got a girlfriend?
     4   Do you think she'll be at the party?

5   1 tell   2 said   3 says   4 ask

6   1   Would you like me <u>to</u> help you?
     2   Would <u>you</u> mind waiting here for a moment?
     3   I was wondering <u>if</u> you could help me?
     4   Is <u>it</u> okay if I use your mobile?

7   1 c   2 a   3 e   4 b   5 f   6 d

Name: _____   **Total:** _____ /40

1 Vocabulary – telephones (1) *6 points*

Complete the dialogues with the words in the box.

got through   mobile   on hold   recorded message
switched off   voice mail

A: Has Laura called yet?

B: No, but my (1) _____ was
(2) _____ for a while. I'll just call my
(3) _____ to see if she's left a
message.

*   *   *

C: Have you (4) _____ yet?

D: No. I've been trying for over ten minutes now, but I
just get one (5) _____ after another.
And then they keep putting me (6) _____ .
This music's driving me mad!

2 Vocabulary – telephones (2) *10 points*

Complete the missing words in this telephone dialogue.

A: Good (1) m_____g. Brown and Sons. (2) C_____n
I help you?

B: Could I (3) s_____k to Toby Brown, please?

A: (4) H_____d on please and I'll try to (5) p_____t you
through ... I'm (6) a_____d Mr Brown is not at his
(7) d_____k at the moment.

B: Okay. Can I (8) l_____e a message for him?
(9) C_____d you (10) a_____k him to call Pat, please?

3 Indirect questions (1) *6 points*

Correct the mistakes in the questions.

1   Have you any idea what time is it?

2   Could you tell me where is the bathroom?

3   Do you know how long does take the job?

4   Can you remember where did I leave my pen?

5   Do you know is Alex in school today?

6   Do you think is my English improving?

4 Indirect questions (2) *4 points*

Re-write the direct questions as indirect questions.

1   What is her phone number?

Can you remember _____ ?

2   Where does he live?

Do you know _____ ?

3   Has he got a girlfriend?

Have you any idea _____ ?

4   Will she be at the party?

Do you think _____ ?

5 Vocabulary – *say, tell, ask* *4 points*

Underline the correct alternative.

A: Did you (1) **say / tell** Joe about the party on Friday?

B: Yes, I did. He (2) **said / told** he's arranged to go out
with Kate. But he (3) **says / tells** he'll (4) **say / ask** her
if she wants to come to the party instead.

6 Offers & requests (1) *4 points*

Add the missing word to these offers and requests.

1   Would you like me help you?

2   Would mind waiting here for a moment?

3   I was wondering you could help me?

4   Is okay if I use your mobile?

7 Offers & requests (2) *6 points*

Match the beginnings with their endings.

1	Would you like me	a)	if you could help?
2	I was wondering	b)	you help me?
3	Shall	c)	to help you?
4	Could	d)	if I help them?
5	Would you mind	e)	I help you?
6	Is it okay	f)	helping me?

The waiting game (p 88)

Listening

1 ▭ **65 SB p 140**

Elicit or explain that the Wimbledon tennis championships take place in London every June. It is possible to buy tickets in advance (and usually necessary in order to see the best matches), but you can also get in to watch the tennis by queuing (standing in line) on the day to get tickets.

Focus attention on the picture. You might like to tell the students that the labelled people in the queue will be interviewed in order. Then play the recording and ask them to answer the two questions.

> a) Hyacinth, Derek, Oona and Maggy.
>
> b) Kati.

▭ **65**

(R = reporter; H = Hyacinth; D = Derek; K = Kati; O = Oona; M = Maggy)

Interview 1

R: *Excuse me, madam, would you mind answering a few questions for London South FM?*

H: *Certainly.*

R: *Well, could you tell me where you come from? Have you come far?*

H: *We don't live far from here. We live in Richmond, actually, so we usually get here very early in the morning. We like to be at the front of the queue, but Derek was slow getting up this morning, and there was a bit of a problem on the underground, so we arrived a little later than usual.*

R: *Could you tell me how long you've been waiting?*

H: *Since about half past eight, something like that, I suppose. So, yes, it's been a long wait. What is it – about three o'clock now? Derek! What's the time now? Derek!*

D: *Yes, dear?*

R: *Do you think you'll get in?*

H: *Oh yes, I think we'll probably get in soon. Won't we, Derek? Derek, stop looking at that girl! You've been looking at her for hours. Haven't you seen enough? She's certainly not interested in you!*

R: *Well, it's a long queue. Do you know how many people there are in front of you?*

H: *I imagine there are about, what, twenty or thirty people. It won't be long now, will it, Derek?*

D: *Huh?*

Interview 2

R: *Excuse me, would you mind answering a few questions for London South FM?*

K: *Excuse me? Can you speak a little more slowly, please?*

R: *Sorry, can I ask you a few questions for the radio?*

K: *Yes, of course.*

R: *How long have you waiting here?*

A: *I have been waiting here since a quarter past eight this morning. I did not know there was a long queue.*

R: *You must be a real tennis fan!*

K: *Ah, so-so. I am a student of English. I have been in London for four weeks, and tomorrow I must go back to Hanover in Germany, and I thought it was a good idea to come to Wimbledon before I go back to Germany.*

R: *Do you think you'll get in?*

K: *Excuse me?*

R: *Do you think you will get in?*

K: *No, I do not think so. It has been raining since half past one. I am wet and cold and I am hungry, and there are many, many people in front of me in the queue. I think I will give up soon.*

Interview 3

R: *Excuse me, madam, would you mind answering a few questions for London South FM?*

O: *Oh, come under the umbrella, dear. Would you like a strawberry?*

R: *Mm, thanks. Have you been here long?*

O: *Ooh, I'm not sure. What time did we arrive, Maggy?*

M: *Mm, about eight?*

O: *Yes, we've been here since about eight this morning. We come every year on the Friday, you know.*

R: *What are your chances of getting in?*

O: *Not very good, I would say. It rained on the Friday last year, too, and we never got in. But*

you never know. There are probably about fifty
people in front of us, but lots of them will give
up and go home soon. Maybe, we'll get the last
match of the day. We live in Scotland, you
know, so this is a big day out for us. We're not
giving up now, not after coming all this way.

R: *Isn't it a long time to wait for one match?*

O: *Ooh, no. We love the tennis, of course, but we*
really come for the atmosphere. We've met so
many interesting people since we arrived. Have
you spoken to that charming young girl from
Germany? We've been chatting for ages – she's
got such good English. And Maggy always
brings her radio, so we've been listening to that.
We've been having a great day, haven't we,
Maggy?

M: *Mm, another strawberry?*

R: *Mm, thanks. Well, good luck with the wait!*

2 This exercise reviews indirect questions. If students have
trouble rearranging the questions, you might like to refer
them back to the Language reference section in Unit 14
(page 87). Allow students to compare notes, but don't
check answers at this stage.

> a) Could you tell me where you come from?
>
> b) Could you tell me how long you have been
>   waiting?
>
> c) Do you think you will get in?
>
> d) Do you know how many people there are in
>   front of you?

3 Play the recording of the first interview again for students
to check their answers to Exercise 2. You may need to play
it again for students to make notes of Hyacinth's answers
to the questions.

> a) Richmond.
>
> b) Since about half past eight.
>
> c) Yes.
>
> d) About twenty or thirty.

Optional activity

Groupwork. Students discuss these questions in small groups.
What sort of things do people wait in queues for?
When was the last time you waited in a queue? (What was it for?)
*What's the longest you've ever had to wait in a queue? (What was it
for?)*

4 The present perfect simple and continuous and the use of
for and *since* were studied in Unit 13. Refer students back
to the Language reference section on page 80 if they have
trouble with this. Allow students to compare notes in pairs
but do not confirm answers at this stage.

> a) You've been looking at her for hours.
>
> b) I've been waiting here since a quarter past eight
>   this morning.
>
> c) I've been in London for four weeks.
>
> d) It's been raining since half past one.
>
> e) We've been here since about eight.
>
> f) We've been chatting for ages.

5 Play the recording again and then check answers with the
class.

6 Groupwork. Students discuss the questions, giving
examples from their own experience and then report back
to the class.

Lexis: describing people (p 89)

1 Remind students of the work they did on describing
people in Unit 11. Allow them to work in pairs or small
groups to complete the descriptions and match them with
the people in the picture on page 88. Check answers with
the class.

> A   miserable, hard-working – Kati
>
> B   wavy, cheeks – Maggy
>
> C   humour, wrinkled – Oona
>
> D   bags, irritating – Derek
>
> E   outfits, teeth – Hyacinth

2 Discourage students from writing anything unkind in their
descriptions. Collect in the descriptions, shuffle them and
redistribute them. Students then try to guess who is
described on the piece of paper they receive.

Lexis: *at* & *on* (p 89)

1 Remind students that *on* is not always used to mean
physically on top of something, eg: we can say *on the phone*.
(You may like to point out that they should not fill the
gaps before the word *minutes* with *at* or *on*. These gaps will
be completed in Exercise 2.) Check answers with the class.

> 1   on
>
> 2   at, at
>
> 3   on, at
>
> 4   on, on, on
>
> 5   on, at, at, on

2 Students should work individually to decide on the
maximum number of minutes they will wait in each
situation. They then add up the total.

3 Students compare their results in pairs or small groups and
report back to the class to find out who is the most patient
or impatient person.

National sport (p 90)

Books closed. Whole class. Ask students to say what they think the national sport of their country is. With multinational groups, find out how many different sports are mentioned. With students from the same country, find out how much agreement there is as to what is the national sport.

Passives (p 90)

1 Remind students of the work they did on passives in Unit 12. Allow them to work in pairs to complete the sentences if they wish. They should then discuss whether they think the statements are true or false and make a decision on each before looking at page 127 to see if they are right. Check answers with the class.

> a) were held
>
> b) is played
>
> c) was invented
>
> d) was climbed
>
> e) has never been broken
>
> f) were beaten

2 Students work individually to make up three more statements. They then exchange them with a partner and decide if the statements they have received are true or false.

Dynamic & stative meanings (p 90)

1 Remind students of the work they did on this in Unit 12 and elicit the difference between dynamic (describing an action) and stative (describing a state). Ask them to choose the best verb forms in the sentences and check answers before they turn to the pictures.

> a) is happening
>
> b) are the people standing
>
> c) are they wearing
>
> d) do they have
>
> e) do you think, come

2 Pairwork. Students turn to their respective pages and look at their own picture. They should not look at their partner's picture, and it may be helpful to have them sitting back to back for this exercise so that they cannot see the other picture.

They ask and answer questions to find as many differences and similarities between the pictures as they can. Check answers with the class and find out which pair found the most things.

Student A's picture

a)   People are waiting for a bus.

b)   They are standing in a group (not in a queue).

c)   They are wearing ordinary (modern) clothes.

d)   A CD discman, a mobile phone, a handbag, a newspaper.

e)   From London. (There are people of lots of different nationalities living in London.)

Student B's picture

a)   People are waiting for a bus.

b)   They are standing in a queue.

c)   They are wearing old-fashioned clothes.

d)   An umbrella, a briefcase, a handbag, a newspaper, a walking stick.

e)   From London (in the 1950s).

Reading (p 90)

1 Allow students to work in pairs if they wish and give them time to read the article for content as well as to choose the correct verb forms. Elicit their opinions on how useful the advice is. You might also like to ask whether queuing is normal in their country. If so, ask them to give the 'rules' for queuing where they come from. Do not check answers at this stage.

> 1 spending   2 to visit   3 to know   4 to keep
> 5 to stay   6 visiting

2 📼 **66 SB p 90**

Play the recording for students to listen and check their answers.

📼 **66**

The noble art of queuing

There is one sport at which the British are always the world champions. Nobody can beat them at the noble art of queuing. The British actually look forward to spending their weekends in a queue, waiting for a shop to open or waiting for a parking space at the furniture superstore.

If you ever decide to visit Britain, you will need to know some of the basic rules of the sport.

First of all, remember that you only need one person to make a queue. If you are alone at a bus stop, for example, don't look too relaxed. Make sure that you are in the queue and look optimistically to your right.

If you want to keep your place in the queue, never leave a space between you and the person in front, otherwise the person behind you will ask, 'Are you in the queue?' (meaning 'Don't you know how to queue properly?').

Conversation is generally not a good idea, and only two topics are acceptable: the weather and the bus timetable. Anything more and you will end up with a complete stranger sitting next to you, telling you their life story.

Unfortunately, the bus does not always stop in the correct place. Try to stay calm and, whatever you do, don't jump the queue. You can be sure that every single person in the queue knows exactly who is in front of them, and who is behind.

Follow these simple rules and you, too, can enjoy visiting the home of the noble art of queuing. But if you decide not to follow the rules, be prepared for the worst.

3 Pairwork. Students work together and follow the instructions. Check the answers to a) with the class.

remember that ...; don't look too relaxed; Make sure that ...; look optimistically to your right; never leave ...; Try to stay calm ...; don't jump the queue; Follow these simple rules ...; be prepared for ...

Optional activity

For a fun activity, ask students to work together in small groups and to prepare a list of hints for foreign visitors to their country, which sound helpful but are not. For example, *In Scotland, the sign for the men's toilets shows a man wearing a kilt.*

Lexis: telephone language (p 91)

1 Pairwork. Students discuss the questions.

2 Remind students of the rules for using *say, tell* and *ask* which they completed in Unit 14 (page 86). Ask them to choose the correct word in each sentence. Check answers with the class.

1 asks 2 asks 3 says 4 asks 5 says 6 tells
7 says 8 asks 9 says 10 says

3 Students match the speeches to the stages in the telephone conversation in Exercise 2. Allow them to compare answers in pairs but do not check answers at this stage.

1 h 2 b 3 f 4 a 5 c 6 e 7 g 8 j 9 i 10 d

4 ▭ **67 SB p 141**
Play the recording for students to check their answers and then give them time to practise the conversation in pairs.

▭ 67

(S = Secretary; MK = Mrs Knightly)

S: *Mr Rogers' office. Can I help you?*

MK: *Oh, hello. Can I speak to Mr Rogers, please?*

S: *Certainly. Could you hold the line, please? I'm afraid Mr Rogers is not in yet, madam.*

MK: *Ah, would you mind taking a message?*

S: *Certainly.*

MK: *Erm, well, it's Joanna Knightly here. I've got an appointment with Mr Rogers at 9.15 and I'm afraid I've missed the bus ...*

S: *Would you like to give me your telephone number, and I'll ask Mr Rogers to call you when he gets in.*

MK: *That's all right, thanks. I'll call back later.*

S: *You're welcome. Goodbye.*

MK: *Thanks. Goodbye.*

Lexis: phrasal verbs (p 91)

1 Students complete the sentences with the words in the box. Check answers with the class.

a) down b) through c) out d) out e) up
f) up, over

2 Pairwork. Students discuss the questions and report back to the class. You might also like to ask whether anyone has ever used any of these excuses and in what circumstances.

3 Pairwork. Give students plenty of time to write their conversations. Invite some pairs to perform them for the class.

Night clubs (p 92)

1 Groupwork. Students discuss the questions and report back to the class.

2 Focus attention on the illustrations of the nightclub and the characters in the sketch (*The Door*). You might like to remind students of the work they have done on describing people and ask them to describe the people in the illustrations.

Pairwork. Students discuss the pictures and answer the questions.

3 ▭ **68 SB p 93**
Ask students who the two men standing outside the night club are and what their job is. (They are called bouncers. Their job is to make sure that only the 'right sort of people' get into the club. They may refuse people if they aren't dressed correctly or if they think they are likely to cause trouble inside. They also deal with any problems that happen inside the club and will throw someone out if they are behaving badly.)

Play the recording and allow students to read the script on page 93 as they listen. Then ask how the bouncers make sure they can leave early.

> They invent stupid rules about the dress code.

4 Groupwork. Students follow the instructions and perform their sketches.

Test

Scoring: one point per correct answer unless otherwise indicated.

1 1 Act your age!
2 Be quiet!
3 Calm down!
4 Cheer up!
5 Don't worry!
6 Take it easy!

2 1 was sold
2 made
3 was baked
4 invented
5 were first worn
6 was produced

3 1 Do you know what time ~~does~~ the party starts?
2 Can you remember what <u>her number is</u>?
3 Do you know if <u>there will</u> be any food at the party?
4 Have you any idea ~~is~~ <u>if</u> Sara <u>is</u> going to be there?

4 1 Can you remember what his name is?
2 Do you think he is a student?
3 Do you know if he speaks English?
4 Have you any idea how old he is?

5 (One point for the correct form of the present perfect and one point for *for* or *since*.)
1 I've known Sue Jones since we were at school together.
2 She's worked here since she left university. / She's been working here since she left university.
3 She's been looking for a new job for months.
4 She's been learning to play the piano since last May.
5 She's wanted to be a musician for years.
6 She's been married since 1998.
7 She's been living in New York for a few years now.

6 1 Would you mind ~~to give~~ <u>giving</u> me a lift to the bus station?
2 Is it okay <u>if</u> I make a coffee?
3 I <u>was</u> wondering if I could borrow this CD?
4 Would you like me <u>to</u> help you for a moment?

7 1 Is it okay if we meet at 8.30, not 8.00?
2 Would you like me to help you?
3 Would you mind waiting here for a few minutes?
4 I was wondering if you could lend me ten pounds until later?

8 1 are you doing?
2 'm looking
3 does he look
4 's
5 smells
6 like
7 are you smelling?
8 think
9 're thinking
10 love

9 1 to study 2 learning 3 to speak
4 to finishing

10 1 b 2 c 3 h 4 a 5 f 6 d 7 e 8 g

11 1 ambitious 2 bossy 3 cheeky 4 easy-going
5 hard-working 6 irritating 7 miserable
8 sociable

12 1 on 2 on 3 of 4 on 5 on 6 at 7 on
8 on

15 Review 3 Test

Name: _____ Total: _____/80

1 Imperatives 6 points

Match the the beginnings and the endings to complete the imperatives.

1	Act	a) it easy!
2	Be	b) down!
3	Calm	c) quiet!
4	Cheer	d) worry!
5	Don't	e) your age!
6	Take	f) up!

2 Passives 6 points

Put the verb into the correct form: active or passive.

1 The first commercial video game _____ (sell) in 1972.

2 Levi Strauss _____ (make) the world's first pair of jeans in the 1850s.

3 The world's first birthday cake _____ (bake) in Ancient Greece, over 2,000 years ago.

4 The Egyptians _____ (invent) paper, around 5,000 years ago.

5 Sunglasses _____ (first wear) by Chinese judges about 1,000 years ago. It was so people couldn't see what they were thinking.

6 The first zip _____ (produce) in 1890.

3 Indirect questions (1) 4 points

Correct the mistakes in the questions.

1 Do you know what time does the party start?

2 Can you remember what number is her?

3 Do you know if will there be any food at the party?

4 Have you any idea is Sara going to be there?

4 Indirect questions (2) 4 points

Re-write the questions with the words in the correct order.

1 is Can you remember his name what ?

_____ ?

2 a student Do you think is he ?

_____ ?

3 speaks if Do you know English he ?

_____ ?

4 how old is he Have you any idea ?

_____ ?

5 Present perfect simple & continuous, *for* & *since* 14 points

Write sentences using the present perfect simple or continuous and *for* or *since*.

We are friends / over ten years.
We've been friends for over ten years.

1 I know Sue Jones / we were at school together.

_____
_____ .

2 She works here / she left university.

_____
_____ .

3 She is looking for a new job / months.

_____
_____ .

4 She is learning to play the piano / last May.

_____
_____ .

5 She wants to be a musician / years.

_____
_____ .

6 She is married / 1998.

_____
_____ .

7 She's living in New York / a few years now.

_____
_____ .

6 Offers & requests (1) *4 points*

Correct the mistakes in the offers and requests.

1 Would you mind to give me a lift to the bus station?

2 Is it okay I make a coffee?

3 I wondering if I could borrow this CD?

4 Would you like me help you for a moment?

7 Offers & requests (2) *4 points*

Re-write the offers and requests so the meaning is the same. Begin with the words given.

1 Can we meet at 8.30, not 8.00?

Is it okay _____

_____ ?

2 Let me help you?

Would you like _____

_____ ?

3 Will you wait here for a few minutes?

Would you mind _____

_____ ?

4 Could you lend me ten pounds until later?

I was wondering _____

_____ ?

8 Dynamic & stative meanings *10 points*

Underline the correct alternative.

A: What (1) **do you do / are you doing**?

B: I (2) **look / 'm looking** for my car keys.

       *   *   *

C: What (3) **does he look / is he looking** like?

D: He (4) **'s / 's being** tall, dark, handsome and very rich.

       *   *   *

E: That perfume (5) **smells / is smelling** nice! What is it?

F: It's called 'Noire'. I'm glad you (6) **like / are liking** it.

       *   *   *

G: Why (7) **do you smell / are you smelling** the milk?

H: It's quite old. I (8) **think / 'm thinking** it's off.

       *   *   *

I: We (9) **think / 're thinking** of going to Paris this year.

J: Lucky you! I (10) **love / 'm loving** Paris.

9 Vocabulary – verb patterns *4 points*

Underline the correct alternative.

1 When did you decide **to study / studying** English?

2 Do you enjoy **to learn / learning** English?

3 Do you need **to speak / speaking** English for your job or studies?

4 Are you looking forward **to finish / to finishing** this test?

10 Phrasal verbs *8 points*

Match the beginnings with their endings.

1	Would you like to take off	a)	smoking?
2	Can you clear up	b)	your coat?
3	Why did they call off	c)	the mess?
4	Do you want to give up	d)	this form?
5	Don't forget to switch off	e)	petrol?
6	Can you fill in	f)	the TV.
7	Did you run out of	g)	some friends?
8	Did you go out with	h)	the meeting?

11 Vocabulary – describing character *8 points*

Complete the character adjectives.

1 am_____ious

2 bo_____y

3 ch_____ky

4 e_____y-g_____ing

5 h_____d-w_____ing

6 irr_____ing

7 mis_____able

8 so_____able

12 Vocabulary – prepositions *8 points*

Underline the correct alternative.

1 Are you going **on / for** holiday this year?

2 When did you last speak **on / in** the phone?

3 Are you in favour **for / of** the death penalty?

4 Do you spend a lot of time **in / on** the internet?

5 Who is sitting **on / at** your right at the moment?

6 When were you last **to / at** a club?

7 Have you ever been abroad **on / in** business?

8 When did you first go **on / at** a date?

16 Lifestyle Overview

This unit is about lifestyles. It covers such issues as what kind of lifestyle promotes longevity, the benefits of health farms, and healthy eating. The grammar focus is on future time clauses and using *will* for prediction.

In the first section the students read a text on the lifestyle of the inhabitants of Okinawa, who tend to live to a great age. Students compare their lives with the relaxed lifestyle described in the text. An opportunity for extended speaking is given in an Anecdote activity in which they tell a partner about the healthiest person they know.

In the next section, students listen to a telephone conversation about a health farm and they discuss what people do at health farms and whether they would like to go to one. They then do some grammar work on talking about the future and making future predictions about their lives.

The subject of the next section is food. Students identify food items in a photograph and talk about their own food preferences. They also examine some popular idioms involving food.

Finally, they read a text from a website offering different ways to cook and prepare bananas. They find words for describing the cooking and preparation of food and describe in detail a meal they have eaten recently.

Section	Aims	What the students are doing
Introduction pages 94–95	*Reading skills:* reading for specific information	Completing advice on how to live longer and finding which of the tips are mentioned in a reading text about elderly people in Okinawa.
		Talking about different lifestyles.
	Lexis: collocations	Completing sentences with words from the reading text.
	Conversation skills: fluency work	Anecdote: talking about the healthiest person the students know.
Health farms page 95	*Listening skills:* listening for gist	Listening to a woman making a telephone enquiry about a health farm.
		Discussing health farms and what people do there.
Close up page 96	*Grammar:* future time clauses; *will* for prediction	Looking at the structure and use of future time clauses.
		Matching future predictions with people.
		Consulting the 'Oracle' to find out about students' future.
		Making personal future predictions.
Food glorious food pages 97–98	*Lexis:* food items	Identifying food items and finding which items on a shopping list have been forgotten.
		Talking about students' own food shopping habits.
	Pronunciation: sounds and spelling	Practising food words which are not pronounced as they are spelt.
	Lexis: food idioms	Reading short conversations and choosing the correct words to make food idioms.
How to eat a banana page 99	*Lexis:* food preparation	Reading a website text about different ways of preparing and eating bananas.
		Finding words in the text for preparing and cooking food.
		Matching food items to ways of preparing and cooking them.
	Conversation skills: detailed description	Talking in detail about a meal students have eaten recently.

16 Lifestyle Teacher's notes

Books closed. Whole class. Write on the board *Growing old isn't too bad when you consider the alternative.* Ask students what they think about growing old. Do they fear it? Are they looking forward to it? What problems do they think they will experience when they are old? What age would they like to live to?

Reading (p 94)

1 Pairwork. Students discuss the options and choose the most appropriate one for each piece of advice. Check answers with the class.

> a)   calorie
> b)   plant, animal
> c)   fruit and vegetables
> d)   80%
> e)   enjoy
> f)   friends

2 Give students plenty of time to read the article and decide which tips from Exercise 1 are mentioned. Gate-ball, mentioned in the second line, is a game similar to croquet, in which balls are knocked through hoops in the ground with a mallet. It is very popular with elderly people in Japan.

> All of them.

3 Pairwork. Students discuss how their lifestyles are different from the one described in the text. You might like to ask the class whether they think they would enjoy the Okinawan lifestyle.

Lexis: collocations (p 95)

1 You could set this up as a race with the first person to complete the sentences and raise their hand as the winner. Check answers with the class. You may need to explain that an *extended family* is one with many members of all generations who keep in close contact, often living together.

> a) brisk   b) lead   c) in   d) extended
> e) networks

2 Pairwork. Students ask and answer the questions in Exercise 1.

Anecdote (p 95)

See the Introduction on page 4 for more ideas on how to set up, monitor and repeat Anecdotes.

Pairwork. Give the students plenty of time to decide what they are going to talk about and to read the questions. They then take turns to talk about the healthiest or fittest person they know.

Health farms (p 95)

Whole class. Focus attention on the photograph at the bottom of page 95. Ask where the students think these women are and what they are doing. (The picture shows two Japanese girls/women at an onsen or hot spring resort. They are enjoying the pleasures and health benefits of bathing in naturally heated mineral-enriched water.) Find out if hot springs occur naturally in the students' countries and if bathing at them is popular. If not, ask about the kinds of places (eg: health farms) people go to for enjoyment or to improve their health.

Listening (p 95)

1 📼 69 SB p 141

Go through the questions before you play the recording so that students know what information they are listening for. Check answers with the class.

> a)   New Life Centre.
> b)   Because she wants to send her husband there as a birthday present.
> c)   He might not like it.

📼 69

(R = Receptionist; W = Woman)

R: *New Life Centre. Can I help you?*

W: *Yes. Could you give me some information about your centre?*

R: *Certainly. Are you interested in losing weight or just improving your fitness?*

W: *Actually, it's not for me. It's for my husband. He needs to lose weight and improve his fitness. I want to book him a week with you as a surprise for his birthday.*

R: *Ah, lucky man!*

W: *Could you tell me something about the programme?*

R: *Sure. As soon as he arrives here he'll take a fitness test to see what sort of diet he needs to go on.*

W: *Right.*

R: *We start every day at 7.30 with a half-hour walk before breakfast.*

W: *Ha ha. He usually starts the day with a cigarette before breakfast!*

R: *Oh dear. If he has a cigarette here, he'll be in big trouble. It's a strictly no smoking area.*

W: *Well, it's a good idea for him to give up smoking. He says he'll give up as soon as he feels more relaxed.*

R: *Oh well, this is the ideal place to relax. We do at least two hours of yoga and meditation every day, and after the morning hike he can have a sauna and jacuzzi.*

W: *Oh, he'll enjoy that. But what's this hike?*

R: *They go for a hike in the morning from 8.30 to 12.30. One of our instructors will take your husband and other people at the same level of fitness for a four-hour hike into the mountains.*

W: *Four hours! His idea of a walk is going from the front door to his car.*

R: *Oh, don't worry. When they get to the top of the mountain, they'll have a twenty-minute break before they come down again. The scenery is very relaxing.*

W: *They'll be starving!*

R: *Oh, don't worry. When they're hungry they'll stop for a healthy snack. The instructor always carries a supply of fruit.*

W: *No chocolate then! And what about the afternoon? Can he relax then?*

R: *No, not really. But he'll have time to relax after the afternoon hike.*

W: *Oh my goodness. I don't think he'll thank me for this.*

R: *Believe me, when he finishes the week he'll feel like a new man.*

W: *If he finishes the week!*

2 Allow students to work in pairs if they wish to complete the sentences. Then play the recording again for them to check their answers and tick those activities that the woman's husband will do at the health farm.

> a) take ✔   b) go on ✔   c) have ✘   d) do ✔
> e) have ✔   f) go for ✔

3 Pairwork. Students discuss the questions.

Close up (p 96)

Future time clauses

1 Pairwork. Students look at the sentences in the table and discuss the questions. Check answers with the class. There is more information and help with future forms in the Language reference section on page 97 and in the Verb structures section on page 130.

> a) Future time.
> b) *will* + infinitive.
> c) Present simple.

2 Students match the conjunctions in Exercise 1 with the functions *a–c*. Check answers with the class.

> a) If
> b) When
> c) As soon as

3 Ask students to say whether they think the alternative sentence structure is also possible.

You might like to ask students to translate the sentences in Exercise 1 into their own language(s) and to say what verb structures they use and what different sentence formations are possible.

> Yes.

4 Ask students to choose the correct verb structure in each sentence. Check answers with the class.

> a) 'll go   b) go   c) finishes   d) have   e) 'll go

5 Students work individually to decide which sentences are true for them and to change those that are not. They then compare them with a partner.

will for prediction (p 96)

1 Students first insert *will* in the correct place in the quotations on the left, then match them with the people on the right. Check answers with the class.

> a) 'Man will not fly for fifty years.' – 2
> b) 'No woman in my time will be Prime Minister.' – 3
> c) 'The internet will collapse within a year.' – 1

2 Groupwork. Establish the meaning of *Oracle* (a place in ancient Greece where a priest gave wise but mysterious advice and predictions of future events). Students turn to page 128, follow the instructions and compare their answers.

3 Students use the topics in the box and the sentence beginnings to make predictions about their own lives in the future. They should do this individually and then compare what they have written with a partner.

Food glorious food (p 97)

Closed books. Whole class. Ask students to name their favourite foods. Is there anything they think they couldn't live without? Are their favourite foods good for them or not?

Lexis: food (p 97)

1 Pairwork. Focus attention on the shopping list and the photographs of food items. See who can find the six items the person has forgotten in the shortest time.

> They've forgotten: apples, potatoes, tomatoes, carrots, sardines and tea.

2 Students work individually to place the items in the correct position on each line for them. They then compare with a partner.

3 Students decide which items they never buy and which they always buy. They add some more things that they always buy and compare notes in pairs.

Sounds & spelling (p 98)

1 🔲 **70 SB p 98**

If you like, you could get students to try to say the words correctly first before they listen to the recording to check. Otherwise, just play the recording for them to listen and repeat.

2 🔲 **71 SB p 141**

Students match the words in the two columns. Encourage them to say them aloud as they do this to practise producing and hearing the correct sounds. Then play the recording for them to check their answers. Elicit which words they find most difficult and give extra practice in saying these.

> a 3   b 1   c 5   d 4   e 6   f 2

> 🔲 **71**
>
> /ɪ/ lettuce   spinach
> /ʌ/ onion   nut
> /ə/ banana   lemon
> /iː/ sardines   beans
> /ɒ/ orange   cauliflower
> /əʊ/ aubergine   tomato

Lexis: food idioms (p 98)

1 Pairwork. Students read the conversations and discuss the questions. Tell them not to worry about the alternatives at the moment. Check answers with the class.

> *Possible answers to a) and b)*
>
> A   Parents talking about their young child.
> B   Two women talking about a good-looking man.
> C   Young son trying to persuade his mum to let him go out.
> D   Friend trying to encourage another friend to ski.
> E   Wife / Mother criticising her husband / son / daughter for being very lazy.
> F   Two friends discussing a very crowded concert.

2 Allow students to continue working in pairs. They choose the correct alternatives to complete the idioms. Allow them to discuss and compare their choices with other pairs, but do not confirm answers at this stage.

> A beans   B tea   C nuts   D cake   E potato
> F sardines

3 🔲 **72 SB p 98**

Play the recording for students to listen and check their answers. You might like to ask students if they know any more idioms using food items or if there are any in their own language.

4 Students work individually to replace the underlined words with the idioms. They then decide if the sentences are true or false for them and discuss this in pairs. Check answers with the class.

> a)   full of beans
> b)   a couch potato
> c)   packed in like sardines
> d)   a piece of cake
> e)   nuts
> f)   my cup of tea

5 Students work individually to decide which sentences are true for them and which are false. They then compare with a partner.

How to eat a banana (p 99)

Books closed. Whole class. This next section is about different ways to prepare and eat bananas. Find out if students like fruit and encourage them to give details of how they eat it. Do they peel apples or eat them with the peel on? Do they eat the apple core? Do they slice them with a knife or just bite into them? Can they peel an apple in one long strip? Do they peel the skin of a banana down in strips (how many), hold it by the end and bite bits off, or do they take the whole skin off and slice it with a knife? How do they peel oranges? Do they eat the whole of a grape or do they peel it first?

Lexis: food preparation (p 99)

1 Students scan the text just to find the dishes and decide which ones they would like to try and which they wouldn't. Find out how much agreement there is in the class.

2 Students read the text more carefully and make notes of the relevant words. Allow them to compare notes in pairs before checking with the class.

> a) peel, cut in half, mix, whisk, blend, slice them in half, chop
>
> b) fry, boil, grill, bake
>
> c) raw

3 You could make this a team game with the team who can come up with the most food items being declared the winner.

4 Students work individually to make notes of their answers to the questions. They then take turns to describe the meal to a partner.

Test

Scoring: one point per correct answer unless otherwise indicated.

1 (½ point each.)

1 banana 2 grapes 3 lemon 4 peach
5 aubergine 6 cauliflower 7 garlic 8 spinach
9 chicken 10 sardines 11 sausage 12 trout

2 1 tea 2 beans 3 cake 4 nuts 5 sardines
6 potato

3 1 on 2 take 3 for 4 done 5 lead 6 having
7 in 8 have

4 1 I'll phone you when I ~~will~~ arrive.

2 I think I'll go for a walk today if it's sunny.

3 He'll come with us when he ~~'ll finish~~ finishes his work.

4 Will you tidy up before you ~~'ll~~ go home?

5 (One point for each verb.)

1 'll give, see

2 'll go, finish

3 have, 'll e-mail

4 will call, finishes

6 1 Next century, everyone will have enough to eat.

2 How many people will there be on Earth in 2050? (Answer: 10 billion)

3 In 2100, half the population of Earth will speak English.

4 Do you think humans will ever live on Mars?

7 1 'll change 2 'll probably learn 3 'll have
4 won't be

16 *Lifestyle* Test

Name: _____   **Total:** _____ /40

---

1 Vocabulary – food *6 points*

Put the foods in the box into the correct columns.

> aubergine banana cauliflower chicken
> garlic grapes lemon peach sardines
> sausage spinach trout

Fruit	Vegetables	Meat and fish
1 _____	5 _____	9 _____
2 _____	6 _____	10 _____
3 _____	7 _____	11 _____
4 _____	8 _____	12 _____

2 Vocabulary – food idioms *6 points*

Complete the sentences using the words in the box.

> beans cake nuts potato sardines tea

1 I didn't enjoy the film. It wasn't my cup of _____ .

2 She's a very lively person – always full of _____ .

3 You can do it. It's easy – a piece of _____ .

4 Stop singing that song! It's driving me _____ .

5 It was so busy – we were packed in like _____ .

6 He just sits on the sofa and watches TV all day. He's a real couch _____ .

3 Vocabulary – collocations *8 points*

Underline the correct alternative.

1 I'm going **in / on** a diet next week.

2 I think I should **take / make** a fitness test.

3 Peter's gone **for / to** a walk.

4 I've never **made / done** any yoga.

5 We all need to **take / lead** a healthier lifestyle.

6 Anna's **doing / having** a sauna at the moment.

7 I can't stop. I'm **in / on** a hurry.

8 How many cigarettes do you **take / have** a day?

4 Future time clauses (1) *4 points*

Correct the mistake in each sentence.

1 I'll phone you when I will arrive.

2 I think I go for a walk today if it's sunny.

3 He'll come with us when he'll finish his work.

4 Will you tidy up before you'll go home?

5 Future time clauses (2) *8 points*

Put the verbs into the correct form: present simple or *will*.

1 I _____ (give) you the book when I next _____ (see) you.

2 I think I _____ (go) to bed as soon as I _____ (finish) my homework.

3 If I _____ (have) any questions, I _____ (e-mail) you.

4 Mr Evans _____ (call) you back when the meeting _____ (finish).

6 *will* for prediction (1) *4 points*

Add *will* to the correct place in each sentence.

1 Next century, everyone have enough to eat.

2 How many people there be on Earth in 2050?

3 In 2100 half the population of Earth speak English.

4 Do you think humans ever live on Mars?

7 *will* for prediction (2) *4 points*

Complete the predictions using the verbs in the box.

> not be change have learn

1 Perhaps I _____ job next year.

2 I _____ probably _____ another language.

3 I hope I _____ two children: a girl and a boy.

4 I probably _____ famous for anything.

Photocopiable

17 Animals Overview

The topic of this unit is animals, both wild and domesticated. The grammar focus is on relative clauses and conditionals, and the unit starts with matching animals to sentences with relative clauses that describe them.

Students then look at some homophones to do with animals before examining relative clauses in more detail. They then read some short stories about animals and use vocabulary from these stories to complete a joke about a clever dog.

In the following listening section, they hear three young people talking about their pets and talk about characteristics that they look for in both pets and people.

Next they do some work on conditionals, making sentences to describe unreal situations and describing what they would do in a series of moral dilemmas.

In the final section they learn about a boy's pet snake and do some work on prepositions after verbs and adjectives. The unit ends with an Anecdote activity in which they talk about a pet they know.

Section	Aims	What the students are doing
Introduction page 100	*Lexis*: animals; homophones	Matching animals with descriptions. Completing a table with homophones.
Close up page 101	*Grammar*: relative clauses	Combining sentences with *that*. Studying the form and use of relative clauses. Making statements about feelings.
Animal tales pages 102–103	*Reading skills*: reading for gist	Matching animals with descriptions. Reading short stories about some special animals. Retelling stories in groups.
	Lexis: vocabulary from the reading text	Using vocabulary from the stories to complete a text about a clever dog. Telling jokes or stories about animals.
Special friends page 103	*Listening skills*: listening for specific details	Listening to interviews about pets to identify the animal described. Listening for characteristics of pets and matching them with the speakers.
	Conversation skills: fluency work	Talking about the characteristics of a good pet.
Close up page 104	Grammar: conditionals	Examining conditional sentences from the previous listening text. Asking and answering questions about unreal situations. Completing sentences describing unreal situations.
	Conversation skills: fluency work	Discussing moral dilemmas.
Reptiles page 105	*Reading skills*: reading for specific information	Scanning a text about a pet snake to explain the connections between figures. Talking about unusual pets.
	Lexis: prepositions after verbs & adjectives	Writing true and false statements and discussing them.
	Conversation skills: fluency work	Anecdote: talking about a pet they know.

17 Animals *Teacher's notes*

Books closed. Whole class. As this unit is all about animals, you might like to begin by finding out what the students attitudes to animals are. Some people are fascinated by them and others want to have as little to do with them as possible. Encourage students to be open about their feelings and their experiences with animals. If you have a pet, you could take in a photograph and tell students something about it and what it means to you.

Lexis: animals (p 100)

Pairwork. Students read the definitions and match them to the animals. Encourage them to discuss and compare results with other pairs before turning to page 124 to check their answers.

Optional activity

If your students are particularly interested in animals, they might like to make up similar animal 'definitions' to test their friends.

Homophones (p 100)

1 Establish the meaning of *homophone* by giving students a couple of examples which are not in the exercise, eg: *sail* and *sale, hear* and *here*. Allow students to complete the table in pairs or small groups if they wish. Do not check answers at this stage.

> 1 tail; tale   2 deer; dear   3 bear; bare
> 4 right; write   5 wait; weight

2 **☐ 73 SB p 142**
Play the recording for students to check their answers. Play it again for them to listen and repeat. Then ask them if they have homophones in their own language(s). If they give examples, ask them to say what the words are in English.

> **☐ 73**
> 1   *Word A: tail – T A I L tail.*
>   *Word B: tale – T A L E tale*
> 2   *Word A: deer – D E E R deer.*
>   *Word B: dear – D E A R dear.*
> 3   *Word A: bear – B E A R bear.*
>   *Word B: bare – B A R E bare.*
> 4   *Word A: right – R I G H T right.*
>   *Word B: write – W R I T E write.*
> 5   *Word A: wait – W A I T wait.*
>   *Word B: weight – W E I G H T weight.*

Close up (p 101)

Relative clauses

1 Go through the example with the class. If your students have difficulty with relative clauses, you might like to go through the Language reference section at the bottom of the page with them first. Give them plenty of time to write their sentences and allow them to compare them in pairs or small groups before checking answers with the class.

> a)   I've got a friend that lives in London.
> b)   I've got a car that isn't very easy to park.
> c)   I know a woman that's got a beautiful singing voice.
> d)   I went to a private school that was a long way from my home.
> e)   My parents have got two dogs that like going for long walks.
> f)   I've got a sister that works in a shop.
> g)   Last week I watched a very sad film that made me cry.

2 Pairwork. Students look closely at their sentences and underline the relative clauses. They then identify the subject of each relative clause. Check answers with the class. You might like to point out the use of relative clauses in the animal definitions exercise on page 100.

> a)   I've got a friend <u>that lives in London</u>.
> b)   I've got a car <u>that isn't very easy to park</u>.
> c)   I know a woman <u>that's got a beautiful singing voice</u>.
> d)   I went to a private school <u>that was a long way from my home</u>.
> e)   My parents have got two dogs <u>that like going for long walks</u>.
> f)   I've got a sister <u>that works in a shop</u>.
> g)   Last week I watched a very sad film <u>that made me cry</u>.
>
> *that* (the relative pronoun) is the subject of each of the relative clauses.

3 Allow students to discuss the questions in pairs and try to work out the rule. Check answers with the class.

You can replace *that* with *which* in sentences *b, d, e, g.*

You can replace *that* with *who* in sentences *a, c, f.*

You usually use *which* for things, *who* for people and *that* for things or people.

4 Students decide which of the sentences are true for them and compare with a partner.

5 Look at the example with the class and then give them time to read through the definitions and cross out the unnecessary words. Go through the answers with the class and then ask them to match them with the words on the right.

a) An animal that ~~it~~ can smell water five kilometres away. – 4 An elephant.

b) A person who ~~he~~ studies birds. – 5 An ornithologist.

c) An animal that ~~it~~ sleeps standing up. – 7 A horse.

d) The only animal – apart from humans – which ~~it~~ gets sunburn. – 6 A pig.

e) A name for people who ~~they~~ are afraid of spiders. – 8 Arachnophobic.

f) The thing that you sit on ~~it~~ when you ride a horse. – 1 A saddle.

g) An insect that you get malaria from ~~it~~. – 3 A mosquito.

h) An animal whose name ~~it~~ means 'I don't understand'. – 2 A kangaroo.

6 Students write three true statements and compare them with a partner. Encourage them to report their most interesting statements to the class.

Animal tales (p 102)

Whole class. Focus attention on the photographs and ask students to name the animals they can see (cat, dolphin, goldfish, cow, mynah bird, dog). Find out if anyone has had any of these animals as a pet or, in the case of the dolphin and the cow, has had close contact with them.

Reading (p 102)

1 Groupwork. Students read the descriptions and try to match them with the animals in the photographs. Do not confirm answers at this stage. They then discuss whether they have known any animals themselves which fit the descriptions.

Possible answers

A: A dolphin.   B: A goldfish.   C: A dog.

D: A mynah bird.   E: A cow.   F: A cat.

2 Groupwork. Working in the same groups, students decide who is A, B and C and read their respective stories. Give them plenty of time to do this. They then match each of their stories to one of the descriptions in Exercise 1.

Student A: 1 D; 2 A

Student B: 1 C; 2 F

Student C: 1 B; 2 E

3 Groupwork. Students now take turns to retell their stories to the other members of the group and say which description in Exercise 1 each one matches. Encourage them to do this without looking at the text. They then discuss the stories and decide which one they like best.

Lexis (p 103)

1 Students work individually or in pairs to complete the text with the words in the box. Remind them that these words come from the stories they have just read, so they can look back to see them in context if they are unsure of the meaning. Allow students to compare their completed texts, but do not check answers at this stage.

1 turned up   2 paw   3 looked into his eyes

4 stayed very still   5 turned round   6 walked off

7 decided to

2 🔲 74 SB p 103

Play the recording for students to listen and check their answers. Elicit their responses to the story and encourage them to tell any jokes or stories they know about animals to a partner. Any really good stories or jokes can be reported back to the class.

Special friends (p 103)

Closed books. Whole class. Find out how many members of the class have a pet now or have had one in the past. Put the names of the animals on the board and see how many different types of pet are represented. What is the most unusual pet anyone in the class has ever owned?

Listening (p 103)

1 🔲 75 SB p 142

Go through the words in the box with the students. You may like to tell them that the people on the recording are talking about their pets, but they don't actually say what they are. The students have to work out which animals they are talking about. Play the recording and allow students to discuss their guesses in pairs or small groups. Play it a second time if there is anything they need to hear again. When they have come to a decision, allow them to check their answers on page 127. Find out if anyone in the class would like to have a spider or a pig for a pet.

◻◻ **75**

a) Tim

(I = Interviewer; T = Tim)

I: Tim, can you describe your pet?

T: She's very fat and not very pretty. But she's got a lovely curly tail.

I: What does she eat?

T: Anything and everything. She's very fond of banana skins.

I: Is she a good companion?

T: Yes, I always go and speak to her when I'm fed up. She listens to my problems when no one else will.

I: When you go away, who looks after her?

T: If I go away for work, my girlfriend looks after her. But if my girlfriend comes away with me, we have to take her over to my parents. She doesn't like that very much because they've got a dog that annoys her.

I: Do you and your pet look alike?

T: I hope not.

I: If you were an animal, what animal would you like to be?

T: I used to say a dolphin when I was younger, but I don't like the sea very much now. I don't know – a giraffe maybe, though I'd hate to be stuck in a zoo.

b) Gus

(I = Interviewer; G = Gus)

I: Gus, can you describe your pet?

G: He's black and has eight hairy legs.

I: What does he eat?

G: Insects.

I: What, he catches them?

G: No, I buy them frozen.

I: Is he a good companion?

G: Yeah. He's like a friend. We have a special bond.

I: When you go away, who looks after him?

G: Well, I haven't been away since I got him and I don't think anybody wants to look after him. Certainly not my mum. He frightens people away.

I: Do you and your pet look alike?

G: I'm not that hairy – but I think he looks cool, like me.

I: If you were an animal, what animal would you like to be?

G: A lion because they're big and tough and they rule.

c) Maxine

(I = Interviewer; M = Maxine)

I: Maxine, can you describe your pet?

M: She's very fluffy and very loveable. My boyfriend doesn't like her because she bit him – she's definitely a girl's girl.

I: What does she eat?

M: Her favourite meals are fresh vegetables, nuts and cereal.

I: Is she a good companion?

M: Oh, yes, I love Page because she's good company for me when my boyfriend is away travelling. Besides, we have the same interests – she loves to sleep all day, eat and then she parties all night long.

I: When you go away, who looks after her?

M: I take her everywhere in her little cage.

I: Do you and your pet look alike?

M: I think that she's better looking than me – who could resist those brown button eyes?

I: If you were an animal what animal would you like to be?

M: I _am_ an animal.

2 Pairwork. Students read the list of pet characteristics and decide which ones they heard in the interviews. Give any help they need with vocabulary.

3 Play the recording again for students to check their answers and write the letters of the speakers' names beside the characteristics. You might like to get them to raise their hands every time they hear one of the characteristics in the list mentioned.

a) TGM b) T d) G f) G h) G i) M

4 Pairwork. Students discuss the questions in pairs. Encourage them to compare their results with other pairs. Find out how much difference there is in the characteristics they look for in a pet and in a person.

Close up (p 104)

Conditionals

1 Pairwork. Go through the question in the diagram with the class and elicit answers to a) and b). You might like to ask students to answer the question for themselves and discuss it in pairs before moving on to Exercise 2. Alternatively, make sure they answer it as one of the questions in Exercise 2. Refer students to the Language reference section at the bottom of the page which has more information and examples of conditionals.

a) An unreal situation.

b) Now. The past tense.

2 Pairwork. Students answer the question in Exercise 1 if they have not done so before and then form other questions using the words in the box and any ideas of their own. You might like to elicit some new ideas from the whole class first and allow them to ask you the questions as well before asking and answering them in pairs. Remind them that the interviewees in the previous section always gave reasons for their choices, e.g. 'A lion because they're big and tough and they rule'.

3 Students work individually to complete the unreal situations in the right-hand column. Go round offering help and encouragement where necessary and check that they are using the verb forms correctly. Students then compare and discuss their sentences with a partner.

> a) If I was a member of the opposite sex, I'd / I wouldn't ...
>
> b) If I was the president of my country, I'd / I wouldn't ...
>
> c) If I had $1 million, I'd / I wouldn't ...
>
> d) If I spoke English fluently, I'd / I wouldn't ...
>
> e) If I could fly a plane, I'd / I wouldn't ...

4 Groupwork. Students read the moral dilemmas and complete them with the correct verb form. Check answers before they start their discussions. Encourage them to report back on their decisions to the class.

> a) found
> b) would you tell
> c) gave
> d) would you look
> e) saw

5 Groupwork. Working in the same groups, students produce two more moral dilemmas for another group to discuss. When they swap dilemmas, make sure each group reports back to the group that set the dilemma on their discussions and decisions.

Reptiles (p 105)

Closed books. Whole class. Tell students that the next section is about reptiles and elicit some examples (snake, lizard, crocodile, etc). Find out what students' attitude to reptiles is. Do they like them? Are they afraid of them? Do they find them repulsive? How many people in the class have ever touched a snake? What did it feel like? Did it surprise them?

Reading (p 105)

1 Go through the figures with the class and ensure they know that they should read the article to find out the links between them. If you want to encourage students to learn to scan a text for specific information, you might like to have this as a race with the first student to find the information to explain the links as the winner. If you do this, make sure you set aside time afterwards for students to read the text again more carefully. Check answers with the class.

> a) Louis had wanted a pet snake since he was 2 years old. He got one when he was 5 years old.
>
> b) The snake was 20 centimetres long when they bought it. It was 1 metre long a year and a half later.
>
> c) Louis left the cage door open for 2 minutes. The snake turned up in the kitchen 3 months later.

2 Pairwork. Students discuss their reactions to the text and answer the questions.

Lexis: prepositions after verbs & adjectives (p 105)

1 Go through the examples with the class. Ask the students to supply the correct prepositions to go with each sentence and check answers before giving them time to write sentences that are true or false for them. You might like to give some examples of your own to start them off.

> a) by b) on c) of d) of e) of f) about
> g) about

2 Pairwork. Students take turns to read their partner's statements and guess which ones are true and which false.

Anecdote (p 105)

See the Introduction on page 4 for more ideas on how to set up, monitor and repeat Anecdotes.

1 🔲 76 SB p 142

Go through the topics with the class first and then play the recording for them to listen and decide which of them Mandy talks about. If students are unfamiliar with the word, the picture to the left shows an iguana, a kind of lizard.

> She talks about all of them apart from the last one.

I know somebody who's got an iguana as a pet. It's a man I work with called Angus. The iguana is called Iggy and it's probably about five years old – that's how long I've known Angus and he got it soon after we met. It was a birthday present from his wife. It's just over a metre long from the tip of its nose to the end of its tail and it's a lovely green colour. Like all reptiles, iguana's never stop growing, so Iggy will get bigger and bigger. It's quite shy and nervous, which is exactly the opposite of Angus who's very outgoing and confident. It's definitely better-looking than Angus though. Iggy doesn't sleep in a cage. At the moment, it lives at the top of the curtains in Angus's living room. When it was young, it ate crickets, but now it's adult it doesn't need so much protein – in fact it's completely vegetarian. Angus takes it for walks in the park on a lead. It's funny – when it's frightened, it runs up Angus's body and sits on his head.

2 Pairwork. Students note down as much information as they can about what Mandy talks about. Allow them to compare with other pairs before playing the recording again for them to listen and check.

3 Pairwork. Give students plenty of time to decide what they are going to talk about and to choose from the topics in Exercise 1. They then take turns to talk about a pet that they know.

Test

Scoring: one point per correct answer unless otherwise indicated.

1 1 ant 2 cheetah 3 dolphin 4 giraffe 5 camel
6 snake 7 spider 8 tortoise

2 1 dear 2 bare 3 right 4 weight

3 (One point for each preposition.)
1 by, in
2 of, to
3 of, about
4 on, with

4 1 The CD ~~who~~ which / that I bought yesterday is fantastic.
2 My friend ~~which~~ who lives in Rome is coming to visit.
3 The man who ~~he~~ lives next door is a vet.
4 The film that we saw ~~it~~ last night was terrible.
5 I've found the keys which I lost ~~them~~.
6 This is the restaurant which I told you about ~~it~~.

5 1 This is my friend who/that lives in New York.
2 Here's the CD which/that you wanted to borrow.
3 I didn't like the pizza which/that we had for lunch.
4 I really like the teacher who/that taught us yesterday.

6 (One point per correct verb.)
1 were/was, 'd buy
2 'd love, could
3 were/was, 'd go
4 were/was, 'd play
5 'd move, could

17 Animals Test

Name: **Total:** _____ /40

1 Vocabulary – animals *8 points*

Add the missing vowels (*a, e, i, o, u*) to complete the animal names.

1   __nt

2   ch__ __t__h

3   d__lph__n

4   g__r__ff__

5   c__m__l

6   sn__k__

7   sp__d__r

8   t__rt__ __s__

2 Pronunciation – homophones *4 points*

Write a homophone for each word.

tail *tail*

1   deer _____

2   bear _____

3   write _____

4   wait _____

3 Vocabulary – prepositions after verbs & adjectives *8 points*

Add the missing prepositions: *about, by, in, of, on, to, with.*

1   'I'm fascinated _____ animals and I've always been interested _____ reading about them.'

2   'I disapprove _____ keeping animals as pets and I've always totally objected _____ zoos. '

3   'I'm tired _____ hearing about the way we're destroying the environment with pollution. I sometimes really worry _____ the future of the planet.'

4   'I bought my son a pet rabbit. At first he was really keen _____ it, but he soon got bored _____ it, and now I look after it all the time.'

4 Relative clauses (1) *6 points*

Correct the mistake in each sentence.

1   The CD who I bought yesterday is fantastic.

2   My friend which lives in Rome is coming to visit.

3   The man who he lives next door is a vet.

4   The film that we saw it last night was terrible.

5   I've found the keys which I lost them.

6   This is the restaurant which I told you about it.

5 Relative clauses (2) *4 points*

Combine the two sentences to make one sentence.

I've got a brother. He is a teacher
I've got a brother who is a teacher.

1   This is my friend. He lives in New York.

    _____ .

2   Here's the CD. You wanted to borrow it.

    _____ .

3   I didn't like the pizza. We had it for lunch.

    _____ .

4   I really like the teacher. She taught us yesterday.

    _____ .

6 Conditionals *10 points*

Put each verb into the correct tense or form.

1   If I _____ (be) richer, I _____ (buy) a better car.

2   I _____ (love) to learn Spanish if I _____ (can) find the time.

3   You look tired. If I _____ (be) you, I _____ (go) to bed.

4   If I _____ (be) younger, I _____ (play) more sport.

5   I _____ (move) to the USA if I_____ (can) speak perfect English.

18 *Weird* Overview

This unit is about strange phenomena and unusual and unexplained incidents.

It begins with a discussion of crop circles and the various theories that have been put forward to explain them. Students then listen to an expert on crop circles talking about one particular group of circles. They match questions and answers and then look at the form of questions with *How*.

The next section presents three 'incredible but true' stories, and students are encouraged to contribute any other strange stories that they know. They then do some work on the past perfect tense and complete a story about a woman who believes she has experienced a past life. In an Anecdote activity, they are invited to talk about any strange experiences that they or someone they know has had.

The final section has a text about the famous UFO crash in Roswell, New Mexico, and students use a guided framework to produce a story about meeting an alien.

Section	Aims	What the students are doing
Introduction page 106	*Conversation skills*: fluency work	Reading a definition of crop circles and talking about what they know or think about them.
	Reading skills: reading for gist	Reading a list of theories about how crop circles are created and discussing which they find most believable.
The mother of all circles page 107	*Listening skills*: listening for specific information	Listening to an interview with a crop circle expert and completing questions.
		Matching answers to questions.
		Talking about what they have heard.
	Lexis: *How* + adjective / adverb ...?	Matching beginnings and endings to form questions with *How* + adjective / adverb ...?
		Interviewing a partner.
		Talking about how long it takes you to do things.
Incredible but true pages 108–109	*Reading*: reading for specific information	Inserting missing sentences from texts about unusual incidents.
	Conversation skills: fluency work	Talking about coincidences and 'small world' incidents.
	Lexis: *have / make / take* + noun structures	Choosing the right verbs to complete sentences and discussing whether or not students agree with the sentences.
Close up pages 109–110	*Grammar*: past perfect	Identifying tenses in sentences from the previous reading text.
		Choosing the most appropriate tenses to complete a story about a woman who believes she has had a previous life.
		Discussing the story and personal experiences which created particular emotions.
	Conversation skills: fluency work	Anecdote: talking about strange experiences.
We are not alone page 111	*Reading and conversation skills*: reading for specific information	Scanning a text about the Roswell incident to find how many explanations there are for the UFO crash.
		Discussing beliefs about the existence of aliens.
	Writing skills: writing a story	Using a framework to construct a story about a meeting with an alien.

18 *Weird* Teacher's notes

Books closed. Whole class. Explain that the title of this unit is *Weird* and that this word can be used to refer to anything strange or unexplained, particularly things of a supernatural nature. Elicit from students any famous mysteries from their country or culture. If they don't have any specific examples, they may be able to talk about TV programmes that they have watched which deal with strange and mysterious phenomena (eg: the American TV series *The X Files*).

Groupwork. Focus attention on the photograph on page 106 and read the dictionary definition of crop circles with the class. Find out if this is a common phenomenon in their own countries. Then ask them to discuss the questions in groups and report back to the class. Refer them to the Language toolbox in the margin for some useful phrases to help them with their discussions.

Reading (p 106)

Pairwork. Students read the list of possible explanations for crop circles and discuss them. They decide which ones they find most believable. Allow them to compare ideas with other pairs before having a class feedback session. You may need to explain that a *hoaxer* is someone who tricks people into believing that something is true when it is not.

The mother of all circles (p 107)

Books closed. Whole class. Draw students' attention to the title of this section and ask them to say what they think the expression *the mother of all ...* might mean (the biggest, best, worst or otherwise most extreme example of something). It may be helpful to give them a few more examples, eg: *the mother of all battles* (= the worst, most ferocious). Ask students to open their books and look at the photo. Elicit that this is the 'mother of all crop circles' because of its size and complexity.

Listening (p 107)

1 📼 **77 SB p 142**
Go through the instructions with the class and ask them to read the questions and predict what the missing words might be before you play the recording. Play the recording and check answers with the class.

> a) long b) big c) many d) long e) long

📼 **77**

(I = Interviewer; KC = Ken Crystal)

I: *This morning the residents of a small village in Wiltshire woke up to an amazing sight. It is the biggest crop circle we've ever seen in Britain. The press is calling it the mother of all circles, and the question everyone is asking ... how did it get there? In the studio with me today is Ken Crystal, a crop circle expert. Ken, how long have you been interested in crop circles?*

KC: *For about eleven years now.*

I: *Can you tell us something about this circle?*

KC: *Well, we're very excited about this crop circle. The design is absolutely amazing, and it's enormous.*

I: *How big is it exactly?*

KC: *It's almost one kilometre wide! We've never seen anything like this before!*

I: *It's a very complex design. How many circles are there altogether?*

KC: *There are more than 400 circles – it really is incredible.*

I: *And do you know who made it?*

KC: *No, I don't, but I believe that this is the work of strange forces.*

I: *What do you mean?*

KC: *It's impossible for people to make something like this.*

I: *But I've heard that most circles are made by people. Is that true?*

KC: *Yes, there are several groups of people who make crop circles. But they didn't make this one.*

I: *How do you know?*

KC: *This circle appeared yesterday morning. The day before that it wasn't there. There were only four hours of darkness that night – there wasn't enough time to make it.*

I: *How long does it take to make a crop circle?*

KC: *Well, a simple circle takes a few hours. But a circle like this one would take several days.*

I: *How long have crop circles existed?*

KC: *The first crop circles were reported in 1980. In the last eleven years, I've visited over a thousand. But I've never seen one like this.*

I: *Ken, a final question. Do you think that this crop circle is the work of aliens?*

KC: *I think it could be a message ...*

2 Pairwork. Students match the completed questions in Exercise 1 with the answers. Allow them to compare results with other pairs before playing the recording again for them to check their answers.

> a 3 b 1 c 4 d 5 e 2

3 Pairwork. Students discuss their own responses to the interview and give their own views on how the Alton Barnes crop circle was formed.

Lexis: *How* + adjective / adverb ...? (p 107)

1 Refer students back to the questions in Exercise 1 of the previous section to demonstrate the use of *How* + adjective / adverb. Students then match the question beginnings and endings. Point out that more than one combination may be possible.

> *Suggested answers*
> a 5 b 3 c 1 d 8 e 6 f 2 g 4 h 7

2 Pairwork. Students take turns to use the questions in Exercise 1 to interview their partners. Encourage them to use some ideas of their own to make new questions.

3 Students work individually to note down how long they take to do each activity in the table. They then guess how long their partner takes and put this in the *Your partner* column of the table. Ask them to take turns to ask each other questions to find out how accurate their guesses are.

Incredible but true (p 108)

Books closed. Whole class. Explain the concept of a coincidence to the class (when two things unexpectedly happen at the same time). Elicit any surprising coincidences they have heard about.

Reading (p 108)

1 Go through the instructions with the class and read the three sentences that have been removed from the texts. Point out that each story has three numbered positions which are possible places to insert the missing sentence. Students have to decide which sentence goes with which story and where it should be inserted.

Give them plenty of time to read the stories, match the missing sentences and decide where they go. Allow them to compare notes in pairs or small groups, but do not check answers at this stage. You may need to explain some of the more difficult vocabulary, eg: *clairvoyant* (someone who claims to be able to predict the future).

> a) Story C: position 1   b) Story B: position 1
> c) Story A: position 2

2 🔲 **78 SB p 108**
Play the recording for students to listen and check their answers.

3 Groupwork. Students discuss the questions in their groups and report back to the class.

Optional activity

A collection of unusual stories might make an interesting display for the classroom wall. Students could be asked to write out their stories and illustrate them.

Lexis: *have/make/take* + noun structures (p 109)

1 Draw students' attention to the underlined sections of the three questions which consist of the verbs *have, make* and *take* + a noun structure. Give them a little time to find the answers in the stories they have just read.

> a) Laura Buxton.
> b) Emily Brown and Peter Baldwin.
> c) Amy Dolby.

2 Pairwork. Students work together to read the statements and choose the appropriate verb for each one. Encourage them to read the choices aloud to get a feeling for what sounds right. Check answers with the class.

> a) take b) make c) have d) take e) take
> f) Making g) make

3 Pairwork. Students discuss the completed statements in Exercise 2 and decide whether they agree with them or not.

Optional activity

You might like to ask students to write down a couple more sentences of their own using *have, make* or *take* + a noun structure.

Close up (p 109)

Past perfect

1 Pairwork. Students work together to look at the example sentence and discuss the questions. Check answers with the class. Direct them to the Language reference section on page 110 and the Verb structures section on page 129 for more information about the form and use of the past perfect.

> a) Past simple and past perfect (simple).
> b) Past perfect.
> c) 1 She knew
>   2 Did she know?
>   3 He hadn't started
>   4 Had he started?

2 The story of Jenny Cockell is presented in two extracts. She was so convinced that she had lived a previous life that she managed to trace the people she believed were her children and convinced them that she was their long-dead mother. You might like to start by explaining or eliciting that a belief in reincarnation is a belief that when we die, we are born again and live an entirely new life. Encourage students to read the first extract quickly, ignoring the verb choices, and answer the question about why Jenny went to Ireland. Check answers with the class. You might like to ask students at this stage for their initial reactions to the story.

> To find out if the children of Mary Sutton were still alive.

3 🔲 **79 SB p 109**
Pairwork. Students choose the most appropriate tense for the verbs to complete the first extract of the story. Then play the recording for them to check their answers.

1	had lived
2	had died
3	were
4	had been
5	had lived
6	realised
7	had died
8	wanted

4 Again, ask the students to skim read the story quickly just to find out the answer to the question. Check answers with the class.

> He thought that she was his mother.

5 🔲 **80 SB p 110**
Pairwork. Students work together to choose the correct tense for the verbs in the second extract. When they have finished, play the recording for them to listen and check their answers. Then ask them for their final responses to the story. Do they find it convincing? Do they think Jenny was telling the truth or was it all an elaborate hoax? (Remind students of the word *hoaxer* from page 106.)

1	found
2	had seen
3	had died
4	met
5	hadn't seen
6	reminded
7	'd caught
8	'd been

6 Pairwork. Go through the emotions in the box with the class first and explain or demonstrate any that they do not know. (Someone who is *on top of the world* is extremely happy.) Students then talk together about the times they have experienced these emotions.

Anecdote (p 110)

See the Introduction on page 4 for more ideas on how to set up, monitor and repeat Anecdotes.

1 🔲 **81 SB p 142**
Go through the topics with the class before you play the recording. Then ask students to listen and tick the topics that Des and Lidia talk about. Check answers with the class.

	Des	Lidia
Who had the strange experience?	✔	✔
Where was the person when it happened?	✔	✔
Were they alone?	✔	✗
Did they see or hear something strange?	✗	✔
Did they meet somebody in a strange situation?	✔	✗
What exactly was strange about the experience?	✔	✔
How did you or the person feel?	✗	✔
What happened after the experience?	✔	✔
What do you think about the experience? Can you explain it?	✗	✔

🔲 **81**

Des's story

I had a strange experience while I was working in Germany.

I was walking down the road in a place called Oberstdorf. I was alone, and I was wearing a coat with a hood over my head because it was snowing.

Suddenly I heard somebody call my name. When I looked round I saw that it was a young woman I'd met the previous summer in Ireland. I live in Ireland, and she had been on holiday in my home town. After the holiday she'd returned to Germany, and I hadn't been in touch with her since then.

She had no idea that I was in Germany and she didn't even live in Oberstdorf – she was just visiting a friend. But somehow she recognised me, even though it was snowing and I was wearing a big hood.

After that we stayed in touch, and in fact she came to my wedding ten years later.

Lidia's story

My sister and my aunt had a strange experience the day after my mother died.

At the time of her death, my mother was living with my sister. My aunt came to stay with my sister to help her make arrangements for the funeral.

In the afternoon, the two women were sitting in the living room when my sister's little dog started barking.

They went out of the room to see why the dog was barking and they both saw my mother's shadow on the wall. The shadow came down the stairs and disappeared.

They said they didn't feel frightened, but of course they felt very emotional.

Actually, my mother's ghost often appears to different members of the family, in different forms.

I think this is because she was such a strong character, and her memory lives on in our minds.

2 Pairwork. Students work together to note down as much information as they can remember about each story. Allow them to compare notes with other pairs before playing the recording again for them to check their answers. Then encourage a class discussion on which story is strangest.

3 Pairwork. Give students plenty of time to decide what they are going to talk about and to choose from the topics in Exercise 1. They then take turns to talk about a strange experience that they or someone they know has had.

We are not alone (p 111)

Books closed. Whole class. The Roswell incident is fairly well-known, and there have been books and films about it. Ask students if the word Roswell means anything to them and if they can tell the class anything about what is supposed to have happened there. If your class knows nothing about it, then have them open their books and read the text on page 111.

Reading & speaking (p 111)

1 Go through the instructions with the class and ask them to read the text quickly to find the information to answer the questions. Check answers with the class and elicit opinions on whether or not they believe any of the explanations.

> There are three different explanations: a flying disk; a weather balloon; a top secret radar balloon.

2 Groupwork. Students discuss the questions and report back to the class. Go round offering help and encouragement where necessary.

Writing (p 111)

1 Pairwork. Students read the framework of a story and discuss ways they can complete the story by answering the questions and adding detail. They should make notes of their discussion.

2 This activity could be set for homework if you have no time in class. Students write up their notes to make a story. Ideally these should be displayed on the classroom wall for other students to read and enjoy and time should be set aside for them to read them. Encourage students to add illustrations if they wish.

Test

Scoring: one point per correct answer unless otherwise indicated.

1 1 make 2 take 3 made 4 take 5 had
   6 make 7 take 8 made 9 has 10 take

2 1 many 2 long 3 far 4 well 5 fast 6 much
   7 old 8 often

3 (Two points per correct answer.)

   1 How long does it take you to get to school?
   2 How long does it usually take you to get ready to go out?
   3 How long did it take you to do your homework last night?

4 1 left
   2 had travelled
   3 was found
   4 climbed
   5 became
   6 had left
   7 were
   8 had been taken
   9 had only had
   10 was
   11 had been
   12 had happened / happened
   13 had got / got
   14 had forced / forced
   15 had been attacked / was attacked
   16 was ever seen

18 Weird Test

1 Vocabulary – *have / make / take* + noun structures
10 points

Add *have, make* or *take* in the correct form to complete the sentences.

1 I want to _____ a lot of money and retire early.

2 Did you _____ many photos on holiday?

3 My essay was terrible. I _____ lots of mistakes.

4 I'm going to _____ a cookery course next year.

5 Have you ever _____ a go at skiing?

6 You shouldn't _____ a promise if you can't keep it.

7 To be successful you need to _____ risks.

8 Have you _____ the arrangements for the party yet?

9 Ask Joe – he usually _____ lots of good ideas.

10 Please _____ a seat. I'll see you in a moment.

2 Vocabulary – *How* + adjective/adverb ...? *8 points*

Complete the questions with the words in the box.

far fast long many much often old well

1 How _____ CDs have you got?

2 How _____ have you been working here?

3 How _____ from school do you live?

4 How _____ do you know your classmates?

5 How _____ can you run?

6 How _____ money have you got on you?

7 How _____ are you?

8 How _____ do you speak English at work?

3 Vocabulary – *How long ...?* *6 points*

Use the words to write complete questions.

How long / take you / get up in the morning?
How long does it take you to get up in the morning?

1 How long / take you / get to school?

  _____
  _____ ?

2 How long / usually / take you / get ready to go out?

  _____
  _____ ?

3 How long / take you / do your homework last night?

  _____
  _____ ?

4 Past perfect *16 points*

Put the verbs into the correct form: past simple or past perfect. Sometimes you need to use the passive.

The story of the *Marie Celeste* is the greatest sea mystery of all time. The ship (1) _____ (leave) the USA for Europe in November 1872 with a cargo of pure alcohol. On 5th December, when the ship (2) _____ (travel) about 500 miles, it (3) _____ (find) by a British ship, the *Dei Gratia*, with no-one on board. When the crew of the *Dei Gratia* (4) _____ (climb) on board, it (5) _____ (become) clear that the crew of the *Marie Celeste* (6) _____ (leave) the ship in a hurry. Half-eaten meals (7) _____ (be) still on the tables. None of the fresh water (8) _____ (take). And the crew (9) _____ (only have) time to launch three of the lifeboats. There (10) _____ (be) blood on the ship's deck and other signs that there (11) _____ (be) a fight.

    There are many theories about what (12) _____ (happen). Perhaps the crew (13) _____ (get) drunk on the alcohol and tried to take control of the ship. Maybe stormy weather (14) _____ (force) the crew to abandon ship. Or perhaps the ship (15) _____ (attack) by pirates. The only thing we do know is that none of the crew (16) _____ (ever see) or heard of again.

19 *Wheels* Overview

This unit is mainly about cars, though the last two sections are essentially about journeys and should provide some light relief for students who are not especially interested in cars. The grammar focus is on *used to +* infinitive for talking about the past and language for giving, agreeing with and disagreeing with opinions, giving advice and making suggestions.

The unit begins with reading texts about people's first cars, and this leads into an extended speaking Anecdote activity in which students talk about their ideal car. Grammar work on *used to +* infinitive follows, and there are frequent opportunities in later sections for students to practise talking about the past.

Students look at the advantages and disadvantages of car ownership and listen to a conversation in which these are discussed. They then do some work on expressing opinions and agreeing and disagreeing with them. This section also has a listening activity which practises giving advice and making suggestions.

Students then read and listen to an account by Bill Bryson of his memories of family holidays in his father's old car. Students talk about their memories and how they passed the time on long journeys when they were children.

The final section has the song *24 Hours From Tulsa* originally sung by Gene Pitney, which tells the story of a man driving home to his partner who meets another woman and decides he would rather stay with her. Students have the opportunity to discuss the lyrics and give their opinions on the story.

Section	Aims	What the students are doing
Introduction pages 112–113	*Reading skills*: reading for gist	Reading texts about first cars and matching texts to pictures.
		Talking about first experiences of cars.
	Lexis: cars	Finding words for parts of a car in the reading texts.
		Talking about important features of cars.
	Conversation skills: fluency work	Anecdote: talking about ideal cars.
Close up pages 113–114	*Grammar*: past time – *used to +* infinitive	Identifying the correct uses of *used to +* infinitive to talk about past time.
		Comparing students' lives now with ten years ago.
For and against cars page 114	*Listening skills*: listening for specific information	Listing the advantages and disadvantages of car ownership.
		Completing a text with words and expressions to do with opinions.
		Listening to three friends giving opinions on car ownership.
		Discussing how much students agree with the speakers' opinions.
Close up page 115	*Grammar*: opinions; advice & suggestions	Studying different ways of giving, agreeing with and disagreeing with opinions.
		Preparing conversations in which opinions on chosen topics are expressed.
		Listening to a radio programme that gives advice on travel problems and identifying the problems discussed.
		Giving advice on travel problems.
A family holiday page 116	*Reading & listening skills*: reading and listening for specific information	Deciding if statements about a story are true or false.
		Matching adverbs with similar meanings.
		Choosing correct meanings of words in context.
		Talking about how students passed the time on long car journeys when they were children.
24 Hours from Tulsa page 117	*Listening skills*: listening for gist and for specific information	Predicting the order of pictures which illustrate a song.
		Listening and completing the lyrics of the song.
		Discussing and giving opinions about the people in the song.

19 Wheels Teacher's notes

Books closed. Whole class. As this whole unit is about cars, it might be worth canvassing students' opinions on cars right at the start. They will have an opportunity later to talk about the advantages and disadvantages of cars, but you could ask students to declare their initial opinions by arranging themselves in a line with people who positively dislike cars standing at one end, those who are fairly indifferent to them and just regard them as a convenience somewhere towards the middle, and those who love them and see them as objects of beauty at the other end. Go along the line and ask for a few individual opinions.

Reading (p 112)

1 Go through the instructions with the class and then give them plenty of time to read the texts, match them with the pictures and answer the question.

> A 2 B 3 C 1
>
> The 2CV (car 2) caused its owner the most problems.

2 Pairwork. Students work in pairs to talk about their first car or their first experience of travelling in a car. Encourage them to report any interesting experiences to the class.

Lexis: cars (p 113)

1 You could set this up as a race with the first student, pair or group to find all nine as the winners.

> bonnet, windscreen, windscreen wipers, sunroof, (white-walled) tyres, engine, boot, steering wheel, seats

Optional activity

Draw the outline of a car on the board and invite students to come up and label the parts of the car they found in the texts, together with any other parts that they know.

2 Groupwork. Students rank the items in the box. When they have finished, have a class brainstorming session on other features that are important in a car.

Anecdote (p 113)

See the Introduction on page 4 for more ideas on how to set up, monitor and repeat Anecdotes.

Pairwork. Give students plenty of time to decide what they are going to talk about and to read the questions. They then take turns to talk about their dream car.

Close up (p 113)

Past time: *used to* + infinitive

1 Pairwork. Students read the extracts from the article and match the underlined verbs with the descriptions. Check answers and then ask them in which case it is not possible to use *used to* + infinitive to talk about the past. Refer them to the Language reference section on page 114 if they need more help with *used to*.

> a 2 b 1 c 3
>
> It is not possible to use *used to* + infinitive to talk about a single action in the past (as in extract b).

2 Pairwork. Go through the example with the class. You may like to point out that in each sentence the past simple has been underlined. Students then work together to replace it with *used to* or *didn't use to* + infinitive where this is possible. Check answers with the class.

> a) used to have
> b) used to drive
> c) didn't use to like; used to be
> d) –
> e) never used to clean; used to smell
> f) –; –

3 Students work individually to change the sentences in Exercise 2 so that they are true for them. They then compare with a partner.

4 Pairwork. Students compare their lives ten years ago with their lives now, using the topics in the box and any others that they are interested in talking about. Go round offering help and encouragement and make a note of any good examples that you can ask pairs to share with the rest of the class.

For and against cars (p 114)

Books closed. Whole class. Find out how many of your students own cars and pair them up with others who do not. Those who have no cars can then interview the others about their cars. Brainstorm some good questions to ask first, such as *How often do you use your car? Did you buy it new? What type of car is it? How many kilometres do you do a year? How much does it cost to run it? Have you ever had an accident in it?* etc.

If your students are too young to own cars, they could interview each other about their parents' cars, using other suitable brainstormed questions.

1 Groupwork. Students should make lists of as many advantages and disadvantages of owning a car as possible. You could make this a timed race, using a chequered flag to indicate the beginning and end of the time limit. The winners are the team with the most items on their lists. Make sure they keep their lists as they will need them in the next exercise. Here are a few suggestions:

Advantages
- privacy
- you can listen to your own music
- liberating
- (in Britain) you can get out to supermarkets (the counter argument to this being that cars have created the culture of big supermarkets out of town)
- cars are beautiful

Disadvantages
- (in Britain) impact on communities – people don't know their neighbours
- (in Britain) limits children's freedom – parents are afraid to let them go out to play because of dangerous streets
- (in Britain) public transport is getting less funding

2 ▭ **82 SB p 143**

You may want to keep students in their groups from Exercise 1 so they can look at their lists of advantages and disadvantages as they listen to the recording and tick the ones that are mentioned. A gapped version of the tapescript of this recording is printed on the Student's Book page. You could ask them to cover this or close their books as they listen. Alternatively, with weaker students, you might like to encourage them to read along with the recording.

▭ **82**

(K = Karen; R = Ron; J = Jill)

K: *You're late!*

R: *Yes, I'm really sorry – I had to wait ages for a bus.*

J: *Why didn't you drive?*

R: *Ah, well. I've sold my car.*

K: *Oh, are you getting a new one?*

R: *No, I'm not getting another car. I've decided to live without one.*

J: *Wow – what made you do that?*

R: *I think there are too many cars, and this town is far too polluted.*

J: *Well, that's true, but a car is useful.*

R: *I don't think so. Not in the city centre, anyway. I can never find anywhere to park, and you spend most of the time sitting in traffic jams.*

K: *But how are you going to get to work?*

R: *By bicycle.*

K: *Don't you think bicycles are dangerous?*

R: *Not really. I don't think they're as dangerous as cars.*

J: *Well, I couldn't do without my car. I have to take the children to school every day.*

R: *I don't think children get enough exercise these days – they should walk to school.*

K: *Well, I haven't got children, but I agree with Jill – I couldn't live without my car. I sometimes have to come home late from the office.*

R: *Why don't you get the bus? Public transport is very good.*

K: *That's not true. The buses are not very regular where I work and anyway, as a woman, I don't feel safe waiting for a bus late at night.*

R: *Okay, I see what you mean, but aren't you worried about pollution?*

J: *Of course, but you don't understand – it's easy for you to worry about the environment. I have to worry about carrying the shopping and children and ...*

R: *Okay, okay, you're right! Come on. Let's get another drink. Hey, what do you think of my new haircut?*

3 Pairwork. This exercise should be quite easy if students read the script as they listened in Exercise 2. If not, give them a few minutes to decide what the missing words are, then play the recording again for them to check their answers.

---

1 think 2 but 3 so 4 Don't 5 think
6 agree 7 true 8 mean 9 right 10 what

---

4 ▭ **83 SB p 114**

Play the recording for students to listen and repeat. Try to get them to reproduce the stress and intonation exactly.

▭ **83**

1 *I think there are too many cars.*

2 *Well, that's true, but a car is useful.*

3 *I don't think so.*

4 *Don't you think bicycles are dangerous?*

5 *I don't think children get enough exercise these days.*

6 *I agree with Jill.*

7 *That's not true.*

8 *Okay, I see what you mean, but aren't you worried about pollution?*

9 *Okay, okay, you're right!*

10 *What do you think of my new haircut?*

5 Have a class discussion about whose opinion they agree with most.

Close up (p 115)

Opinions

1 Refer students back to the highlighted expressions which they saw and practised in the previous section. Allow them to work in pairs or small groups if they wish as they complete the categorisation. Check answers with the class and direct their attention to the first part of the Language reference section at the bottom of the page.

> a) What do you think of
> b) I don't think
> c) Okay, I see what you mean, but …
> d) Okay, you're right.
> e) That's not true.

2 Groupwork. Allow plenty of time for the preparation stages of this activity and for each group to perform their conversation to the class at the end. Go round offering help and encouragement as students prepare their conversations.

Optional activity

Work as a class. Choose the topic the class feels most strongly about from the box in Exercise 2 and organise a class debate.

Advice & suggestions (p 115)

1 **84 SB p 143**

The radio programme students are going to listen to is called *Road Rage*. Ask for suggestions as to what this might mean. (*Road rage* is the term used to describe aggressive behaviour displayed by drivers who are angered – enraged – by other road users. It can range from shouting and gesturing at other drivers, or pedestrians, to intimidation and actual physical violence. A fairly recent phenomenon, it has resulted in a number of deaths and is regarded in the UK as an increasing social problem.)

Go through the instructions and the problems with the class and then play the recording for them to listen and tick the ones that are mentioned.

> *b* and *e*

> 🔲 **84**
>
> (P = Presenter; C1 = Caller 1; C2 = Caller 2)
>
> *And that was of course this week's brand new number one! My name's Dave Darby, and you're listening to 'Road Rage'. Okay, let's see who's waiting on the line. Hello – what's your name, and how can we help?*

C1: *Hello, Dave. Um, my name's Mark, and my problem is traffic jams. I waste too much time sitting in my car in traffic jams in the morning on my way to work and in the evening on my way home, and I'm sick of it.*

P: *Ah, yes. I'm sure lots of people share your feelings, Mark. Why don't you work at home some of the time?*

C1: *I can't do that, Dave – I work in a shop.*

P: *Oh, okay. You could use public transport. Then you could read a newspaper on your way to work, and your time wouldn't be wasted.*

C1: *I can't do that, Dave – I have to use my car at work for deliveries.*

P: *Okay. Well, Mark, if I were you I'd learn a new language! Where do you usually go on holiday?*

C1: *Uh, Spain, Dave.*

P: *Great! You can buy Spanish language courses on CD and play them on your car stereo. They're fantastic, and you won't see the time pass.*

C1: *Uh, Dave …*

P: *Thank you, Mark. Have we got another problem on the line – yes, hello – what's your name, and how can we help?*

C2: *Er, hello, Dave. My name's … I'm, I'm called Sharon and I can't pass my driving test.*

P: *Oh dear, Sharon. Why's that?*

C2: *Well, I'm too nervous.*

P: *Right. How many times have you taken your test?*

C2: *Seven times, Dave. I'm fine in the lessons, and then on the day of the test I fall apart. I start shaking and I can't see the road.*

P: *Oh dear. Well, Sharon, …*

2 Pairwork. Students match the beginnings and endings and then discuss whether or not they think it is good advice. Check answers with the class. This might be a good time to draw students' attention to the ways of giving advice and suggestions in the Language reference section at the bottom of the page.

> a 3   b 1   c 2

3 Pairwork. Give students time to come up with some pieces of advice for Sharon. Then go round the class asking for suggestions. You might like to ask the class to vote on which is the best advice.

4 Pairwork. Go round offering help and encouragement as students prepare their conversations. Ask some pairs to act out their conversations for the class.

A family holiday (p 116)

Books closed. Whole class. Ask students to talk about their experience of family holidays. This is a good opportunity for them to practise the use of *used to* + infinitive, which they studied earlier. Find out where they used to go, how they used to travel and what they used to do. If you choose to do the optional activity below, this initial discussion will help students with ideas to write about.

Reading & listening (p 116)

1 85 SB p 116

Go through the statements with the class before you play the recording, so they know what information they are looking for. Students listen to the recording and read the text at the same time. They then decide which statements are true and which are false and compare with a partner. Check answers with the class and encourage them to correct the false statements. Note: You might like to point out to students that it would be unwise to try out the exploding bomb trick described by Bill Bryson and that modern safety matches have ensured that it wouldn't work anyway!

a) False. He used to go with his parents and his brother and sister.
b) True.
c) False. They made them veer in an amusing fashion.
d) True.
e) True.

2 Students find the underlined adverbs in the text and match them with those in the box that have a similar meaning. Check answers with the class.

quickly – rapidly
casually – in a relaxed way
furiously – angrily
mildly – gently
wisely – intelligently

3 Students should use the context of the words to decide which is the most likely meaning. Allow them to compare their answers in pairs or small groups before checking with the class.

a 1 b 2 c 1 d 2 e 2 f 1

4 Pairwork. Students discuss what they did as children to pass the time on long car journeys. If any of the games they suggest can be played in the classroom, you might like to try some of them.

Optional activity

Ask students to write a short account of a family holiday journey. Encourage them to include at least three of the adverbs in Exercise 1 in their stories. With weaker classes you may want to write some questions on the board to help them to structure their accounts.
a) How many people went on this family holiday?
b) How did you travel?
c) What did the children do to pass the time?
d) What happened as a result?
e) What did your parents do?

24 Hours From Tulsa (p 117)

Books closed. Whole class. In this section students are going to listen to the song *24 Hours From Tulsa*, a big hit for the singer Gene Pitney in 1963. Ask them if they know any other songs that are about cars or car journeys. You might like to point out that Tulsa is a city in the United States.

Song (p 117)

1 Pairwork. Students look at the pictures and try to decide what happens in the story and what order they should go in. Allow them to compare ideas with other pairs, but do not check answers at this stage.

1 B 2 D 3 C 4 F 5 A 6 E

Note: Because the story is told as a 'flashback', the following alternative order would also be acceptable:
1 D 2 C 3 F 4 A 5 E 6 B

2 86 SB p 117

Play the recording for students to listen, read the lyrics and check whether they put the pictures in the correct order in Exercise 1.

3 Students put the words from the box in the gaps in the lyrics. Allow them to compare results before you play the recording again for them to check their answers.

1 home 2 light 3 in 4 something 5 turned
6 closely 7 control 8 this

24 Hours From Tulsa

Dearest Darling,
I had to write to say that I won't be home anymore.
'Cause something happened to me,
While I was driving home and I'm not the same anymore.

Oh, I was only twenty-four hours from Tulsa,
Ah, only one day away from your arms,
I saw a welcoming light,
And stopped to rest for the night.

And that is when I saw her,
As I pulled in outside of the small hotel she was there.
And so I walked up to her,
Asked where I could get something to eat and she showed me where.

Oh, I was only twenty-four hours from Tulsa,
Ah, only one day away from your arms.
She took me to the café.
I asked her if she would stay.
She said okay.

Oh, I was only twenty-four hours from Tulsa,
Ah, only one day away from your arms.
The jukebox started to play
And nighttime turned into day.

As we were dancing closely,
All of a sudden I lost control as I held her charms
And I caressed her, kissed her,
Told her I'd die before I would let her out of my arms.

Oh, I was only twenty-four hours from Tulsa,
Ah, only one day away from your arms.
I hate to do this to you,
But I love somebody new.
What can I do?

And I can never, never, never
Go home again.

4 Groupwork. Students give their personal responses to the song by discussing the questions. Encourage them to report back to the class on their opinions and to use some of the language for giving opinions that they studied earlier. If you widen this to a class discussion, you can also encourage practise of language for agreeing and disagreeing with opinions.

Test

Scoring: one point per correct answer unless otherwise indicated.

1 1 engine 2 sunroof 3 steering wheel
    4 windscreen wipers 5 bonnet 6 boot 7 seats

2 1 d 2 c 3 e 4 b 5 a

3 (Two points per correct answer.)
    1 my parents used to drive me
    2 I didn't use to enjoy having
    3 did you use to have
    4 ✗ (*used to* is not possible here)
    5 I used to have a motorbike
    6 I always used to dream of owning

4 (Two points per correct answer.)
    1 What do you think of
    2 I don't think it's
    3 Don't you think it's
    4 I see what you mean, but
    5 in my opinion
    6 I don't think so
    7 If I were you, I'd
    8 Why don't you

19 Wheels Test

Name: _____   **Total:** _____ /40

1 Vocabulary – cars *7 points*

Add vowels (*a, e, i, o, u*) to complete the parts of a car.

1 __ng__ n ___

2 s__ nr__ __f

3 st__ __ r__ng wh__ __l

4 w__ndscr__ __ n w__p__rs

5 b__nn__t

6 b__ __t

7 s__ __ts

2 Vocabulary – adverbs *5 points*

Match each adverb in the first column with one with a similar meaning in the second column.

1	casually	a)	intelligently
2	furiously	b)	rapidly
3	mildly	c)	angrily
4	quickly	d)	in a relaxed way
5	wisely	e)	gently

3 *used to* *12 points*

Re-write the sentences using *used to* so the meaning is similar. *Used to* is not possible for one sentence. For this sentence, write ✘ in the space.

1 Before I passed my test, my parents drove me everywhere.

Before I passed my test, _____

_____ everywhere.

2 I didn't enjoy having driving lessons.

_____ driving lessons.

3 How often did you have a driving lesson?

How often _____

a driving lesson?

4 I passed my driving test when I was eighteen.

_____ when I was eighteen.

5 I had a motorbike as well as a car.

_____ as well as a car.

6 I always dreamt of owning a Ferrari.

_____ a Ferrari.

4 Opinions, advice & suggestions *16 points*

Complete the dialogues by reordering the words in *italics*.

A: (1) *of What you do think* _____

_____ the new Superhead CD?

B: (2) *think it's I don't* _____

that good really.

(3) *think it's Don't you* _____

very similar to their last album?

A: (4) *what see I mean but you* _____

_____ the new one is much better, (5) *opinion*

in my _____ .

B: No, (6) *don't I so think* _____ .

I much prefer their older stuff.

*   *   *

C: I'm worried about my exam next week.

D: (7) *you I If I'd were* _____

start to study harder. You might pass it if you do.

*   *   *

E: I'm fed up with not having any money.

F: (8) *don't Why you* _____

get a part-time job then?

Review 4 *Teacher's notes*

Big Game Lottery (p 118)

Pairwork. Students read the proverbs. Elicit that the theme of them is fortune and misfortune. In pairs they discuss whether or not they have similar proverbs in their own language and which of them they agree with.

Reading (p 118)

1   Students read the newspaper article and say whether they would feel the same as Mrs Alvarado or not. Have a class discussion and encourage them to give reasons for their opinions.

2   Pairwork. Students read the article again and decide which four verbs they can replace with *used to* + infinitive. Allow them to compare notes with another pair before checking with the class. Elicit why you can't replace the other verbs with the same structure.

> worked – used to work
>
> hated – used to hate
>
> did – used to do
>
> dreamed – used to dream
>
> You can't replace the other verbs because they describe single past events.

Past time: *used to* (p 118)

1   Students replace the verbs with *used to* or *didn't use to* where possible. Check answers with the class.

> a)   –
> b)   I used to live
> c)   I used to share
> d)   I used to watch
> e)   My parents used to give
> f)   –
> g)   I didn't use to enjoy

2   Students work individually to decide which statements were true for them as children. They re-write any false ones to make them true and then compare with a partner.

Listening (p 119)

1   **87 SB p 143**

Students should try to complete the sentences with appropriate prepositions before they listen to the recording. Allow them to compare their answers in pairs or small groups and then play the recording for them to check.

> a) of   b) of   c) about   d) about   e) in   f) about

87

(P = Presenter; A = Amy; J = Jack; V = Vera)

P: *Hi and welcome to 'Speak up!', the radio phone-in where you get the chance to say what you think about the stories in the news today. ... In the news today is lottery winner, Eva Alvarado. Yes, listeners, Eva Alvarado won $198 million but she says she doesn't want to change her life. She loves her job in a children's home and she wants to stay the way she is. Phone us now on 0800 989 8989 and tell us what you think. ... We have our first caller – Amy Wilder. Go ahead, Amy.*

A: *Well, Mrs Alvarado is obviously very fond of the children, but I'm sure she'll give up the job soon. When everybody knows how rich she is, life will be very difficult. Everyone will ask her for money and she will soon get tired of all the letters. So, she needs to think about the future now.*

P: *Good point there. We have Jack Nichols on the line. Go ahead, Jack.*

J: *Well, she doesn't sound very excited about winning the lottery. In fact, she's more interested in the children than in the money, so she'll probably give most of the money away – to the children's home, to her friends, you know? And I think she's right. If you have that much money, how are you going to spend it all?*

P: *Well, Jack, I'm sure I could help her! Right, let's go to our next caller – Vera Baker.*

V: *It's a lot of money, and she'll need a financial adviser. She doesn't have to worry about the future any more, but as soon as she has had time to think about it, I'm pretty sure she'll change her mind about just giving money to the children's home.*

2   Go through the predictions with the class and ask them to raise their hands as you read them if they think they heard them on the recording. Then play it again for them to listen and tick the ones they hear.

> a) ✔   b) ✔   c) ✔   d) ✘   e) ✔   f) ✔
> g) ✘   h) ✔

3 Pairwork. Students decide which predictions they would make about Mrs Alvarado, discuss the questions and report back to the class on their opinions. Remind them of the work they did on giving and responding to opinions in Unit 19 and encourage them to agree and disagree with other students.

Future time clauses (p 119)

1 Students choose the correct alternatives to complete the sentences. Check answers with the class.

> a) finishes b) meets c) gets d) rains e) is
> f) finishes

2 Pairwork. Students discuss in pairs how to change the sentences using names of people in the class to make them true. You could either allow them to ask the people first or make them do it without asking and then find out afterwards how many they got right.

Conditionals (p 119)

1 Students work individually to make the 'facts' true for them. They then complete the 'dream' sentences and compare with a partner. Remind them of the work they did on conditionals in Unit 17 and ensure they are using the verb forms correctly. If necessary, they can look back at the Language reference section on page 104.

> a) If I had $1 million, I'd ...
> b) If I spoke perfect English, I'd ...
> c) If I was / were the mayor of this city, I'd ...
> d) If I could travel in time, I'd ...
> e) If I wasn't / weren't a man / woman, I'd ...

2 Pairwork. Go through the example first to establish the idea of a 'chain' of conditional sentences. Students then work in pairs to try to write the longest chain they can.

It's your lucky day! (p 120)

Relative clauses

1 Remind students of the work they did on relative clauses in Unit 17. Ask them to choose the correct alternatives to complete the questions and then check answers with the class.

> a) is b) are c) brings d) you do e) promised

2 Pairwork. Students discuss the questions in Exercise 1.

Reading (p 120)

1 Give students time to read the e-mail message and discuss with a partner what they would do if they received it. Have a class vote on who would send the message on and who would bin it.

Note: The authors of this book are not suggesting that these chain e-mails are a good thing or that good or bad consequences really occur as a result of sending or not sending them on. Many people who receive them find them intensely irritating and simply bin them without any nasty consequences!

2 Students complete the text by choosing the appropriate verbs. Check answers with the class.

> 1 taking 2 took 3 made 4 had 5 had
> 6 making 7 made 8 had 9 took 10 take
> 11 made

3 Pairwork. Remind students that they studied questions with *How* + adjective / adverb in Unit 18. They complete each question with a word from the box. Check answers with the class.

> a) well b) much c) old d) long e) fast
> f) long g) often

4 Students read the e-mail message again and answer the questions. You may like to ask them if they believe anything in the e-mail message.

> a) She got top marks.
> b) $14 million.
> c) 83.
> d) Only six months.
> e) 15 mph.
> f) Six days.
> g) Every Monday for three months.

Past perfect (p 121)

1 Encourage fast reading by asking students to read the article and put up their hands as soon as they think they can explain the title.

> Because he was late, the man missed the plane that crashed.

2 Pairwork. Students work together to put the verbs into the past perfect and complete the story. The Language reference section on page 110 may help them. Do not check answers as this stage.

> 1 had forgotten 2 had broken down
> 3 had left 4 had left 5 had forgotten
> 6 had changed 7 had already taken off
> 8 had crashed 9 had died

3 🔲 88 SB p 121
Play the recording for students to listen and check their answers.

Anecdote (p 121)

See the Introduction on page 4 for more ideas on how to set up, monitor and repeat Anecdotes.

Pairwork. Give students plenty of time to decide what they are going to talk about and to read the questions. They then take turns to talk about their lucky or unlucky experience.

Let's talk about ... (p 122)

Divide the class into small groups and give each a dice and counters. Make sure that every group has a watch with a second hand. Go through the instructions carefully before they start so that everyone is clear what they have to do.

As they play, go round checking that they are playing correctly and offering help and adjudication where necessary.

Test

> Scoring: one point per correct answer unless otherwise indicated.
>
> **1** (Two points per correct answer.)
>   1 I'll phone you when I get home.
>   2 As soon as we finish university, we're going to get married.
>   3 I'll tell you all about it when I next see you.
>   4 I'm going to learn to ski before I get too old.
> **2** 1 will be / 'll be
>   2 will be able
>   3 won't be
>   4 will live
>   5 will visit
>   6 Will humans ever travel

> **3** 1 The restaurant ~~who~~ which/that we went to was lovely.
>   2 Do you know the people who live next door?
>   3 Where's the magazine which I bought ~~it~~ today?
>   4 The teacher who taught us last week is really nice.
>   5 Do you know anybody ~~which~~ who can speak Welsh?
>   6 This book that I'm reading ~~it~~ is brilliant.
> **4** (Two points per correct answer.)
>   1 The hotel which you recommended was great.
>   2 Do you know the man who I was talking to?
>   3 Is that the woman who spoke to you?
>   4 Here's the CD which you lent me.
> **5** 1 knew 2 'd enjoy 3 had 4 wouldn't do
>   5 wasn't 6 would you do
> **6** (One point per correct verb.)
>   1 lived
>   2 'd left, went
>   3 lived, was
>   4 'd spent
>   5 met, 'd been
>   6 'd known, got
>   7 'd been, had
> **7** 1 used to play
>   2 didn't use to read
>   3 used to eat
>   4 used to get up
>   5 didn't use to go running
>   6 used to eat
>   7 Did he use to play
>   8 did he use to eat
> **8** 1 think 2 don't 3 were 4 see 5 mean
>   6 why
> **9** 1 do 2 nuts 3 in 4 lead 5 by 6 of
>   7 about 8 took 9 had 10 Take 11 made
>   12 far 13 long 14 boot 15 wipers 16 on
>   17 wait 18 cake 19 right 20 make

20 Review 4 Test

Name: _____   **Total:** _____ /80

1 Future time clauses *8 points*

Put the words into the correct order to make complete sentences.

1   I get home 'll when phone you

   I _____

   _____ .

2   finish university 're going to we get married we

   As soon as _____

   _____ .

3   when I tell you all about it 'll I

   _____

   _____ next see you.

4   get too old learn to ski I before 'm going to

   I _____

   _____ .

2 *will* for prediction *6 points*

Complete the sentences using *'ll / will* and the verbs in the box.

| be   be able   ever travel   live   not be   visit |

1   In 2050, there _____ ten billion people on Earth.

2   Half the people on Earth _____ to speak English in the year 2100.

3   Next century, there _____ any more poverty in the world – I hope.

4   Most people _____ to be over a hundred next century.

5   Do you think aliens _____ the Earth one day?

6   _____ humans _____ to another planet?

3 Relative clauses (1) *6 points*

Correct the mistake in each sentence.

1   The restaurant who we went to was lovely.

2   Do you know the people live next door?

3   Where's the magazine which I bought it today?

4   The teacher taught us last week is really nice.

5   Do you know anybody which can speak Welsh?

6   This book that I'm reading it is brilliant.

4 Relative clauses (2) *8 points*

Put the words into the correct order.

1   The hotel which was great recommended you .

   _____

   _____

2   the man I Do you know was talking to who ?

   _____

   _____

3   who the woman Is that you spoke to ?

   _____

   _____

4   the CD Here's lent me you which .

   _____

   _____

5 Conditionals *6 points*

<u>Underline</u> the correct alternative.

1   If I **knew / would know** her name, I'd tell you.

2   If it didn't rain so much, I **will enjoy / 'd enjoy** living here much more.

3   I'd ring, if I **had / would have** his number.

4   If I were you, I **don't do / wouldn't do** that.

5   If I **'m not / wasn't** so busy, I'd go to the party.

6   What **would you do / do you do** if you were me?

6 Past perfect *12 points*

Look at Linda's life. Then complete the sentences putting the verbs into the past simple or the past perfect.

> 1964: born in London.
> 1974: went to live in Paris.
> 1982: left Paris and moved to London.
> 1984: went to art college.
> 1988: left London and moved to Edinburgh.
> 1992: met Steve.
> 1998: got married to Steve.
> 2002: had a baby.

1 Linda _____ (live) in Paris for eight years.

2 She _____ (leave) Paris when she _____ (go) to art college.

3 She _____ (live) in London while she _____ (be) at art college.

4 In 1988, she _____ (spend) six years in London.

5 When she _____ (meet) Steve she _____ (be) in Edinburgh for four years.

6 She _____ (know) Steve for six years when they _____ (get) married in 1998.

7 They _____ (be) married for four years when they _____ (have) a baby.

7 *used to* *8 points*

This year, as a new year's resolution, Tom made several changes to his lifestyle.

> He stopped getting up late at the weekend, playing computer games all the time and eating junk food. He started going running every morning, reading the newspaper every day and eating healthy food.

Complete the sentences about Tom using an appropriate form of *used to*.

1 He _____ computer games all the time.

2 He _____ the newspaper every day.

3 He _____ junk food all the time.

4 He _____ late at the weekend.

5 He _____ every morning.

→

6 He never _____ healthy food.

7 ____ he _____ computer games all the time?

8 Why ____ he _____ junk food all the time?

8 Opinions, advice & suggestions *6 points*

Complete the dialogues with the words in the box.

> don't   mean   see   think   were   why

A: What do you (1) _____ of Sara's new boyfriend?

B: He's okay, but (2) _____ you think he's a bit boring? He just talks about football.

*   *   *

C: Which of these shirts do you prefer?

D: If I (3) _____ you, I'd get the blue one. It's cool.

C: I (4) _____ what you (5) _____ , but the black one's more practical.

D: Okay. So, (6) _____ don't you get one of each?

9 Vocabulary – general *20 points*

Underline the correct alternative.

1 Did you **make / do** any sports at school?

2 Stop doing that! It's driving me **nuts / beans**.

3 I can't stop – I'm **on / in** a hurry.

4 I don't **follow / lead** a very healthy lifestyle.

5 I've always been fascinated **in / by** modern art.

6 I'm really tired **of / for** working here.

7 Stop worrying **for / about** me. I'll be okay.

8 We **made / took** some great photos at the party.

9 Have you ever **had / done** a go at bungee jumping?

10 **Take / Make** a seat. I'll be with you in a minute.

11 Have you **done / made** the arrangements yet?

12 How **far / much** is it from Oxford to London?

13 How **much / long** did it take you to do your homework?

14 Let me put your bags in the **boot / bonnet**.

15 Turn on the windscreen **cleaners / wipers**.

16 I've never been very keen **of / on** Indian food.

17 We had to **weight / wait** in the rain for half an hour.

18 This test is so easy – it's a piece of **potato / cake**!

19 How many of my answer are **write / right**?

20 Did you **make / do** many mistakes in your test?